PRINCE EUGÈNE, THE BEST LIKENESS—AN ENGRAVING OF THE PERIOD

PRINCE EUGENE

PRINCE EUGÈNE

A Man and a Hundred Years of History

by
PAUL FRISCHAUER

Translated by
AMETHE SMEATON
(COUNTESS VON ZEPPELIN)

The child needs neither stars nor planets:
His mother is his planet and star.
—Paracelsus

LONDON
VICTOR GOLLANCZ LTD
14 Henrietta Street Covent Garden
1934

Printed in Great Britain by
The Camelot Press Ltd., Lohdon and Southampton

CONTENTS

PART I. *The Cardinal and His Nieces*
    I.   *page* 9
    II.   20

PART II. *Sun-King and Shadow-Child*
    I.   37
    II. Diplomatic and Military Interlude   51
    III.   56
    IV. Diplomatic and Military Interlude   68
    V.   78
    VI   97
    VII.   112

PART III. *"Austria Holds the Trumps—If She Would Only Play Them"*
    I.   127
    II.   145
    III.   164
    IV.   188

PART IV. *"Genius Wins the Battles—Diplomacy Gains the Territory"*
    I.   205
    II.   221
    III.   239
    IV.   261

PART V. "*Wide Horizons Within Narrow Frontiers*"
    I.   *page* 281
    II.   297
    III.   320
        Conclusion and Bibliography   343

ILLUSTRATIONS

Prince Eugène, the best likeness—an engraving of the period	*Frontispiece*
Cardinal Mazarin *facing page*	24
The Palais Soissons : Eugène's birthplace	44
Triumphal Arch built in honour of Louis XIV. In the background : Paris in the year 1673	72
The poisoner, La Voisin	80
The Palace of Versailles : View from the park. Prince Eugène used the palace as a model for his Belvedere in Vienna	88
Contemporary representation of the advance of the Turkish Army	104
Vienna on the day of the Battle of Deliverance (12th September, 1683)	114
Kara Mustapha, the Turkish Grand Vizier	120
King John Sobieski, during the Battle	128
Victor Amadeus, Duke of Savoy, humbles himself before Louis XIV. A contemporary caricature	184
Prince Eugène's Palace in the Himmelpfortegasse	192
The Battle of Höchstadt (Blenheim). In the foreground, to the right : Prince Eugène and Marlborough	248
Contemporary representation of Eugène's menagerie	300
Prince Eugène's triumph after the capture of Belgrade	312
Prince Eugène lying in state	336

PART I

The Cardinal and His Nieces

CHAPTER I

SIXTY YEARS before the Citadelle of Lille was besieged and stormed by Prince Eugène a gaily beflagged and decorated galleon lay alongside the quay in the harbour of Marseilles. The ship had been placed at the disposal of the Marquise de Sénécé of the house of La Rochefoucauld—till then governess to the ten-year-old King, Louis XIV—for her to convoy from Italy three half-fledged maidens and a youth : one demoiselle Martinozzi, and two demoiselles Mancini with their brother.

Carpets, embroidered with the Bourbon lilies, were spread on the landing-stage ; on the mole, a lady in waiting in gala attire awaited the new-comers, and noblemen and pages were grouped around the carriages on the pier. It was a magnificent spectacle which the Marseillais, however, viewed with mixed feelings. One hundred and fifty years later, a stormy choir of sansculottes would have sung the *Marseillaise* or *Ça ira*, but in 1650 the revolution was still a tamer affair. It called itself the " Fronde," and the populace were insignificant hangers-on, noisy supporters of the Parliaments in their struggle against the Court and against the power of Mazarin, the Cardinal who reigned in the name of the youthful King. His Cardinal's hat was the principal target ; and, inasmuch as the nobility had taken sides with Parliament against the Court, the people of the port were roused to indignation that a Marquise should travel to Rome to bring these little " fishwives " and the " Italian street-arab " to Paris, and that a Duchess should await their arrival on the quay, accompanied by a cavalcade which was equipped, in accordance with the severe etiquette of the time, in a manner to receive Princesses of the Royal blood.

Princesses and Royal blood, indeed !

The three girls who now landed, their hair dressed and their clothes put on in an inadequate attempt at an air of distinction, were anything but the daughters of sovereigns. Their uncle, Cardinal Mazarin, sought, later on, to embellish their pedigree on the paternal side with a baron's coronet, and to prove for their mothers, his sisters, and himself a noble ancestry. But neither the Mancini nor the Martinozzi were of baronial descent, nor was Pietro Mazarini, the father of his almighty Eminence, in any respect a nobleman.

Saint-Simon, in his memoirs, describes the worldly status of Prince Eugène's great-grandfather as follows : " The Cardinal's father lived all his life in Rome in such obscurity that his death would have attracted no attention had not the official circulars maliciously printed a statement containing the following words : ' The Parisian circulars inform us of the death of Pietro Mazarini, father of the Cardinal of the same name.' "

It cannot be supposed that the upbringing of the children of people so unknown and insignificant was such as to fit them for the aristocratic mode of life of the time. Their bearing was self-conscious, and they returned, awkwardly, the curtsy of the lady in waiting and the noblemen's polite greetings. Their embarrassment, in face of the magnificence displayed in their honour, was so obvious that the courtly Madame de Sénécé was several times constrained to exhort them, in a corrective manner, to behave with dignity and self-possession. These events, naturally, gave rise to malicious allusions to the Cardinal, who, on the occasion of his promotion to Minister of State, had announced, publicly, that statues and pictures were the only possessions that he would bring from Rome to decorate the Cardinal's palace in the King's honour. He would, under no circumstances whatsoever, bring his family out of Italy. So much for his promises !

Mazarin was a statesman of the Machiavellian school, and explained that his promise was only valid as long as the circumstances justified it. Since then, circumstances had altered, and his reasons for bringing his nieces out of the obscurity of their Roman homes were far from being personal ones. No action of his was devoid of political significance !

Mazarin did not betray the nature of his motive, but it was an obvious one. Nieces represented, for him, the possibility of acquiring nephews by marriage, and, through them, of allying himself with the great families of the nobility. The relations between himself and the Queen did not suffice to secure for this Italian immigrant the complete establishment of his power. He wished, by means of his family, to strike roots in the kingdom over which, as Minister of State, he virtually reigned ; and to ally himself with the rebellious Princes by indissoluble marriage bonds. It would have suited him better had his nieces been already of marriageable age, so that he were not obliged to wait until they reached maturity.

Unmoved by the hostility shown him by both the nobility and the common folk, he installed them in a princely household, created honours for them, and had them instructed in the dress and demeanour which became the rank that he wished them to adopt.

The Italian girls did not attain this change in their circumstances without corresponding afflictions. For, in those days, the only way to damage the Cardinal was by mockery and insult, and his nieces' arrival was celebrated by jeering crowds, who paraded the streets of Paris carrying effigies of them in Court dress, which were loudly reviled and then publicly burnt. All that was harmless, however, and the demoiselles Martinozzi and Mancini could have felt quite at ease in their magnificent apartments had they had society. But Paris closed its doors to them, and the girls who had learned, with so much trouble, the control of their southern exuberance in conformity with the stiff ceremonial of the French Court found no immediate opportunity of practising it.

At first only rumours were spread about at Court. It was said that the Martinozzi girl was a beauty ; Laura, the elder Mancini, a charming twelve- or thirteen-year-old brunette ; while Olympia, the younger—of whom later the most was to be heard—although she had a long-shaped face, a pointed chin, and small eyes, had plenty of animation, and it could be hoped that with her fifteenth year she would develop further charms.

The pointed chin and the long face were to be inherited by Olympia's son, Prince Eugène ; and as for her charms—from her fifteenth year onwards she made full use of them. She was the most alive of all the nieces, and was well aware that she had not been brought to France merely for her own amusement. She had discussed the matter often enough with the Marquise de Sénécé and asked for a list of the names of eligible cavaliers ; moreover, whenever she encountered members of the Court, she invariably enquired after their standing and circumstances, and, in each case, weighed the pros and cons of an alliance. But Olympia was not the cautious niece of a diplomat for nothing, and decided for none of them. She had become ambitious, and, knowing that she would soon be given the entrée at Court, made up her mind that she would reserve her choice for one from among the King's most intimate *entourage.*

While Olympia and her companions were being presented to the Queen, the Maréchal de Villeroy whispered meaningly to his neighbour, " These little Italians are not rich yet—but wait ; soon they will possess money, lands, castles, and every kind of honour."

Mazarin absented himself from the *salons* during the ceremony which he had brought about with so much effort. He wished, on the one hand, to give the impression that the festive event which introduced his family into the Court circle was a matter of course and of very little moment to him ; on the other, he wished to avoid hearing the contemptuous remarks of the courtiers, who were incensed that these children from the " dregs of the common people " should all at once become of equal, or even of higher, rank than themselves.

The Cardinal's departure from the celebrations, and his apparent indifference to the ceremony, had been carefully thought out. It was unnecessary that his satisfaction should be noticed. His nieces' acceptance at Court, together with the gold bars which were piled up in his castle at Rül and abroad, assured him that he would secure nephews even from the most hostile families of the aristocracy, and they, in their own interests, would continue to mediate between him and his compeers, until, at length, peace was concluded. He could, from every point of view, congratulate himself!

Mazarin strode through his galleries, which were hung with the most valuable pictures of the Renaissance period. He had managed to acquire every costly object offered for sale by Italian and German merchants, and possessed over five hundred works of the world's most celebrated masters. Pictures by Raphael, by Leonardo da Vinci, by Guido Reni, by Giorgione and Correggio, adorned his walls. His galleries were representative of the history of painting up to his own epoch. But his chief passion was for precious stones, and he had bought several million talers' worth of diamonds and emeralds, which he preserved in golden chests. Wealth beyond the dreams of avarice!

When Mazarin, after a tour of his palace and its treasures, retired to his private cabinet and glanced at the map of Europe, he could well believe that he dominated the world outside the frontiers of France. He was proud of his success. He had brought the Thirty Years War to an end with every advantage for his adopted country; France had gained within her frontiers the whole of Lorraine and a part of Alsace. True, he was still at war with Habsburg Spain, but the French armies were intact after the Peace of Westphalia, and held the bled and exhausted enemy in check. The power of the House of Habsburg in Germany was destroyed for a period of many years. Central Europe was a desert which only very slowly crept back to a state of civilisation. Besides this, Mazarin had agents in Hungary, and at the Porte, whose business it was to see that Austria was continually upset by rebellions and insurrections, so that she was unable to think of making war on France. France's ally, Sweden, commanded the north of Europe—England was neutral; Mazarin's power was unquestioned. But while he was making plans of world-conquest, which, in later years, his pupil Louis tried to carry out, he under-estimated the persistent activities of his enemies at home.

This great-uncle of Eugène's, Giulio Mazarini, from whom he was to inherit his diplomatic talent, had a difficult position in France. It is only necessary to turn over the leaves of some amongst the collection of hundreds of books and brochures known as the " Mazarinades," which were written against the all-powerful one, to gain some idea of how much he was detested. Cardinal Richelieu, his predecessor, a powerful despot of French ancestry, had ruthlessly broken the power of the aristocracy, but, nevertheless, bequeathed to his successor nobles who had remained subservient up to the moment that the breath was out of his body, but who as soon as Mazarin stepped into his shoes began to be rebellious. They were known as the " Importants," and at the death of Louis XIII were forestalled by Mazarin in seizing the reins of government. To avenge themselves, they openly published pamphlets of questions, which contained the answers written by themselves.

Who is this Mazarin? it was asked. He was the lover of Anne, the Queen Regent, who, already during the lifetime of her husband, had had a much discussed love-affair with the Duke of Buckingham, the English Prime Minister! This Mazarin, a man of sinister origin, with a still more sinister career, was said to have been a lackey before he took Holy orders. Holy orders indeed! It was not at all certain that he had ever received them; and if he himself had not been a lackey, then his father most certainly had! His grandfather had been a bankrupt and herdsman, of Jewish origin, from the village of Mazare, in Sicily. Hence the name! No trace of noble birth! In Mazare there was neither manor house nor castle such as might be the seat of a noble family! Again, what had been the circumstances of the Spanish journey which this Giulio Mazarini, now Cardinal and statesman, had undertaken as the young and insignificant companion of an abbé of the princely house of Colonna ? Disgraceful gambling affairs, or intrigues with women ? Everyone knew about it. Then there was that extraordinary incident of the notary who had adopted him as his son-in-law, and paid his debts—until Signore Mazarini absconded by night ! This Sicilian vagabond, who remained in France to enrich himself, and to steal, is described in a song of the year 1651 as having " practised roguery from his birth onwards. He had been a rogue in his childhood, a bigger rogue as a man, a rogue in Rome, a rogue while on the lowest rung of the ladder, but, when by an extraordinary stroke of fortune he was raised to the rank of Cardinal, he had become a crimson rogue ! "

Princes, dukes, and counts were not the only people who sang in this strain, for, in their châteaux, academies of verse established themselves, whose object was the debasement of this upstart by means of scandal and insult. Their methods were, as they themselves described, " unscrupulous, undiscerning, of passionate purpose, and entirely without prudence." Open rebellion was preparing—war to the knife against the Cardinal and his supporters, a struggle to the death against the overwhelming, ever more ambitious, power of the State, which, since the time of Richelieu, had been invested in the Cardinal's crimson.

The Gallic wit now became serious. At the head of the rebels—who called themselves " Frondeurs "—were the Princes Condé and Conti. Both Bourbons, their desire to live as closely as possible to the Throne forbade them to tolerate an independent Minister as a connecting link between themselves and the King ; especially when the King was only ten years old and the Minister a man of Mazarin's type, slippery as an eel (not only bodily, as so often described in the " Mazarinades "), washed in all waters (with exception of the holy-water), and painted in every colour. Mazarin's diplomatic ability, developed during his service in the Papal

Chancery, had been trained to extend from the minutest detail to the most complicated combinations. He was a first-class player on the political chess-board, a hardened card-player and card-sharper (a quality that counted as a virtue in those days), and a man of great personal courage who, although his priest's robe became him, would have preferred to parade in the uniform of a cavalry officer.

Richelieu had foreseen his career, and, at the time when Mazarin was Papal Nuncio Extraordinary, had presented him to the Queen, adding, with a Machiavellian smile, " Madame, he is very like Buckingham." Even before the day when the Queen graciously held out her hand, famous for its beauty, to receive his kiss of allegiance, Mazarin had already served the French Crown on several occasions. In the name of Rome—which he frequently made use of without actual justification—he had held out the palm of peace, now to Savoy, now to Spain, and now to France, but, in each case, had furthered French interests. In the intervals between these diplomatic successes, he had provided his patron, Cardinal Barberini, with castrati and female singers for the Italian opera, thereby winning his first spurs in the hierarchy of the Church : the purple stockings, and the title of Monsignore. A mission in Savoy, carried out for Louis XIII, procured him the Cardinal's hat ; and Savoy, that frontier land, half French, half Italian, continued to be the quarter whence the wind of his fortune blew. Thus when, later on, he urged his niece Olympia, Eugène's mother, to marry a Prince of Savoy, his reasons were not merely those of family consideration.

Since the time in the church at Valence when Louis XIII, with his own hand, placed the Cardinal's hat on the still thickly growing brown hair and pronounced him Minister of State, Mazarin had felt himself to be more French than any born Frenchman. The parallel between his adoption of French nationality, and, later, the complete naturalisation of Prince Eugène in Austria, is very striking. The abstract human being for whom the country of his brain becomes his natural home, knows no land of birth : he is a patriot in the country whose frontiers are drawn by his imagination.

During Mazarin's lifetime France had no better friend and patriot than he. Yet, as time went on, his plans were more and more boycotted. The Parliament of Paris finally refused to register them, and, in alliance with the rebellious nobility, declared war on him. This happened at the same historic moment at which the English Parliament dethroned and beheaded the Stuart King, Charles I. In France, however, there was neither Cromwell nor Puritan, and the Importants, who now called themselves Frondeurs, were satisfied with forcing the Cardinal and his nieces to flee the country. Although, nominally, the Queen Mother ruled, in Paris, in the name of the little King, her hands were tied, and, in reality, Mazarin, even while sitting in exile in Brühl, near Cologne, having taken all his treasures with him and having opportunely renewed his diplomatic connections, still remained master of the situation. The Fronde lasted for five years. For five years France was, to a certain extent, turned upside down, solely in order to banish the Sicilian Cardinal ; but, in the end, victory was with Mazarin. A sufficient proof of his irresistible power is shown by the fact that the Duc de Mercœur—with great discernment—travelled to Brühl to ask for Laura Mancini's hand in marriage.

This was the first ray of hope that the nieces had seen for a long time. Actually, a grandson of Henry IV's wanted to marry one of them ! But that was only the beginning. Olympia knew that either she or her sister was being cast by her uncle, as bait, to secure Conti, the brother of Condé— an achievement whereby he would make peace with both princes. She was well aware of her importance to her uncle's plans.

For the moment, however, Mazarin had no urgent need of exerting himself with unpleasant politics ; instead, he filled his sails with wind. " I have been too often to sea not to know that after the ebb comes the flow," he wrote to the Queen in one of the love-letters which exist to the present day, in which, in black and white, he sends promises of kisses and embraces to his lonely one—to the "grass widow," as the Frondeurs called her. The Fronde was breaking up internally; he had known beforehand that it would do so. Mazarin was certainly no phlegmatic personality; he fumed when he heard that, just before the end of the rebellion, not only had his palace been demolished, but the volumes of his beloved library had been auctioned, singly, in order to obtain a worthy price—to be set, by the Frondeurs, as the price on his head. The fact that the swinish mob declared him outlawed did not trouble him. What did trouble him was the loss of his library : "My books," he moaned, "my irretrievable books." For this act he would make them pay in full.

It is interesting to note that, just as, in the future, his great-uncle was to become a model for Prince Eugène in all things, so the Cardinal's library became a model for his own famous library in Vienna.

The Queen had been forced to ban the Cardinal officially; now, however, that the leaders of the Fronde were beginning to go over to his side, she called him back secretly. But he was waging war against his will, when, at the head of six thousand men, whom he had recruited at her bidding, and with the great Turenne on his side, he marched across the French frontiers. This was civil war—his Frenchmen were tearing themselves to pieces. He swore to them that he would make peace; for the blood that would be shed was blood that he needed for his political ends—for war outside the frontiers. He issued manifestos guaranteeing pardon for the misdeeds that had been committed against his person, and even rewards for those who were willing to submit themselves. After his triumph he actually kept his word and suppressed his desire for vengeance.

The people of Paris, who had expected to see the scaffold and the usual spectacle of bloody execution which, in the time of Richelieu, was the invariable sequel to every plot and insurrection, saw, instead, only fêtes and jubilations, in which, for the first time in their lives, the Signorine Mancini and Martinozzi, with their sister and cousin, now Duchesse de Mercœur, were allowed to take part. These monkeys, "round as a ball," as they were described in the "Mazarinades," these "peacocks, this rabble, born of beggars, whom no one dare shelter for fear of being torn in a hundred pieces," were now the centre of the Court activities!

During these festivities, Olympia Mancini was introduced by Turenne to Eugène Maurice de Carignan, a Prince of the reigning house of Savoy.

CHAPTER II

THE PRINCESSE DE CARIGNAN, widow of the Lord High Chamberlain of France, who had died a short while beforehand, was a Bourbon by birth. She had waited at the Porte Saint-Antoine in Paris for the arrival, from Brühl, of the coaches returning with the Cardinal and his nieces, in order to take the girls under her care.

Her Highness did not proffer this hospitality out of affection for Mazarin. By sheltering the demoiselles Mancini and Martinozzi under her paternal roof in the Louvre she was demeaning herself. But she demeaned herself willingly ; she went even further, and on the first evening of their return made full use of her wide connections to organise a magnificent fête in their honour. This she did so that the Cardinal should be forced to recognise the far-reaching influence of the House of Savoy-Carignan. Her logic was quite simple : Mazarin had laid all his adversaries low, and, in her opinion, the future of her second son, Eugène Maurice, was not securely enough established. It was true that he received certain revenues and benefices from Church preferments—without, however, having the slightest intention of taking ecclesiastical office. In those days such arrangements were looked upon with indulgence, and, in any case, he held, among other things, the office of Canon of Lüttich Cathedral. Some idea of the value of these preferments can be gained by considering the fact that, immediately before his marriage, Eugène Maurice relinquished, in favour of his illegitimate brother, all benefices with the exception of the revenue of the Abbaye La Couture—a matter of some six hundred thousand livres !

Eugène's Bourbon grandmother was not merely avaricious, she was ambitious as well. She had married her daughter to the Margrave of Baden, and now she wished to obtain for her son as magnificent a position in the French Army as that held by her son-in-law's brother in the Army of the Emperor. To fulfil this ambition there was only one thing to be done. In France, the way to all appointments led through the Cabinet of his Eminence ; access to the Cardinal was to be achieved by means of his nieces, and Madame de Carignan thought her speculation would be worth twice as much, if, of these nieces, she were to secure Olympia as her daughter-in-law.

In consequence of the relations of Mazarin and Queen Anne—said by reliable contemporaries to have been those of a secret marriage—the Cardinal's family was drawn into the narrowest circle of the Royal household. Their playmates were the King ; Monsieur, his brother ; and Princess Henriette of England, the daughter of Charles I (who was beheaded in the English revolution).

Decked out in the latest whim of fashion, and surrounded by their maids of honour, the Cardinal's nieces, after their return from Brühl, promenaded in the Royal gardens : Olympia, lively in her movements, with the quick eyes of a mouse that peeps cautiously out from behind a cupboard ; Laura, already in her newly acquired dignity as Duchesse de Mercœur ; and Signorina Martinozzi—for whom a reigning Prince was pressing his suit—wearing the airs and graces of a future sovereign. None of the three had wanted the ugly Prince de Conti, so Mazarin saved him up for one of his younger nieces, whom he now, out of " family affection," sent for to join them ! The political business of marriage was well under way. A princely galleon was, once again, sent to Italy, and the Marquise de Sénécé had the doubtful pleasure of fetching three more temperamental Signorine Martinozzi, and yet another Signorina Mancini, of educating them, and of laboriously befitting them for Court life. The zealous Princesse de Carignan assisted in the task.

Her Highness had received an unequivocal refusal from Olympia in the matter of the marriage with her son. She did not dispute it. She had not really thought of Olympia in particular; she had merely decided on one of the Cardinal's nieces. If not this one, then that one : whether it were Hortense, Maria, or Marianne was a matter of indifference to her. She had plenty of choice, her son must make a career, and just the very reason which Olympia had hinted at as the grounds for her refusal made it all the more likely that she would win at least one of the sisters or cousins as a daughter-in-law. "Many thanks for the honour of your proposal," Olympia had said graciously; but explained that she was, unfortunately, already bound. Bound? To whom? For months on end, Madame de Carignan watched, eavesdropped, and enquired. Olympia Mancini bound? If a Prince of Savoy were not of high enough rank for her, then who could it be? Madame de Carignan whispered and gossiped, and discussed the matter with the Marquise de Sénécé who replied that such a suggestion could not be taken seriously. The King? Impossible!

Yet, after all, why not? Olympia was, undoubtedly, the King's favourite. She had captivated him by her gaiety and her winning personality. She devoted her whole existence to him, and spent her time in divining his wishes and tastes. He obviously favoured her, so perhaps, after all, there was some truth in the conjecture.

The attachment of the young King to Olympia soon became an affair of State; the more so inasmuch as, after the marriage of Laura Mancini to Mercœur, the Cardinal had given two other nieces in marriage : Laura Martinozzi to the reigning Duke of Modena, and her younger sister Maria (who thus became entitled to the "hand-kiss") to the ugly Prince de Conti. The Cardinal worked quickly and precisely, and everyone wondered whether he would stop at half measures. It was obvious that he looked with a favourable eye on the relations between the King and Olympia. Did he really intend his niece to aspire to the Throne—to become, actually, Queen of France?

In the Louvre, an atmosphere arose akin to that which had prevailed during the worst days of the Fronde, or at the time of the first arrival in France of the Cardinal's nieces.

For if this marriage really came to pass, then the future sovereigns of France would be the descendants of Signore Mancini, erstwhile coachman and dealer in plaster, who, even now, notwithstanding the exalted rank of his daughters, and the large allowance made him by his brother-in-law, still took fees for reading horoscopes and fortune-telling. Fees! Everyone sniffed and turned up their noses! Olympia's passion for astrology was all at once seen in another light. Of course, she was just her father's daughter. Everyone shrugged their shoulders. Mazarin could employ a genealogist to prove his noble ancestry, if not in the blood, then, at least, on parchment, but that did not suppress the truth. A shabby bourgeois Italian maiden to become Queen of France and successor to Anne, born of the Habsburg blood!

The Cardinal was questioned, but gave no answer, and, while hundreds of notes concerning projects of marriage were sent out from his Chancery (later to be administered by the famous Colbert), he wrapped himself in a mantle of silence, and gave the impression that he was waiting for cavaliers to appear who were inspired by the motive of love alone in seeking his nieces' hands in marriage. To such as these he would not refuse them. When these cavaliers happened to be sovereigns or princes, that was merely a happy coincidence to which he had contributed nothing, and only blessed with his approval by admitting his nephews (whom he treated as sons-in-law) to the highest offices in the State, or by bestowing upon them rich dowries and extensive revenues. He only did this, however, after the accomplished fact of marriage.

Mazarin raised no objection to the inseparability of Louis and Olympia when they were seen openly walking arm-in-arm in the parks of Saint-Germain and Marly, or dancing together in the Louvre. Nor did he contradict her when Queen Christine of Sweden said to him outright: " It is an injustice that these two young people, who suit one another so well, should not be married as quickly as possible." The Cardinal appeared to play a completely passive rôle; but Olympia was so delighted with this encouraging and out-spoken opinion that from that moment she adopted Queen Christine as her model, and thereafter only rode horseback astride—the King, of course, invariably at her side. The last poets of the " Mazarinades " had further inspiration for their epigrams : She would continue to wear the trousers were she to become his wife, they wrote.

But Olympia retained her composure and ignored the insult. She preserved her distance as though she were already Queen. It was her happiest time.

The Court of Louis XIV was then at the beginning of its future brilliance. Mazarin understood the art of increasingly diverting the political passions of the aristocracy by ballets, masques, plays, and tourneys. His predecessor, Richelieu, had spent, during the whole of his rule, three hundred thousand livres on the production and presentation of tragedies : Mazarin spent more than that in one year on the operas which he introduced from Italy. He sent for scenery and scene-shifters from Milan and Mantua ; he organised the performances of the Comédiens Italiens, and insisted that the singers and actors should rehearse before him. He interested the whole Court so much in the theatre that even the young King took part, and, in a ballet entitled the *Marriage of Peleus and Thetis*, played five parts, one after the other—Apollo, Mars, a Dryad, a Fury, and a Courtier. With his craving for being ever in the centre of the picture—a craving which, later on, was forced upon the world—Louis made use of his Royal privilege, and claimed every part for himself !

The rehearsals were held in the Cardinal's palace. Olympia chose the stuffs for the costumes, arranged for the wigs and cosmetics, and, when the bell rang before each performance, it was her duty tenderly to dispel Louis's stage fright ; and afterwards it was she who shared with him the delights of the frantic applause. The world was altogether a pleasant place ; and when the lovers at length took leave of one another, they knew that only the short night parted them, and that their happiness would begin again on the following day.

One morning, however, the whole Court learned that, in the previous night, His seventeen-year-old Majesty—the

CARDINAL MAZARIN

most Christian King—had been seduced, out of hand, by his mother's elderly lady in waiting, Madame de Beauvais! That morning, Louis paid more attention to the memorising of his parts than to Olympia. But she had no leisure to devote to the play. She did not wish her despondency to be noticed; yet every time she looked at the King her sorrow overcame her, so that she had to hold back her tears. Her dream was over, but she did not give way to sentiment. Instead she reproached herself. She should have taken more trouble with the Queen Mother, who had shown her displeasure at the very mention, even in jest, of the possibility of a marriage between the King and Mlle Mancini. Madame de Beauvais was merely the Queen's tool, and Olympia still felt capable of competing with this blear-eyed person who had a son older than Louis himself.

She took the greatest trouble with her appearance—but the result dissatisfied her. True, her reflection in the mirror reassured her that few arms and hands could compete with hers for beauty—but there was that pointed nose, the small eyes, and the olive complexion!

She became reconciled once more with Louis, but it was no longer the complete, absorbing love of former days; and now she had grounds for jealousy. The Court circular could still report that Olympia—*nomen est omen*—gifted of the gods, had engraved her features on the King's heart; but she did not deceive herself. She knew that, even while he sat or stood at her side, he was, all the time, looking out for the most attractive of the Court ladies. Faithfulness! Olympia gave that no further thought. She had lost her illusions, her heart was empty, but she refused to give up her ambition. She sounded the Cardinal as to the state of her marriage prospects, but he kept his counsel. No one ever knew what he thought. Her cousins, Martinozzi, were married, and well married; her sister was a Duchess. Every time now that the King ceased paying attention to her, even for a short while, she feared that she would soon be excluded altogether from the light of his favour, and already on several occasions she had experienced what that meant. Instead of being greeted with respectful cordiality, she had been received, even by her friends, with cool, polite reserve. In the end, she would find herself left without a husband at all. She must force Louis to declare himself. Her woman's instinct told her that she must make him jealous—that that was the only way to win him back. She had intended to work out her plan with forethought, but, in the end, could stand the strain no longer, and, before the night when she had intended to give herself to Louis, asked him what he would say to it if she were to marry.

At that moment she could not have rendered him a greater service than by asking that question. He need, then, have no pangs of conscience on her account? She gave him his freedom without the slightest effort! All the better! Louis behaved in love just as he was, later on, to behave in diplomacy. He had already bound his heart with thin bands, here, there, and everywhere; and, above all, had started a secret affair with Olympia's younger sister, Maria. Without preamble he advised Olympia to get married.

In spite of having been prepared for this, she was despairing. Whom should she marry? The Duc de La Meilleraie, son of the Grand Master of Artillery, who had asked the Cardinal for her hand? Or Prince Eugène Maurice de Savoy-Carignan, whose mother's argus eyes had espied the transference of the King's affections from the one sister to the other, and who now used her knowledge to urge Olympia to marry her son? But Olympia did not want to marry; her heart had become one with her ambition; she pleaded her love for Louis as excuse, and again refused the Princess's offer. This time Madame de Carignan went to the Cardinal in her indignation, and Mazarin sought the counsel of an astrologer, who declared that his secret wish of setting Olympia upon the Throne was impossible of fulfilment. The stars did not foretell that Olympia Mancini was destined to become a Queen. Unrest and change of place were to be her destiny; were she to bind herself to the King, he would share the same fate.

At that time, Charles II, son of the executed Stuart, was

in Paris; a King without a country, who wandered from Court to Court to beg for help towards his reinstatement. This warning example, combined with the readings of the horoscope, worked so effectively on Mazarin that he buried all hopes of Olympia's exaltation, and declared himself ready to accept Princesse de Carignan's son as his nephew. He communicated his decision to Olympia, and awaited an outburst of her violent temperament. But Olympia had renounced her heart's desire, and was now ready to do her uncle's bidding. She became his obedient pupil, trustworthy in all matters that he confided to her. She had recognised that, in the end, her future depended on his power alone, and that Louis XIV's favours were fickle.

She signed her marriage contract in the private cabinet of the faithless monarch.

The title of Comte de Soissons had died out with the Princesse de Carignan's brother. It had been the title of a branch line of Bourbons, and now, for the future husband of a niece of Mazarin's, it was renewed. In this manner Olympia was officially raised to equal rank with the Princes of the blood, and was called simply "Madame la Comtesse." The girl who had come to France, a few years before, poor as a church mouse, now enjoyed, in company with her family, all the privileges of the Bourbons save one: she might not offer her hand, unasked, to one of the real members of the Royal House. Olympia was dissatisfied with this exception, and fought a bitter battle to attain the withheld privilege.

On the occasion of her marriage, a gazette published a poem in her honour, which, in well set-up rhymes, described how the bridegroom had acquired a bride "whose charms were such that Cupid with the arrows from her lovely eyes had penetrated the heart of the great Seigneur himself."

The marriage, of which Prince Eugène was born, took place on the 21st of February, 1658. The newly wed bridegroom received three hundred thousand gold thalers, the command of the Swiss Guard, the government of the Bourbonnais and of Champagne; while Olympia was given the highest rank that a Court lady could attain: the humble-born Mancini became chief stewardess of the Queen's household.

Now for the first time began her real relations with Louis XIV. Hardly a day passed that the King did not appear for a short while in the Palais Soissons. He played cards at Olympia's; he received guests in her palace; she was at his side in all excursions. She was not his Queen, but she was Queen of his fêtes.

Contemporaries, who sought a liaison in Louis's friendship with Madame la Comtesse, had good grounds for their surmise. Louis was certainly no Platonist, and the frantic jealousy which Olympia showed when he courted her sister, and, later on, when he made La Vallière his mistress, points rather to thwarted love than to injured vanity. Her position was not in any way threatened by his amorous adventures. She was unquestionably the lady of highest rank at Court, and if she had not been actuated by simple jealousy would never have plotted the intrigues which were to lead to her downfall. The affair, too, of the love potion, which she obtained from La Voisin for an " illustrious gentleman," points to a past intrigue with Louis XIV which she wished to renew. The question is not an unimportant one, nor merely a matter of the Court gossip of the period: on the contrary, it determined the attitude of Louis XIV to Prince Eugène, as well as the departure of the Little Abbé from his native land, and his subsequent struggle against the Roi Soleil.

With his growing love for Maria Mancini, the King's friendship for Olympia dwindled. The period was a critical one, both for him and for the Cardinal, inasmuch as the political constellation had made it necessary either that France continue to wage war with Spain or that the House of Bourbon ally itself in marriage with the House of Habsburg. But Louis XIV was head over heels in love with Maria Mancini, and declared that he would marry her and no other.

The contemporary chroniclers had once more plenty of material, and new " Mazarinades " were secretly circulated containing ironical poems directed against the King and his Minister, while the flatterers praised Maria to the skies.

The Queen Mother had, up to now, treated the nieces of her most trusted friend (and probable husband) like her own children. It had been her greatest pleasure to be with Maria and Marianne, especially with the youngest, the Cardinal's favourite niece, who afterwards, as Duchesse de Bouillon became the patroness of La Fontaine, author of the famous *Fables*. Now, however, Anne arranged, in conjunction with the Cardinal, to send the two girls away to a well-guarded castle, in order to make it quite clear to Louis that she would hear nothing of such a marriage.

The Cardinal installed a prison *entourage*, who, however, it must be admitted, bound the two young captives with chains of flowers, and set before them, instead of bread and water, the costliest of fares. But he was determined, even in face of the stormy supplications of his Royal pupil, under no circumstances whatsoever to give Maria to Louis in marriage.

Blind admirers of Mazarin assert that he prevented the marriage entirely in the interests of the Crown; and this conviction has much to be said for it. But it is not at all certain whether his strength of character would have been sufficient to forgo such an exaltation for one of the members of his family, had not Maria Mancini set herself in opposition to him. In the case of Olympia, he had assented, even against the will of the Queen; but Maria had aimed at making Louis independent, and at delivering him from the increasing influence of her uncle, in order that she might secure that influence for herself. She had already attained her fifteenth year before she left Rome, and had spent the last years under better intellectual conditions than her elder sisters, who had merely amused themselves about the Court. Maria knew the native poets by heart, was interested in politics, and admired Corneille and his political maxims. Her mature intelligence impressed Louis, whose own literary education was not very profound, although, in all worldly affairs, he had been early, and thoroughly, initiated.

At the victorious battle of Dunkirk in the year 1658,

during the campaign against the Spanish, Louis fell desperately ill, and learned, on his recovery, of Maria's unbounded despair at the news of his illness—news which, incidentally, Olympia received with an indifference for which Louis never forgave her ! Everything contributed to bind his heart to Maria. He broke off, summarily, a liaison which he had had with a lady in waiting, and, when she objected, had her put into a convent. Louis had already, at that time, acquired the ruthless habit of terminating his love-affairs with an abrupt order of arrest.

It was with a similarly autocratic mien that he confronted his mother and the Cardinal with his desire to legitimise his love for Maria. But Mazarin's life's work was at stake. He declared that of course Louis was the King : he could not dispute that ; but he, equally, was the head of his own family, and would put Maria into a convent, or have her poisoned even, rather than give her to the King in marriage ! Louis XIV remained firm in his decision, and promised Maria marriage with every formality. But while the lovers kept up a correspondence, which, without their knowledge, was censored by the Cardinal, Mazarin set an army of intrigues in motion, together with all his state-craft and diplomatic knowledge, to separate them. He organised a meeting between the King and a sovereign Princess, the daughter of the Duke of Savoy, whom he proposed that Louis should marry. Such a marriage would provide, in the first place, a bulwark against Spain in Northern Italy, and secondly, would assure a basis from which, later on, the armies of France could overrun Italy. Inasmuch as the marriage project with Spain had fallen through and the war must be continued, this new alliance was obviously dictated by the *haute politique*. But this plan fell a victim to Louis's opposition. He hardly greeted the proposed bride, and as soon as possible turned his back on her in order to write his daily letter to his beloved. Mazarin was obliged to delve deep into the Queen's jewel casket in order to pacify the indignant Duchess of Savoy ; he only laid hands on his own when it was absolutely necessary !

There now remained for him no other opening against Spain than that of making an alliance with her, and, while the formalities of the meeting with the Savoy Princess were still going on, he busied himself, with a Spanish Ambassador Extraordinary, in composing a marriage agreement between Louis and the Infanta Maria Theresa.

The Spanish House of Habsburg was at that time without a male heir, and the Crown threatened to pass out of the Austrian line. The Cardinal declared that, in the event of a marriage alliance with Maria Theresa, he would, on behalf of his sovereign Louis XIV, forgo all claims to the inheritance of the Crown.

The opinion which Mazarin had relied upon at the time of the Fronde—that the internal disturbances would be smoothed over, and that all the politicians needed was to turn their attention across the frontiers—now proved itself justified. He had entrusted to Olympia the watching over of Louis, who, in Maria's absence, sought refuge in her company. She made him more than welcome; but while he only came in order to keep in some sort of contact with Maria, she worked hard with all her understanding of intrigue to alienate him from her sister. Her sister, who had been the cause of her estrangement from Louis, should not become Queen. Any other rather than she ! Her revenge was successful; she was able to report to Mazarin that Louis's passion was on the wane, and that his stormy love was gradually declining into a sentimental affection. The moment had come in which to force him into a marriage with Maria Theresa.

Louis still continued, however, to write love-letters to Maria. He sent a small dog to Labrouage, the place of exile of his beloved; messengers rode to and fro every day; but all the while, in the Chanceries of the Cardinal and of the Spanish Prime Minister, marriage contracts were being drawn up, the consent of the Spanish King obtained, and the journey prepared with great pomp for the State entry of the Princess.

The result was that the little play-actor of the festive

performances at his own Court suddenly saw his opportunity to play a rôle in the world theatre surpassing in importance that of any previous King of France. Mazarin recited to Louis the words which he was to pronounce on the occasion of the death of the King of Spain, even in the event of the King's having had, in the meantime, a son by a second marriage—a supposition which became actual fact. The concept of mental reservation in the concluding of a pact, by which one party to the treaty asserts that, in his opinion, the limitations of the agreement are not to be considered seriously—in this case, for example, the question of Louis's renunciation of all claim to the Spanish inheritance—was drummed well into Louis's head. Love was a passing thing, a rôle which became older every day, and was only made bearable by variety in women and costumes. But the rôle of a great King was eternal.

The actor in Louis allowed himself to be convinced. The marriage promise to Maria Mancini had been a childish game. He denied having made it, and followed his messenger —who, with great pomp, had left for Madrid—into the Pyrenees, in order to introduce himself to his future father-in-law, the King of Spain. Peace between France and Spain was concluded on the Island of Pheasants. It was the first State treaty which Louis had signed in person, and, thereby, the enmities which had outlasted the Thirty Years War were brought to an end.

Olympia and Mazarin celebrated their triumph together, and Olympia only regretted one thing : owing to the presages of motherhood she could not be present with the Royal family at the celebrations.

During the interval in which the King had ceased visiting his wife, the Comte de Soissons was depressed and fearful for the fate of his career. He was, as Madame de Motteville describes him in her memoirs, a good and thoughtful husband. He did not cavil at the intimate relationship between the King and his wife, and made no objections when the two of them drove out every day in the coach, ate their meals on a rug without getting out, or played *hoc* together. At that time one of the Cardinal's secret agents reported to him, amongst other things, that the King and the Comtesse de Soissons were together for more than three hours in the Archbishop's Palace and performed *media noce*. That was in the year 1659.

During the years before the birth of Prince Eugène, as at the beginning of his intimate friendship with Olympia, Louis was a constant guest at the Palais Soissons. Indeed, as Lafare reports, he visited her every day, even at the time when he was in love with La Vallière. His marriage with Maria Theresa did not take up much of his time, and Maria Mancini's visit to Court after the Royal wedding was of the briefest. She wished to console herself by getting married as quickly as possible, and declined to be the mistress of a man who had not kept his promises of marriage. Moreover, she aimed at sovereignty, and it happened that at that time the young Duke of Luxembourg sought her hand in marriage. But Louis, piqued because she had refused to become his mistress, did not wish her to make a marriage of her own choice. He graciously took note of her wish to marry the Duke of Luxembourg, bespoke the matter with Mazarin, and sent her the old Duke as a bridegroom ! She could not stand such irony, and refused him. But now another marriage proposal came to the fore, and one which flattered the Cardinal, inasmuch as in his youth he had occupied a junior post in the House of Colonna : the Connétable of Colonna became a suitor for Maria, and received her hand. After the consummation of the marriage, he wrote to the Cardinal expressing his astonishment at having found his wife untouched. The reputation of the French Court and its King would seem to have been a worse one than they deserved.

The fact of Maria's virginity almost lends plausibility to the theory that Louis had equally respected Olympia's honour ; but this supposition is rendered unlikely by the subsequent loose career of Madame la Comtesse, who, after she finally renounced the King to Mlle La Vallière, had several

CE

official lovers. Certainly, this happened only after 1661—the year in which Mazarin died, having crowned his life's work by the alliance of his Royal pupil with Maria Theresa.

Olympia's first lover was the Marquis de Vardes, one of the most notorious worldlings of his time. The second, of whom there is definite proof, was the Marechal de Villeroy, —after that, their name is legion.

One memorist of the time reports that Vardes won Olympia's heart at the King's express command. If that was the case, then it must be assumed that Louis wished, thereby, to free himself from Olympia's toils. He was tired of her; even her friendship began to bore him. Vardes had started his affair with Olympia rather for a chance of sharing her influence than on account of her beauty. La Vallière was disinterested; she belonged to no party, and only demanded of Louis a corresponding affection. In consequence of this good example the intriguers at Court feared that their immoral habits would be exposed and, in consequence, defeated. The English King's daughter, Henriette, who in the meanwhile had married Louis's brother, conspired with Olympia to overthrow La Vallière. " Monsieur " was homosexual, and had little time to spare for his wife, while she wished to indemnify herself with his brother. Certainly she had not allowed her sex to suffer, for the Comte de Guiche—of whom Madame de Sevigné writes that he was a " queer personality "—a friend of the Marquis de Vardes, was her lover.

Thus, the four-leaved clover—Olympia, Henriette, Guiche, and Vardes—together forged a plot. In the meantime Olympia had given birth to several sons and daughters, amongst them, on the 18th October, 1663, Prince Eugène. Her friendship with her husband was so secure that on one occasion, when Olympia and Vardes had quarrelled, the Comte de Soissons went and fetched the Marquis and brought him back to his wife! But he had nothing to do with the plot. He was a solid, patient man who valued honour and merit, and who, behind the blinkers of his decency, ignored his wife's amorous adventures. So that when, after the exposure of the plot, he was handed a *lettre de cachet*, which banished him, together with his wife, to his government in Champagne, he endeavoured, in vain, to discover the reason for the Royal disfavour.

The affair was not complicated. Everyone at Court, except the betrayed husband, knew what had happened. Vardes and Guiche, supervised by Olympia and Henriette, had sent the Queen an anonymous report in disguised handwriting, written in Spanish, to the Queen, in which were set forth all details of the intrigue between Louis and La Vallière. The conspiracy blew up. The King was beside himself with wrath : but, nevertheless, his friendship for Olympia was still constant enough for him, in spite of his bad humour, to recall her and her husband from exile after a very short while.

For the next few years Olympia, although still officially about the Court, lived outside the radius of the King's pleasure. The next news of her is after the death of her husband in 1672. He was on his way to join Turenne's forces in Germany, and died suddenly after the passage of the Rhine. All sorts of rumours were circulated about the manner of his death : Olympia's enemies hinted at poisoning, without, however, being able to produce a motive for such a crime.

Eugène Maurice, Comte de Soissons, had proved himself a brave soldier. During his service he had performed a brilliant piece of work when, with Turenne, at the head of his Swiss troops, he overthrew the Spanish infantry. He had also been, at one time, Ambassador Extraordinary in England, and had fought a duel with a nobleman who spoke slightingly of the King of France.

He was an honourable man, by whose death Olympia lost her foothold at the French Court, even as by her marriage she had gained it.

PART II

Sun-King and Shadow-Child

CHAPTER I

THE BACKGROUND of Prince Eugène's early youth was the Palais Soissons, a building in the château style surrounded by gardens, which, a hundred years earlier, Queen Catharine de Medici had had rebuilt for herself. It was a fearful and fascinating place for the growing children; part of the walls had conserved the characteristics of the Middle Ages, and corbels jutted forth as a reminder of the time when the palace was still a fortress. In the courtyard of the building, on the right-hand side of the main entrance, rose a mighty fluted column, 143 feet high, hollowed out and surmounted by an iron lantern in the form of a celestial globe. A spiral staircase within the pillar led to a platform at the top, wide enough for several people to stand on it simultaneously. Catharine had set up the pillar as an observatory for her astrologer Ruggieri; but to Eugène's mother, whose father had been a professional star-gazer and soothsayer, it probably appeared as though this pillar, decorated with secret astrological signs, had been specially built for her. She had a passion for astrology and magic, and the right wing of the palace—the wing dedicated to superstition, which had not been occupied since the time of Catharine—was opened up for her. It contained sinister chambers in which from every corner a death's head grinned down as a reminder of the perishableness and transitoriness of things; and a horoscope cabinet, where the measuring instruments, triangles, and circles, which were spread out on a long table together with the glass retorts and human skeletons, all remained untouched. From this room no magic symbol might be removed.

The furniture was an extraordinary higgledy-piggledy of fashionable *objets* and ancient requisites of magic. Here, Madame de Soissons lived her private life ; and here, only the most intimate members of her family were admitted—and these, again, only with the utmost circumspection. The greatest precautions were taken that none of the seven children to whom Olympia had given birth should knock up against the red-hot coal-pan on which the magic herbs were perpetually brewing. Olympia brewed cosmetics, ointments, and hair dyes from her own prescriptions. Her cabinet of rarities was a cosmetic kitchen, to which she eagerly devoted herself whenever her social duties allowed of it.

Guests came every evening, and were received in the mirrored galleries in the centre wing of the palace, where the children were seldom admitted.

But when both folding doors were thrown open they could see their mother in the great mirrored *salon*, surrounded by her ladies in waiting, and wearing her metre-wide hooped petticoat, the bodice sewn with pearls and cut into a point, the puff sleeves so wide that they touched the imaginary side-line from the head to the lowest edge of the skirt.

It was a strange rigid picture, which very slowly and decorously changed its contours : the man with his flunkey's face at the door, in knee-breeches and silk stockings, and the majordomo, in the livery of Savoy, who smote with his silver-mounted stick on the floor and called out one historic name after another. Then they entered, ladies and gentlemen, one after the other, and walked with measured tread and dignified mien up to Madame la Comtesse. After greeting her, they stepped aside in discreet groups to converse.

Now the whole company seemed to be waiting on some event. The children left their hiding-place to take up a new post of observation. They looked down on the court of honour, which suddenly became alive : cavaliers rode in with a company of musketeers, and then through the portals rolled a great glass coach ornamented in gold.

A young man stepped out with lithe, elastic tread. It was obvious that he would have liked to take the steps of the outside staircase in one spring. But, though the muscles under his silken stockings were taut, he forced himself to a quiet and dignified carriage. He was dressed with exaggerated simplicity; only the buttons of his waistcoat glittered when a ray of light caught and reflected the enormous diamonds. The silken waves of an immense curled wig hung down on his shoulders, giving his head the appearance of a dark-haired lion.

"The King," called out the majordomo, and struck three times with his stick on the pavement.

There was complete silence in the room; every movement froze, and all eyes were focused on Louis XIV, who, without moving a muscle of his face, advanced towards his hostess. She dropped back in a deep curtsy, while every head was lowered until the King, after bowing courteously, addressed himself to Madame la Comtesse.

This scene remained for Prince Eugène the most vivid impression of his childhood : his mother, surrounded by the élite of the Court, and the great King bowing before her. He could forget then his small misshapen body, and wish that his figure might become as upright and dominating, with a carriage as muscularly developed as the King's. He marvelled at the movements, which were closely observed and carefully imitated by all the men in the *salon*. He also tried to imitate them, but his deplorable image in the mirror repelled him. The moment he ceased to allow his phantasy full play, he knew that he could never become the equal of the King, and that the most he could do was to adore his ideal and resolve to serve him.

Whenever Louis made an appearance, the Garde du Corps and the irreproachably turned-out musketeers were the objects of his almost painfully exact and detailed scrutiny. He wished that when he grew up he might at least become a musketeer or one of the Garde du Corps, so as to be near this wonderful being who only needed to appear for all the lights of the Palais Soissons to shine brightly.

Sometimes he would see the King without ceremonial, as a careless horseman throwing the reins to a groom in the courtyard; or again, when, unannounced, he would appear in Olympia's horoscope cabinet. On such occasions the King's expression was naturally bright and gay, enlivened by Olympia's vivacity; and the boy, standing shyly in the room, would wait to see if a glance fell upon him. But usually his mother would dismiss him, with a wave of the hand, before Louis had even noticed his presence.

Olympia knew that the King did not care for Eugène, and that her eldest son Louis Thomas was his favourite. She therefore prevented, as much as possible, his being annoyed by Eugène's unwelcome presence.

Louis's attitude is not to be wondered at, for, if one gives credence to the letters of Liselotte of the Palatinate, the King's sister-in-law, then Eugène was " nothing but a dirty, very debauched boy, who gave no promise of being any good. He had a small, snub nose, his eyes were not bad, and showed intelligence. His mouth was almost always open." On another occasion she writes : " He was fairly small for his age, and sedate."

Such was the appearance, in childhood, of the fifth Prince of Savoy, whose birth resulted from the alliance of the stargazer's daughter Mancini and the House of Savoy. In addition to all that, from the age of five he had worn an abbé's black habit with white collar and flaps, which did not suit his crooked sorry appearance, so that it can well be imagined that the splendour-loving Louis XIV turned the cold-shoulder on this particular boy, especially as it was said at Court that he, the King, was not entirely innocent of Eugène's existence. Louis would never have recognised such an ugly child even if there had been no doubt of his paternity. His vanity suffered with every fault in appearance or behaviour of both his legitimate and illegitimate children :

so much so, that he refused to admit his paternity in any case where faults became apparent; and immediately banished all persons concerned in such an event! That, in spite of this, he gave Prince Eugène the nickname of the "Little Abbé" shows that the King's friendship with the boy's mother was too intimate to allow of his hurting her by a curt rejection; and that the somewhat comic appearance of the lad, if it did not exactly revolt him, at least gave him the opportunity of exercising his wit.

The less interest Louis showed in him, the warmer waxed Eugène's enthusiasm for the King. Louis was the pattern for his phantasy. He saw himself more and more, in his imagination, in the rôle of the King, being greeted by his mother with a low curtsy. But every day his imaginative faculty brought him a new disillusion, for, while he longed to be the centre figure of all around him, in reality, no one took the least notice of him. No one praised him when he stood beside his well-grown and upright brothers. "Poor little fellow," was the most they said, when in a race with his brothers, with teeth and fists clenched, he came in long, long last. No one dreamed that it was only by summoning all his strength that he managed to run at all. When he learned, in history, that children who were crippled and lacking in vitality were left by the Spartans exposed on the mountain of Taygetos, he gasped, "Why not in France as well? Why not me? Why all this bother of living when every movement is such a strain on the weak body that it necessitates taking a deep breath?" After every such moment of despondency Eugène would pull himself together. Because he was too frail to play with his brothers he was dependent upon himself for consolation, and pondered long over what would become of him if he were to overcome his weaknesses and survive his sickly childhood.

Such children mature very early.

Eugène wore his sorry abbé's habit as a cowl of penance. He had been unlucky from his earliest youth onwards. The head of his House, the reigning Duke of Savoy, had, when Eugène was only seven years old, proposed him as Abbé of Casa Nova and San Michele de Cluse. But the nomination was rejected by the Papal Court, the boy was told; and was allowed to infer that the Duke of Savoy had not offered sufficient support for him. He could thus only count on the King of France for his future career.

In whatever plans were discussed for his future, the King of France was invariably mentioned. Casa Nova and San Michele de Cluse, thought the child to himself; and asked to be shown maps. He wanted to see what had been refused him. There was Savoy, the land of his fathers, whose name he bore—the Abbé of Savoy. He followed round, with careful fingers, the frontiers of the various countries, and afterwards drew them in the sand of the park. Louis XIV was King of France: he wanted to be King of Savoy, and not to remain a pseudo-abbé.

His exaggerated sense of pride was wounded because his nomination had not been accepted by the Church, and the next time when the Court barber came—as he did every month—to cut the tonsure in his hair, Eugène defended himself with hands and feet. He had not become a real abbé, and therefore, he would not have the tonsure. But his resistance was useless: it was explained to him that in view of his proposed nomination the sign of priesthood had been cut permanently into his hair, and there it must remain. For, in consequence of his physical backwardness, no other career was to be thought of for him.

It was customary, in those days, for the younger sons of great families to be destined either for the Army or for the Church, since those professions presented the only possibilities of making a career. Such ecclesiastical offices had, however, nothing whatsoever to do with spirituality in any form; they merely presented a roundabout way of acquiring diplomatic and political posts. This had all been explained sufficiently often to Eugène, but he had become distrustful, and refused to believe any longer in his career as a Prince of the Church. He would probably have fallen into a more leisurely way of life, have become less nervously strained, and might have remained faithful to his original vocation, had he not been repelled by the disappointment of his early failure.

But to have a career was essential; conversation in the length and breadth of the Palais Soissons was never about anything else. With open mouth, his precocious gaze fixed on the lips of the speakers, Eugène listened at table whenever the various possibilities in the Army or at Court were discussed. Olympia, as Mazarin's niece and pupil, attracted all influential persons of both actual and potential importance into her circle, and already, in their earliest youth, had discussed with her children their future careers. She was supported in this by her ambitious mother-in-law, who, having promoted her son's *mésalliance*, now wished to have tangible benefits from it. Above all, the whole family had their eyes fixed on Savoy, where the reigning Duke was still without an heir, and his successor, Prince Emanuel Philibert of Savoy-Carignan, was a deaf mute and unmarried. Olympia's eldest son was, without doubt, predestined for the continuance of the Savoy line. But that was only one provided for—what of the others? After all, it was no small matter to bring up and maintain seven children. But, in what paths should their feet be directed? To begin with, Church livings had been provided for the second son, and for the third, who was to be an officer, the governorship of the province of Saluzze in Savoy. The fourth was so frail that his death might be reckoned with at any moment. There remained, therefore, the problem of Prince Eugène, the fifth child, who had begun his ecclesiastical career under such unfavourable circumstances. But the family were not worried about the matter—it was only essential that no possibility for the future be left unconsidered. After all, they had inherited not only money from Mazarin but influence as well, and, through marriages with the nobility and the reigning Princes, had established a network of connections over the whole Court. Olympia did the only thing possible : she left the children to their tutors and their individual inclinations, and began a correspondence with the Margrave of Baden, Eugène's married uncle. A Prince of Savoy to become a

German Prince of the Church ! That was a plan worthy of consideration. The post would provide a diplomatic support for the King in the Empire, out of which a position such as Mazarin's could be developed. But the thoughtful boy had decided otherwise for himself. He received with indifference news of the progress of negotiations in Germany, listened to his mother when she read his horoscope predicting high ecclesiastical honours (which he was in fact to receive later on), and did not read his future in the stars. He contented himself with his reality-nourished phantasy.

Childish wishes for the future are usually determined by overwhelming present impressions. Paris was at that time in a fever of excitement over Louis XIV's preparations for war : the town rang with his successes, and echoed with the extolling of his victorious arms. The Cardinal's crimson soutane, which for half a century had symbolised the power of the State, was, in the imagination of youth, overshadowed by the might of arms. Now it was no longer a question of diverting public attention from military activities by the ostentatious display of diplomatic success : on the contrary, the diplomatic measures were kept secret, while all war-like operations were made known, officially, to the public.

At the beginning of the epoch of Louis XIV, France was so obsessed with the brilliance of his arms, and their victories, that it is not surprising that Prince Eugène became absorbed in the idea of the military profession. It was the town topic, the daily source of novelties and surprises, which, in his family circle were discussed the more frequently, inasmuch as it was the nearest circle to the Court.

But what had happened in France since the death of Mazarin ? As far as was perceptible to Eugène, the emancipation of Louis from all controlling influences was the principal event. Perhaps, during Mazarin's lifetime, the Royal actor had only played to the gallery in filling his time with amusements, much in the same way as his grandfather, Henri IV, had played the part of the worldling before his friends, in order

THE PALAIS SOISSONS : EUGÈNE'S BIRTHPLACE

that, behind the coulisses of a gay life, he might devote himself to serious work.

The conjecture was a true one : the Cardinal had prepared his pupil (to whom he stood in *loco parentis*) for his future destiny. But the preparations had taken place unobtrusively, and had escaped the notice of the mighty ones at Court, so that the whole world was amazed when Louis, on the morning of the death of his fatherly friend, greeted his Ministers with the astounding words : " Gentlemen," he announced, " I have summoned you here to tell you that, while, up to the present, I have been content to leave my affairs in the hands of the late Cardinal, it is now time that I ruled myself. You will support me with your advice, whenever I ask for it, but I forbid you to do the smallest thing—even to sign a passport—without my express command. You will be accountable to me, in person, every day ; and I shall favour no one in particular."

Here was a declaration of government, which, made with a studied nonchalance and an impenetrable expression, did not fail to have its effect. It was, however, still believed at Court—and especially by Olympia, who wished to believe it—that the gay life which the King had led before taking over the reins of government would have the effect of deciding him, now that the whole burden of the State rested upon his shoulders, to abandon any attempt at dealing with it, and to give himself up entirely to amusement. Especially as the state of the world at the moment was such as to demand the closest attention of the diplomats. A young man who, up till then, had only amused himself, would not be capable of dealing with the intricacy of the tensely charged European situation.

Mazarin's nieces, who had grown up with Louis, still saw in him only the playmate of their childhood. They did not believe in his independence : he would soon rely on some Minister again, and could do so with impunity. After all, Mazarin had established order in the country, internally, and had left the King a full exchequer and excellent executive organisations. He was provided with a united France at his back, and all the subsidies for a prosperous reign. But the position outside the frontiers, since Mazarin's death, had become so intricate that only an experienced diplomat could encompass it. It was suggested to Louis that he should appoint Fouquet to be Mazarin's successor. But he rejected this offer with an odd and threatening smile; and soon this young man proved himself more capable of observation and perception than either his predecessor or the would-be successor to the latter.

He began with internal reforms in the most unexpected places. A short while beforehand, Fouquet had invited Louis to one of his castles. The Chief Steward of Finance—after Mazarin, the most influential man in France—had spent 700,000 marks, in the currency of to-day, on the supper which he gave in the King's honour. Louis ate and drank, and took careful note of the magnificence which was displayed on his account, acknowledging it all with an even politeness. Shortly afterwards, Fouquet, a close friend of Olympia's, turned to her for help. She was the only person who could save him. The walls of His Majesty's private cabinet were not thick enough—he had heard of his own imminent arrest. The reason was unknown, but the fact remained.

Olympia hurried to the King—she must speak to him at once. But, nowadays, it was no longer so easy for her, as in former times, to gain the presence of the friend of her youth. Colbert, who had administered her uncle's Chancery, guarded the King's threshold. Instead of the solicited help, Olympia could only bring Fouquet the cynical reply, which Colbert had put into Louis's mouth: "A man who, as subject and official, spends such sums in one evening, is either so rich that one can risk an injustice in confiscating his fortune, or so criminal, that an order of arrest is so much the more justified."

Fouquet's possessions were confiscated. Later, Prince Eugène obtained part of his wonderful collection of pictures, and hung them in the Belvedere in Vienna.

With the Lord High Steward the last great figure

disappeared from the public administration, and a complete re-distribution of posts took place. The officials from Mazarin's Cabinet, who had proved themselves trustworthy, took over the duties of Ministers of authority without acquiring the corresponding rights.

They were administrators who had to prove their worth by achievement, with no privileges of birth to help them: Colbert, who replaced Fouquet, and effected the transition of finance from the casual feudal system to that of commercial exactitude—Lyonne, a theorist of genius, who carried in his head a diplomatic lexicon—and, above all, Louvois, the son of an old functionary of Mazarin's, who, from childhood, had been his young monarch's accomplice in all youthful pranks and follies. He was a cynic through and through; devoid of heart or feeling of any kind; cunning from predilection, and, where circumstances allowed of it, brutal and overbearing. Already, as quite a young man, he had conducted affairs of military and political importance for his father, and, soon after the establishment of Louis's Government, became Minister of War.

Louvois, who organised the French Army, and brought it to a prime of perfection which was only equalled later by Napoleon, was the declared enemy of the family Soissons. It was through his machinations that Olympia was forced to emigrate from France, and, in consequence of his passivity in face of all requests for a post in the Army, that her son Eugène became a fugitive. Personal feelings here decided the issue. Louvois had himself first aspired to Olympia's heart, and then, when he saw that it belonged to the King, to her hand. In each case he had been rejected. For this, however, he had already forgiven the idol of his youth. He was of such low lineage that to his fanatical ambition it seemed quite natural that Olympia should prefer a Prince of Savoy. What he never forgave her was her refusal to give her daughter in marriage to his son, the Marquis de Louvois, thereby denying him the relationship with her dynasty.

The triad, Colbert, Lyonne, and Louvois, were responsible to Louis for the organisation of the State; but he arranged that no single one of them should be independent. He first ensured their mutual discord, and then, in addition, insisted on their reporting to him every one of their decrees in the fullest detail.

Amongst the innovations, the news of which, in consequence of Louis Thomas's preparation for a military career, penetrated the Palais Soissons, was the reorganisation of the Army, which produced the effect of a bombshell in the family. Louvois, this son of a common soldier, who sat in Mazarin's Cabinet, dared to punish members of the highest aristocracy, and actually to cashier them when they were guilty of such small breaches of order as that, perhaps, of disciplining their troops, a trifle autocratically, with the riding-whip ! He dared to deprive Marquises and Dukes of their swords when they neglected their military duties, or when they declared to the authorities a greater number of standing troops than they actually commanded in order to put the extra ration money into their own pockets ! In the end matters would come to such a pass that nobly born young men would be forced to submit to public drill ! Everyone was anxious and listened daily for fresh innovations. Lackeys were sent to copy the public placards from the walls, and to report exactly what the trumpeters—the living organs of official news—announced to the populace in the streets.

When Louvois was silent, Colbert took up the word ; but his decrees were only indirectly felt in the Palais Soissons. Olympia received a fixed income on account of her official position, and therefore had no grounds for combating Colbert's anti-corruptive measures ; she was only affected by the overthrow of the generous Fouquet, whose occasional gifts and financial assistance had been of no little importance, even to such an immense household as that of the Palais Soissons.

Only in the case of governors-general, and lords in waiting of highest rank amongst Olympia's nearer relations, did Louis desist from cutting their incomes, and only these were exempt from the new Finance Minister's decrees.

While their political influence was being more and more undermined, they continued, as before, to eat off gold plate, to pursue their nightly orgies, and to play cards for enormous sums, while each of their children held his little court and had his own tutor, horses, and servants.

Colbert's measures to raise the bourgeoisie to the rank of the smaller nobility gave national economy a fresh impetus, the benefits of which were translated by the Court into carouses and feasts of all kinds. Whoever was drawn into Louis's narrower circle had more than enough to do to ensure that he was suitably clad for every occasion, to wait until the King appeared, to take note of his mood, to observe with whom he spoke, and to hang on whatever marvellous words were formed by the Royal lips.

The high aristocracy were degraded to the status of Court nobility, to Louis's appanage. What happened at Court became the sole object of interest, dispute, and discussion in the princely palaces. The rising and going to bed of His Majesty, the dishes which he partook of, sitting in solitary state, waited on by the highest in the land, were the one and only theme. The King played the Comedy of the Centre, in every version.

To what extent he was, at the beginning of his reign, convinced of his own excellence is not certain; but the fact that later on he left, for his successor, instructions—which reveal an unequivocal contempt for human nature—of how a King should behave, would seem to show that he himself had followed the precepts of government of Mazarin, who had evidently explained to his Royal pupil that only he who places himself at the centre of a circle, and ignores what happens at the periphery, becomes himself the centre of that circle.

It is no wonder that the young as well as the old were obsessed by Louis XIV, and that he became the idol of the rising generation.

Eugène's life, up to a certain stage at least, is one great reaction to the life and deeds of Louis XIV. It can be observed already in his earliest youth, and it is even more

DE

apparent later on when he became leader of the combined enemies of the French King. The habit, which was forced upon him in his parent's house of noting Louis's every movement, and of listening—at least indirectly—to his every word and taking account of it to himself, predestined him to become either a devoted adherent or an enemy.

CHAPTER II

DIPLOMATIC AND MILITARY
INTERLUDE

IT IS UNLIKELY that in his early youth Eugène was capable of pronouncing judgment upon contemporary events, although, when a man at the age of thirty solely by his own efforts becomes a Field Marshal and diplomatic agent in the grand style, it may safely be taken for granted that even as a boy he had had his eyes open. In any case, later on, as a statesman, he was compelled to study the period with the greatest exactitude. The critical and decisive events for Eugène's future happened at that time.

The history of human development proves without any doubt that even the lives of the most talented and active men are dependent upon a finite series of the most varied influences and occurrences. No event can be separated from its context, because each is the consequence of earlier events.

Mazarin had prepared the ground. The rails on which Louis XIV's foreign policy was to run were already laid. He had only to drive in order to drive well. For instance, in the year 1657, when Louis was only nineteen years of age, Mazarin had tried to obtain for him the Crown of the Holy Roman Empire, and had attempted, by exerting pressure and by all other means, to influence the electors in his favour. As is shown in his letters, however, the Cardinal had not the smallest intention of actually obtaining the Crown for his sovereign. His was merely a manœuvre whereby, in exchange for the withdrawal of the King of France again from the narrow circle of candidates for the Imperial Crown, an assurance might be obtained from Leopold of Austria that in the event of a Franco-Spanish war he would desist from rendering assistance to Spain, either in the Netherlands or in Italy.

A year later the Rhine Covenant was accomplished, and amounted to a union of the Rhenish Princes, which included the membership of France. The agreement was one that, for Mazarin, meant nothing more than the means of obtaining for France later on, and under certain conditions, the right of interference in German affairs. These alliances, officially intended to uphold the Peace of Westphalia, were later converted by Louis into a pretext for engaging in his first war. With a vast army behind him, and every frontier secured by treaties, he was in a key position to undertake a war with every assurance of success.

The adults were informed at Court, and the children by their tutors, that His Majesty King Louis XIV was justified in the eyes of God and man when he put his cavalry into a trot, loaded the siege machines invented by his gifted engineer, Vauban, on to mighty wagons, and sent them all to the frontiers of the Spanish Netherlands!

At first Eugène was certainly not aware of the subtlety with which Louis constructed his pretexts for starting a war. It was only later on that, in spite of the cleverly manufactured appearance of legitimacy, he realised that the King's invasion of the Netherlands was nothing less than predatory warfare.

The King of Spain, father of Louis's wife—of whose existence her husband only became aware when questions of inheritance were raised—had died. In Brabant, and in several of the neighbouring provinces, the peculiar legalised custom prevailed whereby rights of inheritance belonged exclusively to the children of a first marriage, and, from the moment of a second union, the actual inheritance immediately passed over, or "devolved" (to use the technical expression) on to them. This entirely local and civilly valid right was transferred to the political sphere.

Now the moment had come when Mazarin's foresight proved itself justified. The renunciation of her rights of inheritance on the part of Louis's wife, the former Infanta, was declared invalid in virtue of the principle of mental reservation—and by Louis's command. He appealed to the fact that the young French Queen, in the first place, had not received the dowry which had been stipulated as a condition of her renunciation, and secondly that at the time of the drafting of the act of renunciation she was a minor, which, according to Spanish law, *eo ipso*, invalidated any renunciation of a right to primogeniture. It can be seen that Louis manipulated law internationally; that is to say, he used the law of each country to his own ends when and where he pleased. He had not married for pleasure; indeed, on the contrary, he had had to give up the pleasures of Maria Mancini at the time of his marriage.

He despatched a manifesto to Madrid, defending the nullity of his wife's renunciation, and placing the soundness of the right of devolution on a moral basis, from which he condemned the immoderacy of a second marriage.

The document, which publicly denounced the immorality of the second marriage of a widower, was signed by Louis at a time when for a long while, besides a legitimate mistress, he had spared no woman at Court who was even passably attractive.

There can hardly be a doubt that, in putting his signature to this document, he wrote it with a contemptuous smile of amusement.

Whether the transparency of this moral screen was perceived at Court and in the Palais Soissons is hard to tell. France was in a state of turmoil, for hardly had the manifesto been despatched than the news of the first victories reached Paris. Several Netherland provinces had been taken without resistance, and the army under Turenne's leadership continued to march forward in the direction which the King had drawn for it on the map.

The power of Spain lay broken, although the Queen Regent still wished to continue with the struggle against Louis XIV. But her declaration of war was merely a manifesto on paper, in virtue of which the Spanish Governor of the Netherlands, to a certain extent as a matter of form, mobilised an insignificant number of troops.

By a brilliant piece of diplomacy the Netherlands were completely isolated and abandoned to their own weakness.

At the Court of Vienna, the French ambassador, Gremonville, had entered into a close relationship with the Imperial Minister, Prince Wenzel Lobkowitz. This relationship benefited both men. Gremonville could boast of being able to accomplish anything he wished at the Austrian Court, while Lobkowitz became one of the richest men in the country. Louis's Minister had a free hand, the more so as he was allowed unlimited access to the State exchequer. Gremonville coolly completed a treaty of partition, which was composed as though Charles II, the minor King of Spain and seven-year-old son of Philip's second marriage, no longer lived; and as though there were nothing to do but to settle the division of territory between France and Austria!

Gremonville treated the conclusion of the contemporary war as unimportant. The whole thing was a comedy. Whenever Lobkowitz introduced—however unwillingly, but from a sense of duty—the question of peace, the French ambassador immediately claimed for his sovereign the whole of the Duchy of Luxembourg, or, if not Luxembourg, then the Tyrol! In his opinion the state of the campaigns was sufficient indication of how the frontiers of France were to be drawn!

England and Holland both heard of the claim. The two sea Powers were compelled, for the benefit of their Parliaments, to protest loudly; although, secretly, they had already promised Louis's diplomatic representatives that if Spain refused to make peace, they would force her to do so—even if Louis did not withdraw from the invaded territories. Louis had no intention of withdrawing: on the contrary, the alliance was a pretext for him to send a new army into the Tyrol! The defenceless provinces were occupied within fourteen days. The Dutch general de Witt, and Charles II, appeared to be beside themselves with wrath. Holland mobilised, and the King of England was voted three hundred thousand pounds sterling by Parliament for the purpose of engaging in war. But the whole game was preconcerted.

In England, a Stuart reigned once more—Charles II, whose relationship with France was compromised by the receipts which he had handed over to French agents in return for a previous declaration of agreement with Louis XIV's enterprises. Jean de Witt was several years later torn to pieces in the streets by the people for his exaggerated submission to France.

Each of these men had fulfilled his duty to his country in effecting peace, and Louis XIV was now ready for peace.

The consequences were obvious. The King of England had no further need to use the three hundred thousand pounds voted him by Parliament for the purpose of raising troops; he could spend the money on his own personal pleasures, and procure for himself mistresses delivered from France! De Witt could send his troops home; France was satisfied with the fortresses she had seized from him, and graciously accepted the territories that were now legally awarded to her.

The Royal actor had shown himself in the most favourable light on all sides. He counted now as the greatest ruler on earth, and his position in the world can best be estimated by reading the report sent by the Venetian ambassador in Paris to the neutral signoria in the doge's palace: " It is certain that the excellent qualities of France have procured for her her present position in the world; and that from there only, may the arts of war be learned. Power and might are to be expected from there. Louis XIV excels his predecessors to such a degree both in heroic qualities and in good fortune that his Government receives its form and power and indeed its whole essence from him alone."

The young Eugène could well be satisfied with his idol.

CHAPTER III

IN A FEW YEARS Paris was transformed and presented a gay and festive appearance. On every corner old houses were pulled down to give place to palaces, and great squares were built around the huge monuments. The whole world talked of a gigantic plan of the King's : to build in Versailles, an hour's distance from the city, in place of the small hunting-box which stood on the marshy land out there, the most magnificent residence that ever a monarch had inhabited.

Louis's activities set the whole population astir ; every day brought a new rumour or a new event. The factory workers forgot what it was to have a holiday ; in the cannon foundries there was a whirl of activity. New troops were recruited unceasingly, and the barracks were filled to overflowing. Every day dozens of horses were broken in, and yet more and more peasants were taken from the plough, and farm horses from the land. In the midst of this feverish production and prodigious preparation for some unknown event, which was heard of outside the frontiers with apprehension and helpless foreboding, everyone in Paris asked themselves : Why ? Wherefore ? War again ? Against whom, this time ? No one knew for certain. Everyone had to be content with the answer : It is the will of the King.

Well, then, war it must be !

If anyone was satisfied with the state of things, it was the young Eugène. He dragged his tutor, Sauveur, more and more frequently to the map of France and the surrounding countries, and tried to understand the meaning of frontiers and the reason of their frequent disparity with the natural constitution of the land. Why, for instance, should they lead over mountain ranges and rivers into countries where foreign languages were spoken and strange customs prevailed ? He wanted to learn the diplomatic multiplication table systematically, and above all to discover how it had come to pass that the geographical and political frontiers so often differed. But Sauveur was Eugène's mathematical tutor, who had gained the post by virtue of being a noted scholar and a pupil of Vauban, the chief engineer of the Army. He was an arithmetician through and through, a theorist who very unwillingly let himself be diverted from his numbers to discuss political problems. He had been engaged to teach Eugène the fundamental principles of arithmetic and geometry ; but this ugly youth had learned those principles with such zeal that, actually, Sauveur ought to have made his adieux and declared his mission fulfilled.

He naturally wished to retain such a lucrative post, but how could he teach politics of which he understood nothing ? No ! But as Eugène was so thirsty for knowledge, and so interested in frontiers, he would talk to him instead out of the mouth of Vauban's school, and explain how home frontiers were defended and enemy frontier forts taken. That was a subject about which he knew something. It was certainly not easy to understand why Monseigneur the Abbé of Savoy should be interested in such things, but there it was ! If he mastered his appointed *pensum* in Latin and in canon law as rapidly as he had mastered his mathematics, then Sauveur's colleague of the other faculty, who instructed him in languages, could also quench his thirst for political knowledge !

But the colleague was a priest who answered his pupil's every question with the monotonous phrase : " Monseigneur, God has willed it so ! " Eugène would have to discover some other way of finding out what he wanted to know. Sauveur advised him : " Do not ask too much, Highness ! Listen rather to what is spoken around you, and draw your own conclusions."

That was a piece of advice which suited the silent, thoughtful, ever-observant youth. But it was easier said than done. The life of a young Prince was almost that of a prisoner in a gilded cage, and, at first, Eugène was thrown back on what he heard in his own family.

That was not much, as he had already realised. Problems of State formed no part of the conversation in the Palais Soissons, which, for the most part, was concerned with intrigues and personal details from the King's life, both of which annoyed Eugène, inasmuch as they showed his idol in another light, and one that in nowise resembled that of the reflected splendour of the sun.

What Eugène did learn in his family circle was not reassuring. Olympia and her seven children were not the only inhabitants of the Palais Soissons. The Count's mother, Bourbon by birth, was the real owner of the palace. She lived in the left wing with her daughter, the Margravine of Baden, who, after six months of marriage, had gone back to her mother, and, after the birth of her son, refused to return to her husband's Court. She pleaded, as excuse for her behaviour, childish obedience to her mother, who, directly after the wedding, had quarrelled with the Margrave, and was only too glad to strike a blow at her son-in-law through his marriage. Although the whole family, the House of Savoy and the Court, were on the side of the Margrave, mother and daughter remained implacable, and when the little Prince was removed by stratagem from the Palais Soissons and taken to Baden both mother and grandmother declared that they wished to have nothing more to do with the child. That was for the world to hear; but the young Margrave, who later became the famous Field Marshal and Eugène's protector at the Court of Vienna, was the cause of incessant strife between mother and daughter. They quarrelled so violently that more than one complaint was made to the King of the thoroughly unseemly conduct of the two Princesses. But whenever a mediator appeared the two combined to form a united front against him, and behaved so disgracefully that soon the left wing of the Palais Soissons was completely shunned. When, in spite of this, the two ladies went to Court, their manner was so boastful and arrogant that they were left standing isolated in the *salons*.

Finally, the King, on the grounds of their indiscreet conversation, forbade them the entrée.

Eugène could hope to gain neither connections nor information from such an aunt and grandmother. Besides, his existence had too little prospect of success to please the two women, who, in spite of their retirement, were filled with ambition for the family. Only a male member of the House of Savoy could avenge them on Louis, who had so completely isolated them. But this misshapen dwarf was no use ! Sauveur's advice could not be carried out. Eugène was not sufficiently important for anyone to discuss weighty matters with him. He was the scapegoat of his environment. The ingenuous Liselotte of the Palatinate acknowledges frankly that as a child he was " often tormented."

Eugène was treated in his family with unfeeling compassion. Nobody as yet believed that his will to live—seeing that he had been put into the world—was strong enough to overcome his inborn weakness. His brothers ridiculed him whenever he announced that he wished to be a soldier, however much, by physical performance, he attempted to prove his capabilities. No one thought it even probable that he would survive adolescence, especially as his brother—one year older than himself, and equally sickly—had died young.

That had been a terrible blow for Eugène, for it left him the weakest and feeblest of them all. During the last days and nights of the hopeless struggle for the life of the elder brother, he never moved out of the sick-room, and held the dying boy's hand as though he would keep him alive by force. Between-whiles he fell asleep, and, half in a dream, saw the pale, wasted face of Emmanuel on his own shoulders ; the wax-like hands became his own, the heart that was too weak to drive the blood through the veins was his. The breathing stopped, and the body stiffened. He imagined himself dying like Emmanuel, lying stretched out in the last state of exhaustion, caressed by his mother's hand, and knowing that the King was coming on tiptoe into the room ! In Eugène's fancy, the King was standing at the foot of his bed, his great curled wig sunk on his breast. Outside, in the

Court of Honour, the musketeers were marching in line, the trumpeters blew the alarm. It was a clear and stirring note, which sounded like the roll-call when, in the barrack-yard, the troops were drilling. Why was his mother crying? The King made the sign of the cross. A priest removed his skull-cap, and there was the tonsure cut round in his hair! But, suddenly, on the right-hand side of the priest's head a flowing wig appeared, and flowed over the shorn hair! It was too strange! The priest's hair on the right-hand side was dressed like a soldier's! A straight parting appeared, and then the left-hand side of the head seemed also to be covered by a wig. The curls, and the pattern of the left-hand wig, were those of a statesman or diplomat of the highest rank. In his feverish phantasy, Eugène saw the symbolic image of his future career. Beneath the Janus-headed wig, instead of the broad, satisfied physiognomy of a priest in prayer, he saw his own narrow, sunken face. The mouth, open, as always, exposed the bare front teeth; in full face, instead of the short, turned-up nose, only the round, dark nostrils were to be seen. His animated eyes looked incessantly to the right and to the left, or were bent on Vauban's plans of forts, which Sauveur was explaining with cold fervour.

Eugène lay for several weeks in high fever, tormented by the fear that he was destined to follow his brother, and would never be able to wear the decorative wig that he had seen in his dream. He intended to go on living, even though the doctors standing around shrugged their shoulders, and his mother cursed the fate that threatened, within so short a space of time, to rob her of two sons.

Her despair made him happy. He had never before experienced such tenderness from her. She had always been, for him, the unapproachable jewelled vision before whom even the King made respectful obeisance. Now she was close to him—very close—and held his wasted body pressed against her. She had long forgotten the superstitious beliefs of her horoscope cabinet, and prayed to God in simple, heart-felt words, in her mother tongue, for the life of her child.

But afterwards, when Eugène was slowly convalescing,

she took up her Court life and habits again, wore once more the stiff hooped petticoat with the pearl-bedecked pointed bodice when she came into the sick-room, and, in the manner of an inspectress, examined the reports of her son's progress. Her astrological secretary, who was said to have long since foretold Eugène's recovery from the stars, followed in her train. Soon she was as unapproachable as before, and, when Eugène childishly begged her to stay, impressed upon him that, after all, she was the stewardess of the Royal household, and night and day was claimed by her duties at Court.

In reality, Olympia had become a passionate intriguer, to the consternation of all the King's official and unofficial mistresses, for at times Louis appeared exclusively taken up with the friend of his youth, and awakened the general belief that he might, after all, go back to his first love. But for the King the evenings which he spent in the Palais Soissons were a welcome rest from the debauches of the Court, and an attempt to enjoy in a family circle festivities of a simpler and more homely character than those at which he was forced to play host in his own palace. But the alleged simplicity can only have been comparative, for eye-witnesses testify to the fabulous brilliance of Madame la Comtesse and her entertainments, and, amongst other things, to the skill of her cook, who was accustomed to prepare for the Royal guest an olive salad of which the single olives formed the stuffing for quails, then the quails for partridges, the partridges for pigeons, the pigeons for chickens, the chickens for sucking-pigs, and, finally, the sucking-pigs for calves, which were then roasted on the spit, so that the stoned olives soaked up the juices from each of the different kinds of meat! It can well be imagined that Louis ate more than one of the olives prepared in this way, and, also, what it must have cost to prepare the salad in sufficient quantities for thirty or forty people—to say nothing of the other luxuries which were served up! But Olympia's sumptuousness was, after all, only that of the average princely house of that time in which the King was a regular guest, and probably did not differ greatly from other households of the same rank.

Another special attraction for Louis XIV was the fact that Olympia considered it a duty and privilege of her intimacy with the King to arrange new love-affairs for him. It was important to banish the gentle La Vallière from the Royal bed, and Olympia suggested a substitute in the person of one, Mlle Lamotte Houdancourt, who, by means of her lovely body and witty letters, held the King's fancy until, one day, he discovered that the letters were written by Olympia, and that the physical charms bored him !

Both she and La Vallière, in spite of all Olympia's intrigues and efforts to the contrary, were replaced by the Montespan, an official friend of Louvois's, who possessed the good qualities of Madame la Comtesse combined with an unusually attractive appearance. Apparently, Louvois, besides his exertions in the Ministry of War, found time to organise feminine warfare ! He did it with circumspection. Eugène's mother fell into one trap after another, and each time lost favour in the eyes of the King, until at length she embarked on a campaign of despair.

In that particular year she had time for nothing else. She was so obsessed with the idea of emphasising her position that she begged her brother-in-law Carignan, the deaf-mute Emanuel Philibert, to look after her children for her. The Prince did not have to bother about his brother's eldest son. He was the Soissons heir—or would be at the death of his grandmother—but, in any case, Louis Thomas would automatically rise in the world. He was liked by the King, who was not only personally attracted to him, but, because he was likely to become a reigning Prince, bestowed upon him every possible favour for which, later, repayment might be claimed. The second brother, Philip, Chevalier of Savoy, had, like Eugène, been destined for the Church ; but already, at the age of fourteen, he was permitted to enter the military academy to prepare for a career in the Army. His life was by no means a model one, and, although he became a soldier, he stayed safely behind the lines, and later, at Court, appropriated Eugène's military successes to himself ! Saint-Simon sums up his life in a few words : " The Chevalier of Savoy died young, over-burdened with Holy livings and debaucheries."

Emanuel sent for the third brother to go to Savoy to prepare himself for war service in his native Piedmont.

And Eugène?

It is evident that all his brothers were assisted, rather than hindered, in their military aspirations, not even excepting the one who had been definitely predestined for the Church. That was another piece of bad luck for Eugène; for, although Philip entered the military academy, he still drew revenues from ecclesiastical posts which he never actually held; and thus nothing was left over for Eugène, whose family, after his illness, had finally decided that he alone of the brothers should become a priest.

His unwillingness to adopt this career, and how unmistakably he showed his dislike of it, can be elicited from a letter of Liselotte's, who appears to have taken careful note of his development : " I knew him very well," she writes. " While he was yet a child, they wanted to make a priest of him and dressed him in an abbé's habit; but I always assured him that he would not remain one for long—and what I said came to pass." Prince Carignan had less foresight than Liselotte. He exerted every effort to acquire for Eugène the Canon's living, either in Cologne or in Luettich —posts which had long been claimed for him by correspondence. The Margrave, Ferdinand Maximilian of Baden, Carignan's brother-in-law and husband of the obstinate Louise Christine, had played the part of mediator; but, in spite of all efforts, this further attempt towards an ecclesiastical career for Eugène was condemned to failure.

An exchange of letters between the Margrave of Baden and the Prince Carignan, as well as reports from Knörr, the Councillor of the Crown Lands of Baden, to Baron von Greifen, High Chamberlain of the Court of Baden, then resident in Turin, testify to this early failure of Eugène's.

But the refusal came just at a time when Olympia was in a position of complete isolation at Court—the result of her disfavour in the eyes of the King. Had Louis discovered some harmless intrigue of hers, or surprised her in some act of betrayal of confidence ? Or had Louvois and the Montespan definitely achieved the upper hand and defeated her once and for all ? She did not know. She only realised that she had become as air to the King—that he did not seem to notice her presence, and neither spoke to her nor visited her any more. She felt guilty, but decided that her real crime could not possibly have been discovered, or there would have been a *lettre de cachet* at least, if not an order of arrest, as a result of the discovery. It would be better for her not to show herself again until grass had grown over the plot which she and the midwife Deshayes, a person of disrepute called La Voisin, had hatched. The " poisonous " Catherine, to whom Olympia had turned in her need and affliction, was a fortune-teller like Madame la Comtesse herself—a worthless counterpart to the father, Mancini. But La Voisin did not confine herself to reading the stars. She was of very earthly mould, sold love potions, and, above all, " heritage powders," with the aid of which unwanted relations could be despatched into the Beyond !

At the onset of the King's disfavour, Olympia preferred to banish the thought that the plan which she had fabricated with the " poisonous " Catherine could ever be brought to light. She pursued an ostrich policy, and told herself that the incessant struggle for power had left her tired and exhausted ; and that instead of continuing with it she would retire from Court for a while. During this time of exclusion she found an unexpected friend. Eugène had ripened in years during his convalescence. He felt now an inner conviction of having passed through the danger zone for his health, was certain that his body was strengthened, and that now all he had to do was to develop his brain in order to achieve the object on which, in his taciturn, reserved way, he had silently set his heart. His youthful programme was the subject of a letter which, nearly sixty years later, he wrote to the then twenty-two-year-old Frederick the Great, fully conscious that he represented the historical connecting-link between Louis XIV's epoch and that of the representative

Prussian king. "Always set before you a higher aim. Make your plan as wide and comprehensive as possible, in the knowledge that one is always a long way behind one's goal. Meditate unceasingly on your handiwork, your own enterprises, and those of earlier commanders. Such meditation is the only means by which a quickness of decision can be achieved, which grasps the situation at once, and devises all the practicable possibilities which the conditions afford." With such a credo in his heart, and, above all, in his head, a man becomes very easily clairvoyant about what happens in his immediate environment. Eugène was certainly no mother's boy, although at the time of his weakness he would gladly have been one. But his inward aspirations made of him a conscientious son. From her distractedness he had deduced that his mother was in need of help. Why had she ceased going to Court, and why did the King never come to see her now? The Palais Soissons was deserted: why were there no more guests? Eugène sought out the lonely woman in her magic cabinet, and asked her questions. At first she answered him unwillingly, then more and more frankly, until, at length, the feeling grew upon her that the Little Abbé who stood before her, apparently concentrated on the horoscope tablets, and only casually letting questions fall, yet in such a way that an answer had to be given—that this young man in the priest's robe was her uncle Mazarin himself, or, at all events, a being of his quality and domination.

Her subtle intelligence, which had come into contact with the greatest diplomats of the period, appreciated the precocious political talent of her youngest son, and, above all, recognised that she could have confidence in him.

Now a strangely stirring time began for Olympia. She could, as it were, soliloquise in his presence, and pour out all the repressed bitterness and bad humour that was in her. Her listener remained unmoved, only here and there putting a casual leading question which contained the answer to all her statements. The whole life of the Court, as well as her personal life, lay spread out before Eugène. He understood it, and reviewed it all, without betraying by a sign that he recognised it as the life around him and the reality which he breathed.

Only once did she see emotion cause the pale cheeks of the Little Abbé to redden—and that was when she spoke too vehemently of the King. Perhaps it had only been the reflection of her red velvet dress! But she became cautious. The slim, nervous, childish hands had all too suddenly and noticeably busied themselves with the retorts and glasses on her table. The King, then, was the vulnerable spot in the boy's phantasy? Here was his Achilles' heel! The King, with whom she was in disfavour, who did not call her to his side, who neither asked after her nor came to see her!

In the stories she told him, she lifted ever more the exalted ermine: Eugène should learn to know his future King in all his vanity, in all his ruthlessness—the man as he really was. But she must be careful—very careful—not to give herself away, even in the smallest degree, to her son, in case she should afterwards become reconciled with Louis! He was, after all, the King, and in order that Eugène might approach him dispassionately he must first learn to know him and his faults, so that he might not burn his fingers at the fictitious spotlessness of the Roi Soleil.

But Eugène saw through her caution, and evolved the formula out of his head. But he kept it to himself. The King was a man. This *constatation* carried nothing depreciatory with it. "A man like myself, made of flesh and blood," he reflected. The comparison with his own bodily inferiority counted so much in the King's favour that, in spite of everything, the ideal was nourished by the blood of the boy's admiration of physical beauty. He still experienced an enthusiastic affection for Louis, slightly tinted by his own Platonic idealism.

He did not worry about it. His programme of work had been so much enlarged by the results of the encounter with his mother that time was now very short. He was so full of thoughts and plans that he would have to eliminate his own person altogether. Olympia had told him more than once that, beside her eldest son, she had set her greatest hopes on him. He must manage to achieve as much as Louis Thomas, who on account of his seniority, was almost certain of attaining a throne. He must manage to achieve not only as much, but more—far more. But how? That "how" tormented his brain.

Yes, he would even consider the ecclesiastical-diplomatic profession which they were trying to force upon him—he would leave nothing out of account, and would learn everything there was to learn! But the time of Cardinals was over. Had not Louis XIV begun war again, in spite of all the diplomatic bolts which had been pushed home for him? What was the might of a Prince of the Church compared with that of a Field Marshal? It was plain for all to see that the might of arms was supreme.

He held animated conversations with his mother until he forced her to agree to his reading history, making himself acquainted with the biographies of famous commanders, and learning the theory of strategy.

Olympia did this with no thought of her backward son himself ever becoming a general. She merely thought that it might be of use to him to understand the military operations which formed the basis of diplomatic negotiations. Unconcernedly she let him go into raptures over the sound of trumpets and drums, and made no objections when he watched military parades rather than processions, and read reports of battles and sieges rather than the breviary.

CHAPTER IV
DIPLOMATIC AND MILITARY INTERLUDE

Eugène only studied the history of past wars for comparison's sake. He read Cæsar's *De Bello Gallico*, and the histories of Roman battles on the banks of the Rhine, but held his gaze firmly fixed on the movements of the French armies, who now, seventeen hundred years later, marched like the Roman legions in the direction of the Rhine. On further meditation the comparison must hold a deeper significance : The Rhine was, surely, more than a mere geographical boundary between two States—was it not rather the symbolical dividing-line between two worlds, the centres of eternal strife ?

When Sauveur appeared in the ceremonial garb which was *de rigueur* for the tuition hours of His Highness, the Little Abbé, who was otherwise so controlled in his demeanour, would seize him boldly by the pockets, and ask anxiously whether he had brought new plans or models of the siege machines ? Was there any fresh news ? The best troops had been despatched to the north ! " Holland is being attacked, Monsieur Sauveur—Why Holland ? " A definite reason was lacking ! Was it only because enlightened Holland was a republic, and a supporter of world peace ?

Certainly the public thought otherwise than the democratically minded Sauveur. No one knew anything of the secret agreement which had been made previously between the King and de Witt. The leaders of the Dutch Government were looked upon as presumptuous tradesmen, and propagandists of all manner of republican institutions, who deserved an exemplary chastisement on the part of the great King whose victorious progress in the Netherlands was hindered by their pretended alliance with England.

The true state of affairs was quite different. Colbert had not only improved the State institutions, created the mercantile system with protecting tariffs to prevent the import of foreign goods, improved the roads and constructed new canals, he had also founded colonies in the Little Antilles, in Canada, in Cayenne, Louisiana, and Pondicherry, increased the Navy, created a mercantile fleet, and now saw himself faced on all seas and in every colony with the competition of the Dutch fleet of merchantmen. Indeed, the Dutch Navy was far superior to the budding French sea trade, especially overseas, where the great Dutch monopoly companies often suppressed by violent means the efforts of foreign Powers to gain a foothold on the other side of the ocean.

Thus it happened that the Most Christian King felt himself constrained, in the name of the Church, to organise a crusade to overthrow Protestant Holland.

That was, of course, merely propaganda to win confederates, a clumsy trap in which most of the Catholic States obligingly allowed themselves to be caught, while, in spite of the attack on their faith, the neutrality of the Protestant States was bought with cash and the double-tongued explanation that the religious war was merely a pretext.

As in the case of his predatory war engagements, Louis XIV had protected himself by preliminary treaties, the most important of which was made with the Emperor, who thereby bound himself not to interfere in any war that took place outside Germany or Spain, and to lend no assistance to any of France's enemies.

This treaty was a piece of diplomatic ingenuity on the part of Gremonville, the French Ambassador, who took advantage of the Imperial Prime Minister's fear of his own Government by threatening him with exposure of his earlier traitorous correspondence with France if he did not succeed in concluding the agreement. Once more, Lobkowitz renounced, on behalf of Austria, the rôle of a great Power, to the advantage of her most dangerous enemy.

Now there was only the conclusion of an agreement with Sweden to be achieved, and the last remaining State would be won over in the struggle against Holland.

But the Dutch were also aware of this fact; and there followed a regular bargaining of the worst kind for the coveted support of Sweden. It was just an auction, which promised success to the highest bidder—and Colbert had made ample provision beforehand that his sovereign should be the highest bidder.

Louis was so sure of his success that he actually started hostilities before the treaty was signed!

One hundred and twenty thousand men stood in readiness —troops who marched past the Palais Soissons with trumpets and drums and flags flying, and caused the heart of the war-loving Little Abbé to beat faster.

"That is Vauban's doing," explained Sauveur, when, within a few days, the French troops had taken all the forts of the Duchy of Cleves, which, although they actually belonged to the Elector of Brandenburg, were held by the Dutch in pursuance of a claim for the repayment of old debts.

The Dutch were powerless. It seemed as though Nature itself were on the side of their overwhelmingly powerful enemy. The summer was hot and arid, and the great rivers, behind which they had imagined themselves unassailable, dried up into shallow, easily fordable rivulets. The downfall of Holland seemed certain.

That was Louis's opinion also—a single campaign should be sufficient to end the war. Already, in Paris, the names were cited of the French officers whom he had chosen to command the Dutch forts before even they were besieged; and already the conquest of the entire Spanish Netherlands, the subjection of the left bank of the Rhine, and, in fact, the complete subjugation of Europe, were expected.

Madame de Sévigné, who reproduces very faithfully the moods of the French Court, wrote at that time : " The King's success is so complete that in future he will only have to announce which piece of European territory he desires and it will be given to him willingly, without its being necessary for him to go to the trouble of marching at the head of his armies."

But, of the Germany that was enervated as a result of the Thirty Years War, Louis XIV had forgotten one State, which lay rather outside the radius of his politics, and which, perhaps as a consequence of the Thirty Years War, had grown to be an important Power. In Brandenburg, over the territory of the Prussia of to-day, the Great Elector reigned.

Simultaneously with France, Frederick William had undertaken a reorganisation of his State, had concentrated all resources, and was the only reigning Prince to recognise that in Holland not only the lesser interests of the great German confederation must be defended, but the existence of Germany itself. The occupation of Cleves, his own territory which had been distrained by the Dutch, provided him with a pretext for offering his alliance to Holland. The panic-stricken de Witts hardly seemed to take note of his offer, and the Elector was obliged to force the Covenant upon them. Not only that : he then forced the House of Habsburg, in the person of the Emperor, whose part it was to summon *him* to protect the Empire, to tear up the treaty which he had made a year previously. Lobkowitz was deposed, and the Brandenburger succeeded in making an agreement with the Emperor which would secure the terms of the earlier-concluded treaties.

It was high time that something happened : the French troops had crossed the Rhine for the first time.

A triumphal arch was erected in Paris, and Boileau, and a number of other hymn-writers who aspired to be Court poets, praised Louis's deeds, and set him up above Cæsar as a great captain. They pointed out how colossal the effort had been for the great Roman to cross the Rhine, and how easily Louis XIV had achieved it !

But the unresisted advance had been witnessed by the whole army. The excessive praise of the flatterers evoked secret mockery on the part of the officers and men of the army. They knew better than Boileau and his colleagues (or, as well, at any rate) that the valiant crossing of the Rhine had not been much more than a stroll across well-built boat-bridges, which, without a single enemy in sight, had been thrown elegantly across the river. In the eyes of sober critics an advance made with such overwhelming superiority of strength was no war : it was nothing but the annexation of an almost disowned property. Napoleon later described this heroic deed of Louis's as a fourth-rate operation.

The Parisians, when the King was once more within their walls, suppressed their mockery ; but Louis felt himself a hero, and would not have been the least affected by Napoleon's criticism. The laughter of the disrespectful did not reach his ears. He only recognised one fact—that the war had been, from every point of view, a successful one, and particularly from the material standpoint !

There exists, to this day, a note of Louis XIV's containing a command which culminates in the words, "*manger le pays*," meaning, " to consume the occupied territory." War levies, foraging expeditions and sequestrations were the order of the day. There is also a letter in existence, from Louvois, the War Minister, to the Marshal of Luxembourg, which runs : " Although the King is firmly convinced that you have robbed him well in the land from which you have come, yet His Majesty is quite content with what you have left him."

Such letters were common property in the French palaces. Louvois's enemies, headed by Olympia, endeavoured to undermine the moral credit of the all-powerful War Minister by the circulation of the contents of these letters. Louvois and his orders were held up as a warning example in the Palais Soissons, and Eugène, in later years, in dealing with subjugated territories in his own campaigns, took this warning example to heart, and firmly forbade any kind of plundering.

Just the pitilessness of the French troops in occupied territory had the effect of setting the whole of Europe against

TRIUMPHAL ARCH BUILT IN HONOUR OF LOUIS XIV. IN THE BACKGROUND: PARIS IN THE YEAR 1673

Louis. The able French diplomacy proved weaker than the panicky fear of the European dynasties that they would be subjugated, not only at the conference table, but in entirety. The King was forced to the decision to evacuate Holland. His German confederates deserted him and allied themselves with the Emperor ; and finally, the Holy Roman Empire declared war against France.

But European unity was unity only on paper ; and while the Allied States were failing to agree amongst themselves on a plan of campaign—on the principle that too many cooks spoil the broth—Vauban, under the nominal supreme command of the King, suddenly attacked the Tyrol. In six weeks the conquest of the province was complete, and, at the same time, Louis succeeded in raising enemies to attack the Allies from the rear.

Eugène's future was thus prepared for him in Turkey and in Hungary. The Imperial armies which embarrassed the French King on the Rhine and in Holland would now be needed in the east of the Empire more than in the west.

This plan of Louis's indicated Eugène's converse plan when, twenty years afterwards, the Prince of Savoy did battle in the east against his erstwhile King, on the same piece of territory where Louis XIV was now stirring up trouble in order to draw off the Imperial armies. Eugène's later plan was to make the east safe for the Empire, so as to have the full complement of arms released for the war with France.

Turkey and Hungary, whom Louis incited to rebellion, had already been Mazarin's guests at the French Court. Already at that time, the Cardinal had sent his agents to Prince Rakoczy in Upper Hungary, and to the Sultan in the Sublime Porte. He had foreseen that an attack in the rear of the Imperial Power would be necessary in order to lessen France's burden, and he had prepared the ground in such a way that his Royal pupil only needed, as it were, to press a button in order to set the insurrection in motion.

Certainly, Louis XIV had himself contributed a certain amount to the preparations in the east. With his assistance

John Sobieski had become King of Poland, and partly through his French wife, but chiefly on account of a yearly income, he had been won over to the side of France. Emmerich Tökölly, a twenty-year-old nobleman, became the exponent of the French agitations in Hungary, which were reinforced from Poland. But the clumsy behaviour of the Imperial officials was the greatest help to French diplomacy.

Soon the whole Magyar population was in mutiny. The Rhine was very far from Vienna, and the Emperor, in order to protect his own residence, was obliged to withdraw troops from the French front and hurl them on to the lower Danube.

The breathing spaces between these military operations, which Eugène followed on the map with the keenest interest, afforded him an opportunity of drawing comparisons between the heroes of antiquity and the generals whom he saw at work. His favourite literature was, at that time, Q. Curtius Rufus and the Latin biography of Alexander. He took the career of the young Macedonian as a pattern. But Alexander's actions were very different from Louis's. In Curtius, Eugène read of the phalanx at the head of which Alexander the Great cut through the Persian battle lines, always risking his own life whenever it was necessary to do so. But what of Louis XIV, the man of laurel-wreaths, who built triumphal arches, and in whose honour hymns of praise were written? He had ordered a new attack in the Netherlands, and the news of the fall of one fort after another reached a jubilant Paris. The King was to join his army in person, it was said. Everyone hoped that news would soon arrive of the final, decisive battle. But the French troops expected William of Orange to lead the Spanish and Dutch forces, and it was subsequently learned that Louis, with his experienced army, advanced boldly against the enemy, followed him up to within cannon-range—and then cautiously retreated!

Eugène would like to have stood at the head of the army at that moment; *he* would not have been held back by Louvois's advice not to let " his authority risk the chance of a set-back," and would not, like Louis, have deserted the troops. So his idol was that kind of a leader ! The King could, however, self-righteously assert that his presence in the field had been of decisive importance, for hardly had he departed than the Allies gained ground, and, if the riots in Hungary had not demanded the attention of the larger part of the Imperial army, the scales would have turned to Louis's disadvantage. At any rate, he now showed himself inclined to consider the Dutch offers of peace. But the Allies' conditions were too severe for His All-Christian Majesty to accept them without great loss of prestige ; and so Louvois was forced to double his feverish activities. A short winter campaign was staged whereby the province of Artois and the whole of Hennegau were won for France. Louis thought that he could now dictate peace terms. But he had still to wait : he had under-estimated the diplomatic capabilities of the newly appointed Captain-General of the Netherlands, Prince William of Orange, whose talents as a commander Louis had, a short while beforehand, avoided putting to the test. For the Prince, the matter of liberating Holland from French domination was less important than that of bringing England—whom, later, he was to rule—into the war, and of delivering her from the French influence which, under his uncle, Charles II, had brought her almost to a state of vassalage. Charles must be forced to unite with Holland ; the whole of Europe must rise, as one man, against France !

The partisans of the Coalition triumphed. If Orange succeeded in winning over England, then victory and the humiliation and weakening of France were a certainty.

At this moment, Louis's army was stronger in numbers than it had ever been. Three hundred thousand troops were put in the field—an enormous number in comparison with the armies of forty to fifty thousand men with which Richelieu won his great victories. But Louis now chose to give up warfare, and concentrated entirely on diplomacy.

The survey of these complicated political circumstances was only possible from the desk of the French Foreign Minister. Eugène only realised them in historical perspective— as a political critic, initiated in the circumstances. It happened, for instance, that Sobieski, King of Poland by Louis's grace, suddenly concluded an unfavourable peace in order to lead the forces of Poland to the support of the Hungarian insurgents. The Imperial troops were entirely defeated: Upper Hungary was seized from the Emperor. Already, in Vienna, everyone was in terror of the onset of Hungarian horsemen; it was quite impossible to send Imperial regiments to the Rhine. But even the secrecy of the French diplomatic measures could not prevent coins being minted, on the edge of which the inscription was engraved, " *Ludovicus XIV, Galliæ rex, defenser Hungariæ.*" These coins, which were shown in the Palais Soissons, were another indication to Eugène of the place where, in later years, Louis XIV, his life's great enemy, was to be vulnerable !

Another elegant French cavalier was honoured with an audience with Charles II, who tried to force upon him an agreement whereby he was assured the payment of the sum of six million French livres for three years if he were to prevent the convocation of the Parliament that had already voted for a declaration of war on France.

Six millions livres, even for Louis, involved a call on the exchequer which he turned over several times in his mind before he allowed it to be paid out. He held Charles's letter in his hand, and declared that he would, of course, make the payment, but at the moment was unable to fix a date for settlement. In any case he would not hesitate to publish the letter at the first signs of any hostilities on the part of England !

He had not waited for Charles's reply, but, in Nymwegen, the place that had been chosen for eventual peace negotiations, had handed over his ultimatum in which he set out the concessions that he would make for each of the Powers separately. He fixed a date, beyond which he would not consider himself bound to those concessions.

The people of Europe, who were unaware of the intrigues whereby Louis had covered his retreat, saw, with astonishment, how this one man dictated laws to a world apparently united against him. Louis's position was mightier than it had ever been.

A characteristic caricature, which was circulated after the conclusion of peace, shows his hand appearing from out of a cloud. On each finger dances a marionette dressed as a Prince. The inscription runs : " *In te vivimus, movemur et sumus.*"

CHAPTER V

NOT ONE of Olympia's sons, even of those who were already qualified for the colours, was actually serving. Louvois had hermetically sealed the War Ministry against her house. As long as he remained Minister of War he would sign no officer's patent for any member of the Soissons family.

But the successful conclusion of the war seemed to have caused him to change his mind. Perhaps he sought a closer relationship with Savoy ? Or, had he alienated himself from the Montespan ? The agent whom Olympia received in her horoscope cabinet could tell her nothing. He merely cautiously announced that Louvois was disposed to make peace with Madame la Comtesse. That was a day of rejoicing in the Palais Soissons, and the future appeared in the rosiest light, particularly for Eugène, who had often pondered over how he could, in his mother's, and, above all, in his own interests, effect a reconciliation with the all-mighty Minister of War. Now at least he would be able to lay aside his hated Abbé's habit, and wear the beloved uniform of a cavalry regiment to which his Prince's rank entitled him. When his mother, in her costliest dress, climbed into her most magnificent coach, he accompanied her to the doors, and begged her not to forget that he wished to be a soldier and nothing but a soldier. He begged for the smallest regiment, and, if that were not possible, then for a company at least.

Olympia was so happy that she promised everything : the wretched time of exile had come to an end. Once reconciled with Louvois, she was protected. In her lively phantasy, she saw herself once more on terms of intimacy with the King, in the proved splendour of her position as first lady of the

Court. She would ask for regiments for her sons Louis, Thomas, and Philippe; but, in a confidential moment, she would beg her old and now once more her submissive friend Louvois to explain to her fourth son that an undergrown youth with such a weak constitution could not stand up to the wear and tear of a military career. She would talk to the King about Eugène, and would request for him the post of ambassador in some foreign country, preferably in Spain, where her little friend Marie Louise of Orleans was the young King Charles's Queen. She told the coachman to increase his pace. But, an hour later, the gilded coach with the quarterings of Savoy drove back into the courtyard of the Palais Soissons. Madame la Comtesse had not even been received by Louvois!

On the evening of that day, Olympia invited all the nearest members of her family to come and discuss the measures to be taken in this case of unheard of discourtesy. Even her mother-in-law left her sulking-corner. The insult had, after all, been directed at a Princess of Savoy, and, moreover, it presented a good opportunity of picking a quarrel, of plotting intrigues, in short, of forcing the Court, which wished to have nothing more to do with her, to recognise her existence, born of royal lineage.

The consultation took place. The nobly born ladies and gentlemen conceived a plan which should bring about Louvois's downfall, and, after an animated discussion, sat themselves, as usual, at the card-table. Eugène, too restless to stay with his books, stood behind his mother's chair and handed her out the ducats which she invariably lost. Presently the Duke of Bouillon arrived, and begged Olympia to retire with him into her private cabinet. A few minutes later, she called Eugène, and explained to him that she must either leave France or be imprisoned in the Bastille!

What had happened? What had put Mazarin's most gifted niece in the position of choosing between these alternatives? Eugène only heard the explanation on the following day. At the time he had to return to the guests and tell them that his mother was obliged to dine out, and that something had happened which prevented her from fulfilling her duties as hostess !

Not even the nearest relations learned the reason why, within an hour's time, the whole of the Palace, with exception of the reception-rooms, was in a state of upheaval. Menservants and maids were doing up packages. Olympia, dissolved in tears, called one child after another to her, packed money and jewels into her bags, and ordered the servants and coachmen to put on their grey travelling clothes and to harness eight horses to the coach. Whoever asked her what was the cause of this precipitate departure received the answer that no one was to trouble about her, for she was innocent. Only Louvois and the villainous Montespan had taken pleasure in compromising her.

It was only in the early hours of the morning, when the curiosity of the Princesse de Carignan outweighed her annoyance at being left alone in the card-room without adequate apologies, that the children learned the truth of what had happened.

La Voisin—the " poisonous " Catherine Deshayes—had been arrested, and at her trial had named amongst the distinguished people who had visited her house, in the first place the Maréchal de Luxembourg, the Comtesse de Soissons, and her sister, the Duchesse de Bouillon.

The warrant for the search of La Voisin's house had been issued at the instigation of the Archbishop of Paris ; for news of many cases of poisoning had reached the ears of the priests of his diocese by way of the confessional. Four years had passed since the trial of Madame de Brinvilliers, whose numerous poisonings had evoked such horror, and yet her subsequent execution had not deterred La Voisin from practising the black arts.

The Maréchal de Luxembourg was secretly arrested, and taken to the Bastille, where he remained for nearly two years.

But in the case of Olympia, Louvois had reserved for himself the pleasure of first playing cat and mouse with her by obliging her, once again, to ask favours of him. He had

THE POISONER, LA VOISIN

waited nearly two years for the moment in which he might refuse to receive Madame la Comtesse, and with this humiliation he began his revenge. He knew perfectly well that the King would never seriously punish the playmate of his youth and the widow of a Prince of a sovereign House. A serious punishment? Louvois wished to banish Olympia from Court, once and for all, and to ostracise her and her family, who had considered him unworthy of being related to them.

While the light-hearted Duchesse de Bouillon declared that she feared neither the Devil—whom she pretended to have cast out—nor his representative who sat in judgment over her, Olympia was intimidated, and fled. Already, at the time of the death of her husband, the rumour that she had poisoned him, had frightened her, and now, she explained candidly, " Monsieur Louvois is my deadly enemy. He has enough influence to be able to condemn me. He has false witnesses, and, moreover, one who has decided to arrest such a person as myself will certainly complete the crime, and either bring me to the scaffold or else imprison me. I prefer to flee, and will vindicate my action afterwards."

The vindication did not follow, for the matter never came to a direct accusation. That a case was instituted against Olympia is certainly authenticated: it was thus brought to light that she had questioned La Voisin about the King and his mistresses, and also that she had begged for a love potion for an "illustrious gentleman." Madame de Sévigné wrote to her daughter : " Up to the present, nothing very black—indeed nothing that could even be called grey—has come out of all this nonsense of which Madame la Comtesse is accused. If really nothing further is discovered, then the whole thing is an annoyance which persons of her standing might have been spared. Madame la Maréchal Laferté, out of her kindness of heart, accompanied Madame la Comtesse to La Voisin's house, but did not go up with her. She has to thank this caution for an infrequent pleasure : they tell her that she is innocent ! Madame de Soissons asked La Voisin how she could win back a lover who had deserted her. This lover was apparently a great Prince, and it is insisted that she said that if he did not return to her he would rue it. This statement was supposed to refer to the King—and everything is momentous that might refer to such a great personage."

Louvois's plan of destruction was based on the circulation of such stories, and, during three whole days, Prince Eugène experienced the misery of hearing street-criers and trumpeters, in front of the Palais Soissons, demanding, in tones so loud that everyone in the neighbouring streets could hear, that his mother be brought to justice.

In the meantime, Olympia had left France; but Louvois's persecution followed her even beyond the frontiers. The Abbé de Choisy reports that she was refused shelter by the large inns in all the towns and villages through which she passed. She was obliged to sleep on straw, and to bear with the curses of the mob, who reviled her as a witch and poisoner. " Louvois sent a Calvinist Captain to Brussels, who distributed money amongst the ragamuffins so that they should insult her by songs of calumny and abuse; and, on one occasion, she was obliged to sleep in a Beguine convent, whither she had gone to buy lace, on account of the crowd of more than three thousand people who had collected at the door to tear her to pieces."

It was a melancholy sojourn. La Rochefoucauld writes that " in Brussels, Madame la Comtesse was obliged to leave the church in secret, for the most appalling Sabbath had been arranged, consisting of a dance of cats all tied to one another, with the mob shrieking that these were the devils and sorcerers that followed her. The whole thing was so horrible that Madame la Comtesse was forced to quit the place to let this madness pass. It is certain that the gates of Namur, Antwerp, and many other towns in Flanders are closed against her, as no one desires a poisoner in their midst."

But soon better news reached Paris. The Governor of the Netherlands had received Olympia, and, in Brussels, a small Court was established about her. Maréchal Villar's mother wrote to Paris : " The Prince of Parma is in love with Madame la Comtesse. He is not a handsome lover, yet, were he to possess three hundred thousand gold francs in his coffers, he would be more generous in spending them on his lady than any other man in the world."

Olympia did not need money—Mazarin's niece had taken care of that. She had taken three hundred thousand thalers with her in her flight, and, when she realised that she would not be permitted to return very soon, she sold her position as stewardess of the Royal household for a further three hundred thousand thalers. That was an enormous sum, with which she could easily instal herself in Brussels in a princely manner.

The family left behind in Paris did not fare so well from the material standpoint. No one in the magnificent Soissons palace held a position at Court, no one drew allowances from the King : they were all dependent on the fortune of the Princesse de Carignan, who, crazy in this, as in all other matters, thought twice about every penny before she gave it out. Small sums were now and then forthcoming from the reigning House in Savoy, when the young Princes urgently begged for them. But even their petitioning letters passed through the hands of their grandmother, who had, at last, arrived at dominating the whole palace.

Under such circumstances there was nothing left for Eugène to do but to attach himself to strangers. He had been brought up with unlimited means, was accustomed from childhood to luxury, and now incurred debts on the strength of his hopes of a future career. Finally, the tutor to the young Dauphin—for whom the work was specially written—lent him Bossuet's *Universal History*, to help him to continue with his studies, and, further, the works of Mabillon on diplomacy, from which he gained a survey of political events from the time of the Middle Ages.

No one continually absorbs knowledge and information without finding use for it eventually. A review of his own epoch had formed itself in Eugène's precocious imagination, to which his youthful observations of earlier years made their contribution. The extent to which, with open eyes, he had followed the course of events is proved by his future actions.

Now that his anxious mother was no longer at home, Eugène had, in the true sense of the words, a free hand to wield the sword, to fight on an equal footing with his brothers, and to steel his body after the fashion of the famous men whom he read of in history. He slept no longer in the high bed, as was the custom of Princes, but, wrapped in his cloak, lay on the bare earth like any soldier in the field. The saddle-horses of all the retainers were at his disposal, and soon he rode like a cavalryman. From the reports that came in from the various theatres of war, he learned of the feats of horsemanship of the Imperial Croats and of the Turkish Spahis ; and, in spite of his crooked shoulder and thin arms and legs, he trained like any circus-rider. Everyone in the district must have laughed at the sight of the shabby young man as he rode through the countryside, clad in his worn abbé's habit, and perched like a small black monkey on the huge chargers of the Soissons stables. Now and again injunctions came from his mother to take care of himself. He took care of himself, it is true, but in his own way. He developed his faculties for the great future which, despite all predictions to the contrary, he had determined for himself.

All the same, it must not be thought that the young Eugène was a prig who occupied himself exclusively with methodical preparations for his future, boldly and yet deliberately answering for himself the question as to whether he would become a soldier or statesman by deciding for both. On the contrary, as a friend, he must have been companionable ; otherwise he would not have appeared so often in the society of the Contis, the Commercys, and Vaudémonts, and would not have become such an intimate friend of the King's son-in-law, Armand de Conti.

It must never be forgotten how revoltingly ugly he was. Everyone who knew him spoke repeatedly of his nose, which hardly deserved the name, and of the huge, black nostrils surmounting the upper lip, which was drawn up revealing his two enormous front teeth.

But, in spite of his ugliness, the charm of personality of the Prince, who, since his mother's flight, had occupied a somewhat dubious position in society, was overwhelming. He was even drawn into the " Cabala of the Temple." His friends had formed a society for the purpose of holding, regularly, a series of orgies, which were attended by the young man with the tonsured head and the abbé's habit. Another abbé akin to Eugène was the young Choisy, who describes his life's history in shameless memoirs. Choisy was admittedly so feminine that he bought a small house, where he established himself as a woman, and lived a dual existence. He attended Court as a cultivated abbé, but at home " Madame " received ladies and gentlemen—amongst them many gentlemen to whom " she " afforded the opportunity of convincing themselves of her sex!

Prince Eugène left behind him no indiscreet publications concerning his youth. But the pleasures in which he took part were by no means harmless ones : even the French Court, which could hardly be accused of rigorism, was roused to moral indignation. The young Princes carried their friendship for one another too far. This can be confirmed without having recourse to Liselotte of the Palatinate with her ever-ready pen, for there is a Court register which records these events. Liselotte writes of the young Eugène thus : " As soon as he cast aside the clerical habit, the young people all called him Madame Simone and Madame Lansiene." That in itself would have been harmless ; after all, the young Princes might have given a masked ball or amused themselves in disguise. But the next sentence in the letter divests the youthful masquerade of its harmlessness : " Yes, when he was quite young, he was called Madame Simone and Madame Lansiene because it was suggested that he played the part of a woman amongst the young people."

A later letter of Liselotte's gives the explanation quite bluntly.

But even if Liselotte's somewhat officious letters had been

lost to the world, or had never existed, the Court register provided information enough of the details of the life of the youth at Court. It was a sensation for the initiated when Louis XIV extorted disclosures from his fifteen-year-old son, the Duke of Vermandois, to the effect that, in his most intimate circle, a homosexual clique had established itself, to which nearly all the young Princes of the blood and their nearest friends belonged. The Cardinal de Bouillon, brother-in-law of Maria Mancini, the youngest and most poetically inclined of Eugène's aunts, was another member of the group.

Louis could not exterminate the whole rising generation of the aristocracy : he had to satisfy himself with threats and severe reprimands. Besides, he had no time to spare for the further moral cleansing of his Court : he was himself too much taken up with immorality of the normal kind !

How much Eugène was involved in these affairs it is impossible to establish. It is only known that one day he laid aside his abbé's garb and donned the lace-trimmed suit of a Prince of a sovereign House. He called on his grandmother, and had himself announced as the Chevalier de Carignan. But he was not well received by the old lady : she hardly noticed what kind of cavalier he was, but, raising her crutch, bade him leave her house for ever unless he returned to it as an abbé !

The house-government, after the flight of her daughter-in-law, had turned out otherwise than the old lady had anticipated. Prince Eugène was the second of her grandsons whom she had put at the door. A year before, the eldest, Louis Thomas, had wished to bring into the house a certain Mlle de Beauvais-Cropté, whom he presented to his grandmother as the daughter of the Prince de Condé's Master of Horse, declaring that he intended to marry her and no other. Neither insolence nor the proof that the girl was the illegitimate daughter of a lady in waiting (who, even if she had been legitimate, would only have been the daughter of a Master of Horse) availed the old lady in the very least against such determination : he was not even moved by the assurance of his grandmother that as long as she lived such a person should never take up her abode in the Palais Soissons.

Louis Thomas took the girl to Court, and the King gave his consent to the marriage. Louis did not do this without malice, for he knew that if Louis Thomas succeeded to the Throne of Savoy, he was bound to be dependent upon Louis as his only sovereign kinsman. Apart from that, the new Comtesse de Soissons was more than usually lovely, and the King was having a boring time. He had sent the Montespan away, replaced her with a Mlle de Thianges, who became his mistress for a short while, and afterwards was very near to becoming religious at the instigation of his most recent amour, the widow of the poet Scarron, composer of the wittiest of the " Mazarinades." The young de Soissons pleased his taste. After the established manner, he made the Count an allowance, which, although it was not adequate for his position, yet enabled him to bring his young wife to Versailles, where the King then openly pursued her with attentions.

The family Soissons had no luck in France at this period. The young Comtesse was virtuous, and all the opportunities which she might have opened up for her family were spoiled by her prudishness. Louis XIV could not tolerate this : he reduced her husband's income below the range of any valid excuse, and soon found a pretext to remove her altogether from him.

But the outraged grandmother had a sudden inspiration : she wished to demonstrate her power to the grandson who had refused to obey her. One mounted messenger after another left the Palais Soissons and rode in the direction of Turin. The letters which her deaf-mute son Philibert de Carignan received were full of injunctions to the effect that the time was come when he should think of getting married. The letters which her nephew Victor Amadeus, the young reigning Duke of Savoy, found on his table also contained injunctions to the effect that it was high time that he got married. Emmanuel Philibert, who felt lonely, was only waiting for the hint. A Princess of Modena was ready to marry him. A few months later, Louis XIV learned that Louis Thomas was no longer the next heir to the Dukedom. On that day the Count was deprived of his income. He was dependent, with his princely household to maintain, on the miserable twenty thousand livres sent him by his uncle in Savoy.

But, notwithstanding this, he was in a better position than his youngest brother, who received nothing at all from home. A certain Bagneur—of whom history even in its most secret documents has nothing to record beyond his homely middle-class name—had the doubtful honour of harbouring a lodger who possessed nothing but one shabby suit which he wore on his back, darned stockings, black shoes with buckles from which the gold had long worn off, a sword without a single precious stone, no baggage, no horses : nothing but the name, unsuited to an abbé, which he had arrogated to himself—that of the Chevalier de Carignan.

It was a sad cavalier who, as Sourches reports, was seen about in rags, having perhaps one silver thaler piece in a month which he could call his own, and yet holding on to his determination not to remain an abbé, nor to exchange his beret even for a Cardinal's hat.

He was urged on all sides to submit. Even his grandmother let him know that if he came back as an abbé the way was always open for him to return to a life of luxury and magnificence. The Prince de Carignan pledged him the livings that had been refused him earlier. But what was all that worth compared to the silver thaler, with which he fought for his existence certainly, but fought for it in his own way ?

Such obstinacy is either mad or heroic. Mad when the fact is taken into account that Eugène with his miserable equipment could not so much as enter the inner courtyard of the newly built Palace at Versailles to seek to obtain a military post for himself, and still less penetrate into the King's audience chamber, and in the presence of the monarch, to whom no one might address an unsolicited word without His Majesty's condescension, advance his petition !

THE PALACE OF VERSAILLES : VIEW FROM THE PARK. PRINCE EUGÈNE USED THE PALACE AS A MODEL FOR HIS BELVEDERE IN VIENNA.

However, later on Prince Eugène gained access to the audience chamber, was presented to the King, and had the opportunity of making his request. But at the time immediately after the forced departure of his mother he was deterred by the determination not to beg for anything. Eugène was filled with a profound indignation ! The man whom, in his childhood, he had seen daily in his mother's house, at her card-table, taking part in her entertainments and expeditions, whom he knew to have been the playmate of her youth, who had attained his power (on the strength of which he thought himself divine) thanks to Eugène's great-uncle—this man had permitted her to be banished in disgrace and dishonour. The brilliance of his idol was tarnished for ever. Louis ceased to be his ideal. Eugène had heard that the King had forbidden Cardinal Mazarin's name to be mentioned in connection with his diplomatic successes. So that was the position ! His great-uncle, the mighty diplomat *ad majorem regis gloriam*, denied ; his mother in a foreign land, persecuted to such a degree that an order had been issued to all French travellers forbidding them to visit her house in Brussels, as the King did not wish homage to be paid to her ! After such an experience a young man who had deliberately suffered privation and distress for conviction's sake would think well and long before asking favours of such a monarch !

But, after all, a man cannot go on eternally preparing, steeling his body, making his brain dexterous, absorbing knowledge, and fencing like a master, merely in order to walk the streets in Paris like a ragamuffin or a thief, with no prospect of achieving anything. Besides which, Louis had started war again. Again, as in his childhood, the princely vagabond saw preparations in the streets, increased activity in the barracks, the rounding-up of horses, the piled-up bales at the workshops and clothiers—which left the warehouses in the form of finished boots and uniforms—the galloping messengers, the marching troops and parading colours. How could a man stay still, with his sword in its scabbard, while the victorious French armies marched away ?

Now that he no longer belonged to the elect, who received

all the news, official and unofficial, direct from Court—the former reporting the successes, the latter from which the truth could be learned—Eugène was thrown back on what information he picked up in the streets, and on which he made his own comments. For, during his hard times, he kept away from his high-born cousins and illustrious friends. Now he learned vaguely that the King had instituted chambers of reunion in Metz, in Besançon, and in Breisach.

What was a chamber of reunion? Eugène had great trouble in finding out. At the time of the last peace negotiations, French diplomacy had purposely left the question open as to whether the territories ceded to a victorious France should be measured in accordance with the existing frontiers, or whether the question should be interpreted in a remoter, historical sense. Every disinterested person naturally considered that the existing divisions, the *status quo*, must be continued. Certainly, at the time of the agreements, the French diplomats had left no room for doubt that they favoured the opposite interpretation. Louis had already reduced to subjugation ten Imperial cities and the Knighthood of the Empire, which in earlier days had belonged to Alsace. He now demanded that all territories which had stood at any time in the remotest relationship to the provinces ceded to France at the conclusions of peace should be reunited with these provinces. Lorraine, for instance, having been ceded to France, would include all territories which had ever been in any way connected with Lorraine—such as the former feudal tenures of the Bishops of Metz, Toul, and Verdun.

The territories belonging to Alsace subjected themselves without protest, with the exception of Strasbourg. The Princes concerned, who were thus robbed, in time of peace, of their thousand-year-old possessions, protested vehemently to King and State. But, in place of an answer, Louis took Strasbourg—Strasbourg, of whom one hundred and fifty years earlier Charles V had said : If Strasbourg and Vienna were besieged simultaneously, he would march first to the defence of Strasbourg.

This statement of Charles V remained a theoretical one, for Louis, before he invaded Strasbourg, had arranged for the subsequent siege of Vienna, so that the Emperor might have no opportunity of defending Strasbourg !

The Most Christian Monarch staked everything on keeping Hungary in a rebellious condition, and in getting the Turks to advance to her support. With a Turkish war in sight, the Emperor's hands were tied.

Louis XIV now turned his attention to Mantua and took the fortress of Casale. On all frontiers French hands reached out to grasp a strip of territory. There was the Dukedom of Zweibrücken, which Louis annexed, but which belonged to the King of Sweden. Charles XI indignantly broke off an alliance with France which had existed for more than fifty years, and concluded with Holland—that is to say, with William of Orange—a covenant for the protection of the peace of Nymwegen. The Emperor joined with Hanover and a number of other Imperial States, for the purpose of combining with Sweden and Holland to chastise France.

But France had also found confederates and, most important of all, had succeeded in neutralising England and Brandenburg. The Great Elector had no desire to pull the chestnuts once again out of the fire for the Empire, and to have his fingers burnt in so doing. The Elector of Cologne and the Bishop of Münster united with France. Tökölly concluded an agreement with the Porte, became Prince of Upper Hungary, and was provided with ample funds by Poland at the instigation of France. But the King, Sobieski, only remained on Louis's side, and helped Tökölly up to the moment when he heard of the covenant between Tökölly and the Turks. From that instant he broke finally with France and attached himself to the Court of Vienna, where the Emperor pledged himself to provide him with subsidies for forty thousand men.

As soon as Poland's secession from France became known in Paris, Prince Eugène turned to the Prince de Conti. His moment seemed to have arrived. For, after all, France was threatened, and there was no point in condemning himself to inaction purely on private grounds when he could be of assistance to his native country.

But he over-estimated the value of his person when, dressed up in borrowed clothes, he set out for Versailles, in the Prince de Conti's coach, and drove in a great sweep into the Court of honour. The lackeys made way, and the two Princes of the blood, Eugène and Conti, were accompanied by Chevaliers d'Honneur up the great staircase. Conti was not only a Bourbon : he was also the husband of the Demoiselle de Blois, Louis's natural daughter by La Vallière, and therefore son-in-law to the All Mighty One. He had the right of free entry to the King's private apartments, and whoever enjoyed his protection was certain of success. Eugène had saved him up as a last resource. If anyone could help him to the command of the smallest company—he would be satisfied with the meanest unit although he had educated himself, theoretically, for the command of great armies—then it was Conti.

A free space was cleared in the reception-rooms. Everyone wanted to know who the small snub-nosed, dressed-up cavalier was whom Conti had brought with him. " The Abbé of Savoy," they were told. " The Little Abbé ! " Disdainful smiles, but hardly a greeting accompanied Eugène's progress.

At last the audience chamber was reached—the last room before the threshold of the King's private apartments. Now he stood in the presence of His Majesty. He saw, before him, a strong, broad-shouldered man, who, after being greeted by his son-in-law, turned a well-nourished, slightly bloated face in Eugène's direction.

" The Chevalier de Carignan," announced Conti.

Louis's features remained unmoved. He showed by no sign that he had known Eugène's face for twenty years, that he had seen him for the first time in his cradle, at a time when the child's mother had been the person he cared for most in the world.

" The Chevalier de Carignan," began Conti, " does not

wish to remain an abbé, Sire. He is inspired with enthusiasm for the arts of war, Your Majesty. He wishes to become a soldier, as his father was. He has learned fencing and riding with me, Sire." He broke off apologetically as he saw that Louis still moved no muscle, and merely looked away over Eugène's small, slightly trembling figure as though it were made of air. "The Chevalier de Carignan begs for a company!"

Louis made no reply.

There was nothing left for Conti to do but to make a sign to Eugène that he must go—that he must disappear, inasmuch as the King had not even looked at him much less greeted him. But it needed a vigorous tug on Conti's part to get Eugène to move from the spot.

Eugène stood and gazed through the lace jabot—right through the body of the great King. He saw himself at the head of a galloping squadron which, leaving the masses of foot-soldiers behind, rode away into wide spaces. Fortress walls appeared, catapults exploded: he saw the turbans of the Turks, the horse-tail standards of the pashas, French uniforms, and captains who bowed themselves before him. He saw his mother, Olympia, in her pearl-bedecked dress, greeting the man who stood unmoved before her.

He looked penetratingly at the King. "I shall come again," he decided, and now became aware of Conti's hand pulling him away.

Eugène received a present of money from Conti, fitted himself out, and took part in the orgies of his cousins and friends. For a short while he became a dandy, but, what he did, he did with clenched teeth and fists, awaiting the moment which would afford him the opportunity of causing that unmoved countenance of the King's to be convulsed. His Majesty had not condescended to see him: well, he would open His Majesty's eyes!

He had made his plans. All at once he ceased to take any further interest in the events either at the French Court or in the French armies. As far as he was concerned, they could devastate the Palatinate, take possession of the province of Chiny, blockade forts, and fight battles! He fixed his gaze on the east and waited for a signal.

It came in a tragic fashion.

Eugène's decision to become a soldier had been ten times strengthened by the example of his brother Louis. Certainly, Louis's path had been smoothed for him; he had had the advantage of education in every department of military knowledge, had been deputy-governor of a town and province in Savoy, and had a straightforward career before him. But it appeared to be the fate of all Olympia's children to be unable to accomplish anything without some misadventure. The Chevalier of Savoy, as he was called, had had a quarrel at the Court of Turin, in which he had openly insulted a favourite of the Duchess's. He should have apologised, but, instead of doing so, he wrote a letter to his cousin, Ludwig of Baden, and, before there was time for an answer, appeared at the Court of Vienna and begged for the command of a regiment.

As soon as the Savoyard Ambassador, Baron Sbarra, heard of his arrival, he placed himself at the Chevalier's disposal. But the councillor of the Crown lands of Baden, Knörr, the man who in Eugène's interests had played the part of mediator with the Margrave of Baden, advised him to have confidence in his master and not to trust the Savoyards. Knörr appears to have given good advice, for a Viennese, "hand-written journal," dated about a month after the arrival of the Prince, reports the foundation of five foot, two dragoon, and three Croat regiments. The one dragoon regiment was commanded by the Duke of Croy, who had hurried to Vienna from his service in the Danish army, and the second by the Prince Louis de Soissons, who was no other than the Chevalier of Savoy.

In Vienna, feverish preparations were being made. Louis had accompanied his cousin, the Margrave of Baden, to Upper Hungary to fight against the rebels there. At the end of December he received the news that he had been made colonel of the Imperial dragoons. In the winter there were no campaigns, and soon the regiment was formed with the aid of older officers and men, who had been furnished by other regiments. The colonel had time to visit his mother in Brussels, and his uncle in Turin. It was then, just before his audience with the King, that Eugène heard of his brother's success.

But the Chevalier of Savoy had evidently not been born under a lucky star in spite of all his mother's blessings, and the favourable horoscope which told her that one of her sons would become an Imperial captain, be victorious on all battlefields, and avenge her on Louis XIV ! Hardly was the Savoyard Prince back in Vienna, than one day, while out driving, his carriage turned over, and he was badly hurt in the leg. On account of this he could not proceed at once to the army. His regiment was one of the last to go into the field, but, in return for that, it had the honour, before its departure, of being inspected by the Emperor and Empress, who were, at that time, still able to stay in Vienna up to the last moment.

Prince Eugène knew very few of the details of the Turkish war, which, fanned by Louis, had broken out in flames. In Paris it was said that the Imperial Crown was beginning to sink under the blows of the Crescent. An immense Turkish army was marching towards Vienna under the leadership of the Grand Vizier, Kara Mustapha.

The Imperial troops were commanded by the Duke of Lorraine, who had decided on an offensive, and had already begun the siege of Neuhäusel. But the superior forces were overwhelming : he was forced to give up the siege of Neuhäusel, and even to retreat on Vienna. Prince Louis, with his regiment, took part in the retreat. He formed part of the division of the Margrave Ludwig, and the dragoons were chosen, on account of their fighting capacity, to cover the retreat against the wild, swarming Tartar hordes. On the 7th of July, the Tartars penetrated the column of artillery drivers near Petronell, and caused a panic in the Imperial army, which equally infected the Emperor's dragoons. The troops fell back. Louis was trying to pull his regiment together, when his horse fell dead under him in such an unlucky way as to cause the pommel to penetrate his body. The badly wounded man was brought to Vienna, and died six days after the encounter.

A Savoyard diplomat finishes his report to Turin with a sentence which almost exactly corresponds with the horoscope reading which Olympia had made for her son : " He gave hopes of becoming the bravest general of our century."

A copy of this letter was sent to Prince Eugène in Paris.

CHAPTER VI

ON THE MORNING of the 23rd of September, 1683, Prince Eugène was handed the news of the death of his brother. On that same morning he succeeded in communicating with Knörr, the councillor of the Crown lands of Baden, who was just then in Paris. Knörr had come from Vienna, and Knörr must know whether, through the death of his brother, there were any prospects of his getting the command of Louis's regiment of dragoons.

The Margrave's worthy councillor and factotum advised him to set off at once. He was convinced that his master would support Prince Eugène's wish. An Imperial dragoon regiment for a Prince of Savoy should not be difficult to obtain, especially as Vienna had been so satisfied with his brother.

Eugène would have liked to start without delay, but he had neither a horse nor money to buy one, nor even the means of maintaining himself in the humblest inn on the road to Vienna. What was he to do? He *must* start; the longed-for moment had come, but to whom could he turn for help? Whom could he trust? Eugène ran through the sunny streets of Paris, his cap in his hand, obsessed by the problem of how to obtain money. How much did he need, and who would lend it him? He was head over ears in debt, and had no credit. Above all he needed a horse. Would the lackeys of the Palais Soissons prevent his taking one out of the stables? He would sell his birthright to some Jew for a thousand louis d'or—for less even—for the simplest field equipment, and a couple of silver thalers with which to keep himself from starving on the road to Vienna. " Your future heritage, Monseigneur ? " was the sceptical query that greeted his suggestion. Everywhere he was sent away

GE

empty-handed ; for, although genuine respect was felt for the House of Soissons, yet the family was in disfavour, and, in addition to that, Eugène himself had been cast out by his family. The money-lenders kept their coffers closed. The Little Abbé's prospects were not even worth a charity offering. For Eugène, in despair, had even stooped to begging people to help him out of kindness of heart, out of pity for a fallen Prince, for the worthy cause of Christendom in the war against the Turks. Scorn was concealed under polite phrases, but the answers all had but one meaning : if Christendom were dependent upon Eugène's help, then it would go badly—very badly—for the good faith. He was thanked for the honour of his visit, but hardly had he turned his back than the laughter, which had with difficulty been restrained during his presence, broke out.

But this youth of twenty did not lose heart. In the glaring sunshine he hurried through the great city, from house to house, from door to door, up and down endless steps. Someone must help him ! He was quite exhausted when in the afternoon he stormed into his cousin Conti's palace. But, although bodily worn out, he was so filled with the urgent necessity of his immediate departure at all costs that, after an hour's discussion, he succeeded in persuading Conti, who was happily married, to accompany him, and in forcing him to agree to an immediate departure. They wished to set off that very evening, but they had first to prepare their journey in secrecy. Above all it was imperative to persuade the young Princess that it was Armand's duty as a knight and a Christian to take part in the Turkish wars and prevent the fall of Vienna. All Paris was aware of the danger, and a slight feeling of revulsion was aroused in the population by the indifferent attitude of the Most Christian Monarch, who casually left his army at rest in its field quarters, its fortresses and barracks, while the Turks surrounded Vienna, and planned a world-empire in Europe. With tears in her eyes, the young Princess agreed to the necessity of Armand's departure.

At ten o'clock at night, Conti and Eugène, without

farewells, and accompanied by a single page, left Paris, and drove with the mail coach in the direction of Senlis.

By the following morning the news of their departure had reached the King's ears. He fell into a rage, and sent out eight couriers to bring Conti back. No one mentioned Eugène. Only Louis himself, in the evening, said ironically to the Duke of Orleans, " Do you think that I shall suffer a great loss if the Little Abbé does not return ? "

In the diaries of the Abbot Gallus Wagner, of the cloister Schwarzach, there is a note describing the homeward journey of the prior of the Cistercian monastery in Alsace. The prior had been visiting his Abbot of Ibbetsheim, who was taking a cure in Baden-Baden, and wished to cross the Rhine to return to his own monastery, close at hand. But the ferryman refused to take him over : the King of France had forbidden, with threats of corporal punishment and on pain of death, that anyone be permitted to cross the Rhine. A messenger had ridden to Baden-Baden—that being the nearest residence of a German Prince to the French postern gate—to communicate this order to the Seneschal von Greiffen. But von Greiffen had known of it already, and feared that it might be an indication on the part of the French of another blow at the shield—this time of an attack on Germany from the west whilst she was being threatened by the Turks from the east. He informed Max von Starhemberg, the Imperial governor of Phillipsburg, and sent out spies. A few days later his fears turned out to have been unfounded : the Rhine passage had been closed for the purpose of holding up the Prince de Conti and forcing him to return to Paris.

A King's courier overtook the two fugitives in Brussels, but that nobleman, in order to accomplish his master's mission, was obliged to disobey his commands. For Conti and Eugène were Olympia's guests, and, before he could gain access to them, the courier had, not only to set foot in the house whose threshold was forbidden to all Frenchmen, but, more than that, was obliged to pay respectful and devoted homage to Madame la Comtesse.

Eugène lay in bed. The violent exertions of the journey had been too strenuous for his wasted body. But the emissary had orders to take no notice of Eugène. Drily he delivered his message : His Highness the Prince de Conti could only obtain His Majesty's pardon if he were to return without delay. Otherwise he must give up all thought of seeing France again. At this point Olympia joined in the conversation, and exhorted the two young men to return. Eugène's bodily condition, which had been weakened by the privations of the last few years, caused her great anxiety. How could this frail, almost crippled youth stand up to the hardships of the Turkish war when her elder son, Louis, who, at least, had been trained for military service, had succumbed to them ? The mother proved stronger than the politician. Since she had been so cruelly disappointed by her son Louis's horoscope, Olympia believed no longer in her family's future. Eugène must return to Paris : if, after his flight, he were to show himself repentant and submissive, then the King would grant him his wish and give him a company. After all, he had shown—if only in a negative manner—that he was capable of independent decision !

But before even Conti, that spoilt but dutiful Prince, whose own situation gave him food for thought (for, after all, he was the colonel of a regiment, absent without leave, and faced with an explicit command from the King to return without delay), could open his mouth to answer, Eugène had replied to the King of France's noble emissary that, in spite of his illness and feverish condition, he, personally, intended to proceed at once on his journey. His cousin was, naturally, free to return, but he was going on— and with a side-glance he added that he was sure that his cousin would go with him !

The nobleman wished to give the Prince time to reflect ; but Eugène urged their departure so vehemently that even his mother had no time to ask whether he had sufficient money by him. The two young men were already in the saddle, the page behind them, riding post-haste from town to town, snatching a hasty meal at an inn, a few hours of sleep, and then on again. In Frankfort-on-the-Main, as they were hastily swallowing their mid-day meal at an inn, M. de Raglie, a gentleman of the bedchamber of Louis XIV's, galloped at full speed into the courtyard. Conti sprang to his feet: he knew what Raglie's arrival meant. Covered with perspiration, and without a word of explanation, Raglie handed him a letter.

The contents of the Royal missive are not known. At all events, Conti had his horse brought out of the stable, and gave his page the order to pack his wallet. Eugène went on with his meal. He exchanged no greetings with Raglie, and accepted Conti's farewells with cool politeness. Now he was alone—alone in Frankfort-on-the-Main, without means. What should he do? In any case he must at all costs reach the Emperor's army. But without money, how was he to do it? For he intended to give the wallet containing the thousand gulden and the diamond ring, which Conti had pressed upon him, to the inn-keeper in payment of the reckoning. However, common sense reasserted itself. A thousand gulden together with the diamond ring were almost enough to enable him to fit himself out—indeed, they were almost enough to allow of his presenting himself at the Emperor's Court in a more fitting manner than that in which he had appeared at the Court of Louis XIV.

Eugène's ride to Regensburg was, in the spiritual sense, the ride of a Don Quixote setting forth against the world-domination of France. The lonely young man, who only by a superhuman effort withstood the strain of the long unbroken hours in the saddle, was combating the world-empire in the west, and setting out to subjugate the empire in the east. *In te vivimus, movemur et sumus?* He wished to show Europe how unnecessary it was to live, move, and have its being under the sign of Louis XIV. He would cause the throne of the Lord of the World to totter; but first the

Crescent must be expelled from European soil, and be driven back into Asia. Europe must be delivered, for all time, from the Turks. The return to Paris was forbidden him? At the head of an army he would force his return. . . .

He arrived at the shores of the Danube. He had studied maps, and knew the course of the river right down to the Black Sea. The new Imperial Austria, to whose assistance he was hurrying, should arise from the basin of this great river. Then, when Austria was once more in safety and no longer threatened by the Turk, he would begin the struggle against Louis's power, and the attack on the France that had cast him out!

But the news which greeted Eugène in Regensburg seemed as though calculated to disappoint his dreams. The Imperial army, which he was rushing to join in order to fight the Turks as an officer of dragoons, had been forced to retire on Mähren. Hysterical rumour had raised the number of Turks who were besieging Vienna into many hundreds of thousands. The garrison was said to consist of a handful of men only, so that any day the city must capitulate. The Emperor had taken to flight, and now held his Court in Passau—that is, if the confusion of the numberless, indiscriminate conferences that took place daily could be called a Court. If all the troops were added together that had been despatched to the defence their number would not amount to a tenth of the strength of the Turkish army; and the might of the Turks appeared to be inexhaustible. As in the time of the migration of peoples, fresh hordes of Asiatics poured unceasingly through the Dardanelles. If Vienna fell, then all was lost. Only Louis XIV could help now; and no one dared to call upon him for assistance. If Vienna were to fall, then the German Emperor would be faced with the alternative of becoming either French or Turkish.

Perhaps any other man in Eugène's position would have turned back, having recognised the hopelessness of his flight from France. But Eugène had read history, and had learned how to calculate. He knew what it meant when fugitives came up the Danube with tales of the atrocities of the Turks and Tartars, of the irresistible strength of the janizaries' assaults, and of the inexhaustible wealth of the Grand Vizier, who had at his command as many provisions and as much war material as he could possibly need. To Eugène the atmosphere of the German town was only too easy to understand : it was an atmosphere of panic, which exaggerated everything.

Yet Count Tarini, who happened to be staying in Regensburg at that moment, confirmed the truth of the rumours which were causing such consternation in the town. Yes, it was true that Vienna was on the verge of capitulating ; it was true that, without the assistance of the Most Christian King, the Christian army would be lost, and it was true that Europe lay exposed to the Turkish menace. It was a question whether even His Most Christian Majesty would be able to save the situation, for the news of the humiliation of the French Ambassador at the Porte had been circulated in the world. In Germany it was related, with a certain satisfaction, that Louis XIV had been obliged to apologise at the Sultan's Court for the victory at sea of his Admiral Dufresne over pirates who were sailing under a Turkish flag. The position seemed despairing.

However, Count Tarini's hopelessness was not of long duration ; in consequence, his dependence on Prince Eugène was all the more lasting. In Regensburg, without provisions, thrown back on the power of his own personality, a seeker after a position, Eugène made the first friend in his new life— and a submissive friend at that—who believed in his glorious future. At first Tarini was mistrustful of a Prince of Savoy found in such a dubious situation without servants or *entourage* of any kind—a fugitive from the French Court. Was this little man with his vast plans really a Prince, or merely a crook taking advantage of the chaos of the times ?

Tarini was one of the young Duke of Savoy's numberless agents, and a diplomat who wished to obtain information about everything, to know everything, and to experience everything, so as to be in good time to trim his sails to the wind. He was the liaison officer of a small army of agents whom the Duke had sent to Germany. Why, then, had he not been informed from Turin of the arrival of a Prince of Savoy in Regensburg ? He endeavoured to trip up the false Prince, and to expose the supposed swindler, but he was disarmed, and yielded to the feelings of sympathy which the young man inspired in him.

At last, on the 20th of August, an agent from Savoy, Carocchio by name, arrived in Regensburg. Tarini breathed again. Carocchio had brought a message for Eugène from the Duke, reminding him that he belonged to the House of Savoy, and might depend for assistance upon the head of the House. He sent a very gracious letter, an encouraging document which Eugène would like to have exchanged for a sack of gold coins. Almost at the same moment a messenger from Eugène's mother arrived in the person of a nobleman who brought letters of introduction for him to the Emperor, to Ludwig Wilhelm of Baden, and to the Spanish Ambassador in Vienna, the Marchese Borgomaniero. But even Olympia had not thought of his material needs. In her letter she again tried to deter him from his decision. She wrote that " although his idea was worthy of his nobleness of heart, yet it was unsuited to his weakness and youth." The mother's anxiety was still paramount. Yet Olympia left a loophole for ambition : in case Eugène really intended to present himself to the Emperor, and to serve in the Austrian army, then he would find the introductions useful. Might they serve him better than her maternal advice !

Eugène had now three cavaliers in his train, and felt himself a Prince once again. More letters arrived, this time from his grandmother, and from his aunt, the Margravine of Baden. Eugène's optimism knew no bounds. His revolt against Louis XIV had decided the two ladies to recommend him to the Emperor. They hoped, thereby, to cause the French King a small annoyance. If they had lived to witness the amount of harm which, later, Eugène was to inflict upon him, they would, in spite of their meanness, have written the letters of introduction with golden pens !

CONTEMPORARY REPRESENTATION OF THE ADVANCE OF THE TURKISH ARMY

On the 29th of August, Eugène and his cavaliers arrived in Passau. Here the Emperor held his Court, and here Eugène would be presented to him by the Margrave of Baden, who would request for him the command of his brother's regiment. He saw himself already as a colonel of dragoons riding to Vienna to the relief of the city! But it was not so easy to find the Margrave in Passau. The Court had dissolved—already the upheaval caused by the flight had loosened the stiff etiquette. Thence the despairing rumours that were circulated daily. Every moment brought a new message or a new rumour. The Turks were said to have closed in upon Vienna to an extent that caused the defenders' breath to give out. The enemies' trenches now extended as far as the ramparts, the Turkish guns bombarded the walls unceasingly, and mines were being laid, while within the garrison the powder was threatening to give out.

In Passau a constant stream of people passed in and out of the Archbishop's palace, where the Emperor lived. While he was searching for his cousin, Eugène saw the Emperor for the first time. He was appalled. Was this flabby, sickly, bowed figure, this man with long-drawn face, hollow cheeks, and gross underlip which, like a damp red sponge, hung down almost to his chin, to become his future Emperor? In the person of Louis XIV, Eugène had seen the personification of Majesty, the embodiment of the ruling principle. How could he compare this nervous, uneasy man, who before he mounted his horse looked first to right and then to left as though to reassure himself that he were not threatened from either side, with the personality of Louis, who only at his own inclination condescended to be aware of the presence of a third person? Was this man really to become his Emperor?

Filled as he was with the ideal of manly beauty, and disappointed by the feeble stature of the Emperor, Prince Eugène forgot his own appearance. When, however, a few days later, he was presented to the Emperor, Leopold, in his turn, was little less astonished as he gazed at the thin little Prince of Savoy whose upper lip was almost entirely absent, and whose black nostrils filled him with revulsion. This misshapen young man wished to become a colonel of dragoons ? If his own situation had not been so tragic, the Emperor would have laughed outright at the idea. As it was, he was dependent both upon Eugène's cousin, the Margrave of Baden, who commanded his armies, and upon Eugène's uncle, who was President of his War Council. He, therefore, gave an inaudible, but evasive answer.

Once again, Eugène's appearance, this time at the Austrian Court, was not a propitious one. There was no question of his being promoted to the colonel's rank upon which he had built his hopes. His brother's regiment had been given to an officer, already proved in the Emperor's service, by the name of Donath Heissler. There was no post free for Eugène, and no one had time to give attention to the matter.

The Margrave told him that, at the moment, the plan was quite impossible of fulfilment ; after having received him with the utmost friendliness ! But it was merely the friendliness of a far-removed relation. Ludwig listened to stories of the Palais Soissons, from which, as a child, he had been abducted, but, however much the contrast between Eugène's ugliness and his attractive personality intrigued him, in these agitated days he could spare but very little time for his future friend. Eugène was sent away, graciously, and with all manner of promises. He might, for instance, join the other volunteers of rank who had come to Passau, and had been allotted to the Corps of the Elector, Max Emmanuel of Bavaria. That was not much, but it was something. It would be Eugène's first opportunity of distinguishing himself, and of demonstrating to a commander his usefulness as a soldier.

His disappointment on the following day was unbounded. The Prince of Anhalt, two Princes of Pfalz-Burg, two of Saxe-Altenburg, two of Holstein, one Prince of Eisenach, one of Hohenzollern and one of Hessen—all these, together with other Princes of lesser significance, only needed to open their wallets to bring forth the number of ducats needed to obtain the uniform which distinguished the volunteers of rank from the regular troops.

Actually it was no great exaction when Princes of reigning Houses were requested to keep two servants and four horses, and to wear light blue braided uniform and headgear ornamented with waving plumes. But for Eugène these requirements were equivalent to the impossibility of his appearing in company with his equals in the field. He pawned Conti's diamond at a Jew's, but the amount that he received was not enough for the equipment, and he had long broken into the purse with the thousand gulden. The necessary equipment was beyond his means.

The Elector Max Emmanuel, who led the Bavarian army down the Danube, was disappointed that the young Chevalier of Savoy, with whom he had had pleasant conversations about the French Court, was not to be found among the volunteers. His sister was the Dauphine ; French culture and customs were his ideal, and he had found pleasure in the diplomatically subtle Eugène. He asked after him ; but the twenty-year-old young man had vanished in shame and confusion.

At the beginning of September, eleven thousand men, together with the guns for twenty-six regiments, marched down the Danube. Compared with the vast numbers of the Turkish army, and the reinforcements that were rumoured to be pouring out of Asia, it was a small, indeed, a *very* small, army which Eugène watched marching out of Passau.

He did not as yet know whether he would succeed in finding any corps to which he could attach himself in order to march to the relief of Vienna. But his optimism held fast, and he announced to Count Tarini that during the few days more of waiting he intended to learn all he could of the situation of the Christian relieving army. He enquired, he listened, and gained entry to the improvised offices of the War Council. He wanted to know about the army marching against the Turks ? Well, it consisted, in the first place, of twenty-seven thousand Poles under the command of Johann Sobieski : twenty-seven thousand strong, they were, instead of the forty thousand settled by agreement, and now, at length, at long length, they had joined the Imperial army in Tulln. And the Imperial troops ? Eugène, who was familiar with Louis XIV's armies, could hardly regard them as an army at all. The whole Christian relief army, which had been scraped together in Germany by every possible means, counted, together with the Bavarian troops, seventy thousand men, hardly one-third of a corps which the Roi Soleil sent into the field in order to invade a province ! True the overwhelming numbers of the Turkish army had been exaggerated. The five hundred thousand men that rumour spoke of were reduced in the spies' reports to one hundred thousand, and if the secret *communiqués* were to be trusted, then the besieging army was not more than one hundred and twenty thousand strong, of which, again, only thirty thousand were janizaries, the chosen troops of the Ottoman Empire.

The military situation did not seem to Eugène to be a hopeless one if the Turks could be forced to fight simultaneously on two fronts—against both the besieged and the relieving forces. It was only a question of tactics, he declared to Count Tarini ; and the panic in Passau was just as unfounded as the panic in Regensburg had been. Everything depended upon the morale of the troops.

But the morale of the troops was not good. In the seventeenth century, the image of a Turk was, for the terrified population, synonymous with the image of a murderous, violating, destructive barbarian—a figure taken out of the nursery tales. In Germany, and in the rest of the world, the old atmosphere of the Turkish wars of a hundred years earlier was revived. The priests declaimed from the pulpits ; " new newspapers " and other " pamphlets " reported the atrocities of the Turkish bloodhounds, and wrote of the threatened downfall of Christendom ; while in all villages the Turkish bell tolled. When it rang, then, according to the instructions, everyone whether at home, in the streets, or in the fields, was asked to repeat a fervent paternoster, and to entreat God with heartfelt sighs to remove the great danger !

The Grand Vizier, Kara Mustapha, the leader of the Turkish army, was especially famed for his cruelty. In the war against Poland, for instance, he had stormed the fortress of Human, and was said to have slaughtered the inhabitants so unmercifully that the streets ran with blood. He had had the Christian prisoners flayed alive, their skins stuffed and sent to the Sultan as war trophies. The rumours that arose were Tartars' rumours in the true sense of the word !

In any case the Turks were not dependent upon the resources of the invaded territories, and could, without harm to themselves, lay waste the lands which they conquered. They carried the necessary means of subsistence with them in their baggage, and, therefore, had no need to spare the inhabitants of the country in order to be fed by them. They made war with the customary fervour of the Mohammedan, who does what he does thoroughly, and, since he does not spare himself, does not see why he should spare his opponent.

The internuncio Caprara's companion, who was obliged to travel with the Turks during part of the campaign, gives a description of the Tartars. " In appearance, they are more like savages than men," he says, " both in their clothing and in the form of nourishment that they take. The latter consists of raw meat, including horses' meat. They pride themselves on robbing and stealing. Their weapons consist of arrows and swords. They possess horses of good breeding who can go all day without food and can swim rivers easily. The Tartars are useful for the purposes of plundering and burning, and provide the camp with many necessities."

The report of the diplomat Renninger, who had conducted negotiations in Constantinople, was no more encouraging : " What I have seen ought to be witnessed by all Christians, and particularly by the higher potentates. The enemy is mighty, swift, and cruel."

But even worse than this were the reports on the Turks' allies, the Magyars, the rebellious subjects of His Imperial Majesty, who had brought about the Turkish invasion. The bands who had instigated guerilla warfare in Upper Hungary since the year 1670 consisted of a wild and rapacious people—of Heiducs, or Hungarian foot-soldiers, and rabble of all kinds. They were called " Kuruzzen " and made war to the accompaniment of every bloody outrage dictated by passion.

The Turkish commanders-in-chief and their officers were descended from the cultivated Orient, whose way of life was, in those days, far more advanced, more refined, and more degenerate than that of civilised Western Europe. But when a Christian commander of the fortress of Kaschau, as a warning to the Turkish army, suspended from the walls the body of a Turk which had been roasted on the spit, it could hardly be expected that the Turks would wear deerskin gloves in handling their Christian prisoners! Atrocities were committed on both sides, and the young man in Passau, who compared the reports, came to the conclusion that in a war, when one side starts committing outrages, then the other inevitably follows suit. Eugène's directions in his own campaigns, as to the methods of conducting war in enemy territory, prove that he knew how to apply the observations made in his younger days.

In the diplomatic circles in Paris—where the extraordinary fact was often discussed of the friendly footing on which the All Mighty Sovereign stood to the Turks—Eugène learned that the Orientals, far from being barbarians were the perpetrators of Byzantine culture.

Thirty years later, Lady Montagu, the wife of the then English Ambasador at the Porte, was Eugène's guest at the Belvedere in Vienna. She told him about her sojourn in Constantinople, and described the fabulous splendour of the harems, the mosques, and the palaces; and of the refined mode of life of her Turkish hosts. Eugène then showed her, as a jest, the bindings of some of the books in his magnificent library. " These books," said he, " are bound in the skins of Turks."

With that, the modest, retiring little man smiled. His smile reflected the memories of the atrocities which, in the year of the terrible siege of Vienna, had caused an anxious world to hold its breath with fear.

CHAPTER VII

At last, in the early days of September, Eugène succeeded in joining the relieving forces : his cousin, the Margrave of Baden, took him into the Army.

It was a stroke of luck for Eugène, for, after his failure to attach himself to the Elector of Bavaria, he had modestly decided to become one of the many insignificant members of the Emperor's bodyguard when Leopold went to join his Army. But the Emperor remained in Passau ; he was not temperamentally fitted for the encouragement of troops, and his father confessor expressed the wish that His Majesty should await the decisive moment at a distance.

The ride to Vienna led Eugène along the shores of the Danube, through historic Austria. The road is the ancient Nibelungen way, the road that had existed throughout the early history of the country whose frontiers Eugène was to push back far unto the east and into the south. The little horseman in plain clothes rode alongside the walls of Pöchlarn, the stronghold of Rüdiger von Bechlarn, the trusted swordsman who had been King Etzel's envoy to the Burgundian Kriemhilde of the Nibelungenlied, and to Medelike, the present-day Melk. But, just now, history was not so interesting to the young Eugène, who, though so much a child of his own age, was yet looking beyond it into the future. For the moment, the present absorbed his interest. In Melk he entered war territory for the first time. Swarms of Turks from the besieging army had pressed forward, right up to the fortified monastery, and had attempted to take the little stronghold. Here Eugène heard cannon-fire for the first time, but no turban was visible to the excited youth who raised himself in his stirrups the better to look out for the enemy, loosened his sword in its scabbard, and gripped his pistol-holster. Instead, with tonsures cut in their hair and crucifixes held on high, a group of monks approached the horsemen, while from inside the monastery the sound of trumpets and kettledrums made an accompaniment to the rhythmical cannonade. Melk was celebrating the passing of each division of troops of the relieving army.

Eugène now saw the traces of devastation: hastily shovelled mounds that were the graves of the war victims, and spoil, consisting chiefly of bent swords that had been taken from the slain Turks and turban cloths still sticky with the caked blood of their fatal wounds.

The Margrave had no time for delay. A hastily served drink from the cellars of the monastery of Melk, and then they were away again across the Danube by the ferry, and down the river between the vine-covered hills of the Wachau, and past the castle of Dürnstein, where Richard Lionheart had lain in prison before he was set free by his servant Blondel. They rode past fabulous strongholds a thousand years back into history, into the time of the invasion of Asiatic hordes when the Germanic race had succeeded in stopping their advance and in driving these blood-lusty forerunners of the Turks from the soil which their colonists had laboriously tilled and made fertile.

Eugène! During a ride like this, when your native land seems strange and distant, and when your phantasy turns from the chivalrous France of your childhood; during a ride like this, when, in silence, you absorb in a glance the history and development of the country which is to become your own—during such a ride, in a single moment of time, you will become a patriot!

The country became flatter now, and the broad Danube flowed through a plain strewn with tents. From afar, the immense masses of men looked like an ants' nest. Tulln, a small town to the north of Vienna, was the assembling-point. Here the Polish and Bavarian troops had collected. The Imperial army had united with them—and, at the Margrave's side, Prince Eugène rode into the general's tent.

It was the 10th of September. The troops were beginning
HE

the advance. A motley army set out from Tulln and marched across the plain to the foot of the mountains. It consisted of regular regiments and a mass of " inexperienced, ragged, weary, and badly nourished soldiery," as a contemporary wrote of the Polish infantry. " Besides their swords, they had either muskets, guns, or half-picks, as well as clubs with iron prickles." They marched either to the accompaniment of drums and pipes or in silence. They marched in a regular order or in no order at all, and looked more like gypsies than soldiers."

This ragged soldiery was a contrast to the compact and well-armed French troops whose march past the Palais Soissons Eugène had watched with so much pleasure.

In the commander's tent he met the Elector of Bavaria again, who greeted him cordially and explained to him the plan of the march. The King of Poland had already given the *ordre de bataille*. It was the first plan of campaign Eugène had set eyes upon. The army was first to surmount the Kahlenberg, or " Naked Mountain," a mighty chain of hills that lay to the north of Vienna, and then push forward into the plain that surrounded the city. The infantry and guns were posted to the fore, with the cavalry in the rear holding itself in readiness to fall upon the enemy and then retire once more behind the infantry. In order to afford a better protection for the foot-soldiers, the Spanish horsemen were to be used. These consisted of obstacles made out of wood and barbed wire, which were so named in ironical allusion to the Spanish relief troops which had failed to arrive !

It was a simple plan of battle, which allowed of no counter-action on the part of the Turks—a plan of attack which left out of account any defence on the part of the enemy. Eugène wished to raise objections, and to ask whether the terrain had been reconnoitred, and why the greater number of guns had been left behind ; but the Elector anticipated his questions and said, " The command is disunited, *mon Prince*." The Margrave gave the same answer. On the other hand, the commander-in-chief of the Imperial troops, the Duke of Lorraine, appeared to be a commander after

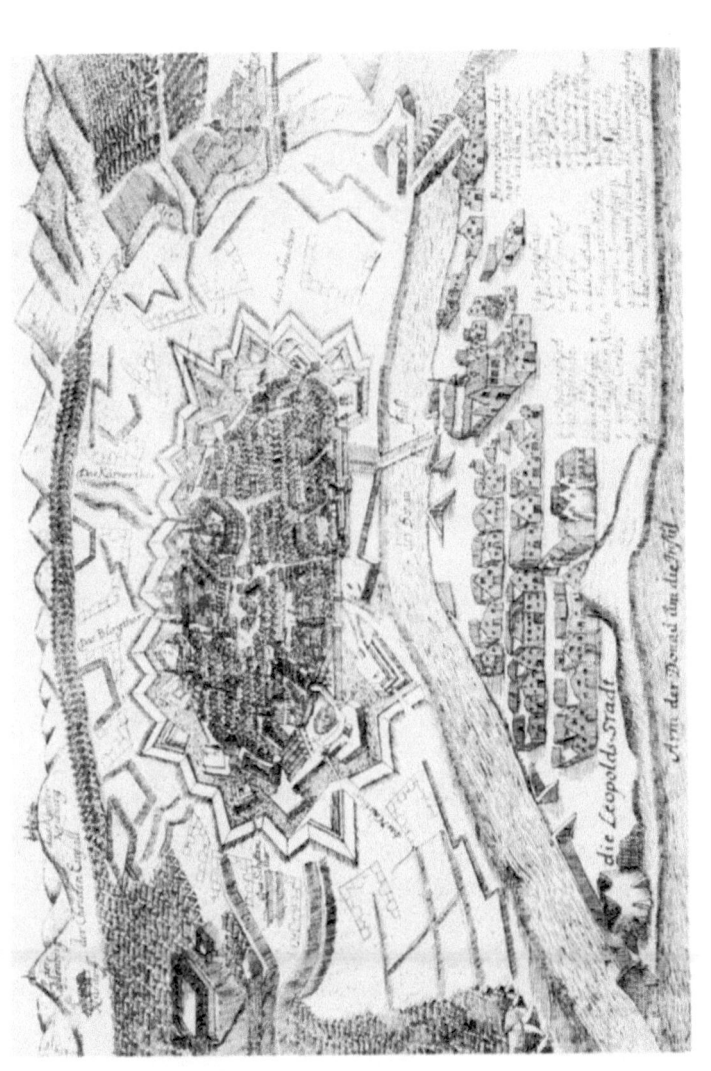

VIENNA ON THE DAY OF THE BATTLE OF DELIVERANCE (12TH SEPTEMBER, 1683)

Eugène's heart, for he encouraged his men, spoke to them in a friendly manner, and, even at long, long last, sent out an expeditionary force to explore the heights which were described in the plan of campaign as a bare range of hills.

The expeditionary force, which was the first to climb the Kahlenberg, consisted of three hundred men and the dragoons commanded by the new Colonel Heissler. He led the regiment which Eugène had coveted. Would Eugène, as a completely inexperienced soldier, have been capable of commanding this critical raiding party ? Would he have sent back patrols with the message that for an army in close formation the mountain would be arduous to climb—in no wise as easy as the *ordre de bataille* had assumed ?

Feverishly, and repressing with the greatest difficulty his trembling excitement, Eugène listened to the first report that came into the headquarters tent. Heissler's regiment had reached the summit and had arrived only just in time ; for from the other side a detachment of Turks was on the way to take possession of this salient point, from which the whole Imperial army would be exposed to their view. Was this the first decisive encounter before the critical battle ? Now the next message came : the arrival of the Imperial troops had decided the Turks to turn back !

Supposing the mountain had been occupied ? The chain of hills flanked the north-west side of Vienna. It would have been impossible to force the advance along the narrow road by the Danube, and would have necessitated a retreat probably, and an attempt to raise the siege from the south. But would the garrison have been able to hold out for so long ?

Strange to say, and contrary to every prediction, nothing hindered the army's advance, and nothing and no one threatened the party on the Kahlenberg ; not even when the colonel, in order to signal to the Viennese that the relief had arrived, planted at the top of the mountain a huge blood-red flag of defiance, with a cross in the centre.

Here and there swarms of Tartars appeared on the open road, but these were immediately driven back by the cavalry.

The night was short, and at daybreak the advance was continued. The soldiers were enjoined not to spread themselves out, but to proceed cautiously, in close formation, across the hills and through the forests, on account of danger not only from the enemy, but also from their own ignorance of the country.

The march was a particularly trying one, as the roads were completely devastated and impassable. According to a contemporary chronicler, the soldiers had to beat paths through the thickets and overcome the difficulties of precipices and narrow passes. If the enemy had occupied these dangerous positions, the advance of the relief army would not only have been hindered but would have been rendered quite impossible.

During the critical hours, Eugène stayed at his cousin's side. Now and then he was sent with a message to the Duke of Lorraine, who asked after his mother, Madame la Comtesse, and after Maria Mancini-Colonna, whom he had, at one time, wished to marry. Eugène marvelled at the Duke's cold-blooded calmness on the eve of the critical battle, for he himself was breathless with excitement. He was overtired, and began to be hungry. The left wing of the army now reached the top of the mountain, and towards eleven o'clock in the morning Eugène arrived on the Kahlenberg, and saw Vienna for the first time.

Even to-day, the loveliest view of the city is from the Kahlenberg. Certainly the view which Eugène enjoyed on that day was quite different from the view which he was to enjoy several years later from the summer palace that he built for himself on the south side of the city; for the Belvedere was built on the gently sloping hillside which exactly faces the Kahlenberg.

Had Eugène chosen this place for his summer residence because it happened to be the first that met his eyes, and because he had thought of it as the most favourable starting-place for the decisive battle? Would he have refused to undertake the raising of the siege from the Kahlenberg on account of the hardships of the road across the chain of hills, which Sobieski had only chosen because he had put his faith in the literal meaning of the word Kahlenberg?

" Disappointments are irritating," wrote the Polish King to his wife. " There are woods, precipices, and a large mountain to overcome, besides five or six narrow passes of which no one gave me an account."

It was a long time before the army reached the heights, for violent rainstorms rendered the climb difficult, but at last, by evening, it was accomplished. Now the whole of the relief army was in sight of Vienna.

The Frenchman Dupont, an engineer in the service of King Sobieski, describes in his memoirs the view from the heights of the Kahlenberg over the city at that historic moment. " What a scene was revealed to our eyes from the crown of the hill ! " he writes. " The great space was covered by tents—for even the island of Leopoldstadt was hidden by them. The frightful thunder from out of the mouths of the enemies' guns, and the answering fire from the walls of the town, filled the air. Smoke and flames enveloped the city to such an extent that only the tops of the towers were visible in between."

A letter headed " Within sight of Vienna, the 11th of September, 1683," and signed by his " humblest, most devoted and true servant, Father Marco d'Aviano, Capuchin, father and poor sinner," was received by the Emperor, in which the father confessor reassures his penitent : " . . . Leaders and Princes are all united here, and everything is proceeding in order. His Most Serene Highness, the Duke of Lorraine, neither eats nor sleeps, but works uninterruptedly with the greatest industry. He inspects the sentries in person, and fulfils in the best possible manner the functions of a good general. To-morrow, I hope, if it please God, the attack will begin. . . ."

To-morrow was the watchword of the evening ! Under the hastily roofed-in remains of the walls of the burnt-out monastery which served as a dwelling-place for most of the commanders, at the guards' fires, at the sentry posts, and in the cavalry lines, everyone was in readiness. To-morrow! Eugène looked out impatiently over the burning city. Would Vienna be able to hold out until morning? He offered himself to the Margrave for patrol work or sentry duty with the troops. But the war-accustomed Ludwig smilingly ordered him to get some sleep before the battle. Eugène did not sleep; he gazed out again and again over the city from which, unceasingly, burning sheaves were tossed up in the sky. Would her martyrdom be at an end on the morrow?

For sixty-two days, since the 15th of July, when the Turks brought their first guns into position, the cannonade had never ceased, except during heavy rainstorms. From the 23rd of July until the 10th of September, twenty Turkish and twelve of the garrison mines had been fired. The garrison had been stormed fifty-three times, had driven the enemy back each time, and had itself made thirty-six assaults. During nine solid weeks the town had been the object of unceasing attack from cannon-balls and firebrands. . . .

The commandant of the town, von Starhemberg, had ordered that all the shingled roofs in the town be torn off, so as to prevent fires, and also in order that, later on, the great beams on which the roofs rested might be used for palisades. All available timber was dipped in lead and used for the illumination of the city trenches at night, to prevent attacks by stealth. Most of the buildings were damaged; the Hofburg was pierced by holes and the tower of the Minoriten Church was robbed of its steeple. More than fifty shots had penetrated the tower of St. Stephan and bombs had exploded, even in the interior of the church. In the town, owing to the segregation of so many people within such a small space, the filth in the streets and squares had become unbearable. Horse dung and decaying rubbish spread pestilence abroad. Such was the report that Eugène read. Was such to be the appearance of his future home?

On the following morning—it was the 12th of September—King Sobieski sat down at an improvised writing-table, and took up his ever-ready pen to write a last letter to his wife before the battle. "I spent the night with the infantry of the left wing," he wrote. " From there one can see right into the Turkish camp. The noise of the guns makes it impossible to close one's eyes. On Friday and Saturday we were so starved out that the enemy could easily have hunted us with deer ! The horses are in a worse condition, as they have only had the leaves off the trees to eat. Of the promised provender for men and horses there is not a trace ! "

The thunder of cannon from the left wing of the relieving army prevented Sobieski from continuing the letter. With his son Jacob, he hurried to the Duke of Lorraine's headquarters in the burnt-out monastery on the Kahlenberg.

The 12th of September, 1683, was the 14th Sunday after Whitsuntide. The Catholics call it " *Dominica Protector Noster* " (the Sunday of Divine Providence). Spasmodic firing between the enemy outposts on the left wing of the Christian army had begun at dawn. But, in the Camaldolese monastery the assembled Princes and army leaders, amongst them Prince Eugène, attended Mass. Father Marco d'Aviano celebrated Mass on a hastily improvised altar, and blessed the Christian arms in their struggle against the unbelievers. Here the last details were discussed : it was the war council on the eve of battle, and, for the first time, the question was raised :

Where had the vast Turkish army remained hidden up to this time ?

Two days before the battle the Grand Vizier, Kara Mustapha, called the pashas into his tent. He did so very unwillingly. Only the repeated insistence of his generals decided him to hold a war council. A war council ? The generals could come and talk as much as they liked ; in the end his will would decide the issue. And even the Sultan would not dispute his will, although he had reproached him for not having first taken Raab and Komorn, two small forts on the road to Vienna, before laying siege to the Imperial city. What did the Sultan know about it? The town which Kara Mustapha held in an iron vice could not slip out of his grasp; it must fall. Why, therefore, waste strength in besieging smaller forts which must of themselves capitulate once Vienna ceased to be an Imperial city?

Kara Mustapha could not rid himself of the conviction that Vienna would fall to his arms, and that nothing could now prevent his victory. When he received the first news of the approach of a Christian army, he refused to pay any attention to it. But the messengers ran the risk of paying with their lives for the delivery of the news. In the end, however, Mustapha shared the general unrest which the unexpected *communiqué* spread amongst his troops. But up to the very last moment he refused to admit that a Christian army was approaching, and declared that the pashas were allowing themselves to be alarmed by a figment of the brain. However, he could scarcely refuse to believe the official reports that were brought to him of the fugitive-like departure of Turkish soldiers from the camp!

During the war council, the old pasha, Ibrahim, rose and, after flowery eulogies of the Grand Vizier, declared that of course Vienna would fall—there was no doubt of that. But first the camp must be raised, the mountain passes protected by barricades, batteries mounted, and the relief army attacked during its advance march. The Turkish troops were too exhausted by the long ordeal of the siege to be capable of fighting on two fronts simultaneously. First the advancing enemy must be driven back, and then the city would be forced to yield itself to their clemency or inclemency, as the case might be.

If Ibrahim Pasha's advice had been taken, then the relieving army would never have been able to surmount the Kahlenberg, nor would it have been possible for them to force the decisive encounter in such a short time; in consequence, the final outcome of the battle would have been doubtful.

But Kara Mustapha ordered that the siege be continued. The Turkish forces would attack the oncoming army as it

KARA MUSTAPHA, THE TURKISH GRAND VIZIER

descended from the mountain and drive it back. Vienna would then be compelled to open her gates to the victors.

But at the last moment the Grand Vizier decided otherwise.

The Viennese, Lieutenant-Colonel Gschwind, reports : " On the 6th, the garrison had observed a commotion in the Turkish camp. We did not know the cause, and prepared ourselves for the worst. We placed the houses lying immediately behind the two bastions that were being attacked in a state of defence, barricaded the streets, and put up chains. During the afternoon of the 11th the Turks left the camp and marched in the direction of the mountains. The troops in Leopoldstadt struck their tents and marched towards the Kahlenberg."

That was the division of troops which had allowed itself to be turned back from the Kahlenberg by the timely appearance of Colonel Heissler's patrol.

Kara Mustapha felt now that his life was at stake. He stationed both cavalry and infantry on the chain of hills below the Kahlenberg, mounted guns, and waited for the attack.

On the morning of the 12th of September, five cannonshots, fired one immediately after the other, broke the short, expectant silence. It was the Duke of Lorraine's prearranged signal for the opening of the battle.

Eugène found himself with the right wing. For the first few hours of the encounter, in company with the Margrave of Baden, he negotiated the descent from the mountain, and thus had no opportunity of witnessing the skirmishes which took place either on the steeply sloping terrain, intersected by torrents, in the narrow, deep valleys—which in some places became actual ravines—and in the vine-gardens of Grinsing and Sievering.

The descent lasted for four hours. In Vienna, from the bastions, and from all other points of vantage, the population gazed across at the Kahlenberg. Välkeren wrote : " Hardly had the dawn appeared than we saw the hills swarming with men who, advancing in a long, broad line, in unbroken close formation, gradually and slowly let down and drove before them several cannon pieces, which they continually fired off at the Turks standing underneath. Then, so as to be able to re-load, they waited to allow time for the troops following to join up more and more closely with them. They then advanced again, keeping their guns to the fore, through bushes and shrubs, through hedges and undergrowth, down through the vineyards, to within forty or fifty paces of the Turks. There they fired again—and again remained stationary until those following overtook them. In this way they came gradually to the foot of the mountain where the Turks were stationed.

" Then the fray began ; and when the Turks saw that the Christian peoples, for the most part, were provided with coats of mail, harness, armour, helmets, swords, rapiers, guns, pistols, and all other imaginable weapons, and perceived that there was no end (for ever more and more men crowded forth from the brushwood), as they became aware of this unceasing advance of troops, and remarked that, in the rear, from the bastions of the town, the noble commandant, von Starhemberg, was causing his guns having the longest range and heaviest calibre to play unceasing and cruel havoc upon their rear, they resolved, rather from motives of despair than of bravery, to attack the Christian host and to engage them in an encounter."

As this eye-witness relates, the Turks took up the battle against the garrison as well as against the relieving forces. But the whole of Kara Mustapha's army did not take part in the encounter. Lieutenant-Colonel Gschwind notes, in his diary for the 12th of September : " The violent cannonade which was directed against the bastions of the town led us to fear the worst. Everyone was expecting the mines to explode and the enemy to storm the city. Yet, as had been observed already in the early morning, many hundred wagons and as many men from the enemy's camp moved off in the direction of Schwechat."

The flight—or what at first appeared to be the retreat only of a part of the Turkish army—began in the early morning of the 12th of September, before the onset of the battle.

The Grand Vizier left the janizaries in the camp before Vienna. With the aid of dispirited Seimens and Spahis alone he began the struggle against the relieving army.

The only important encounters took place in the two wings of the army. It was just midday, and still, from the left wing, no sign could be detected of the arrival in the battle-line either of the centre or of the right wing. At last, towards two o'clock, as all eyes were directed towards the place where the Poles were to break forth from the wood, Sobieski's winged horsemen, in coats of mail, appeared in gleaming armour and waving plumes, with their long spears and fluttering pennants. They were greeted by shouts of rejoicing from the Imperial troops. In spite of heat and thirst, and in spite of all their previous hardships, the men were so impatient for the combat that they wished, without waiting for the order, to hurl themselves upon the enemy. In some places, indeed, the officers were obliged to force them back with the flat blades of their swords. Sobieski, with his son Jacob, rode at the head of the cavalry division. Seven thousand mailed horsemen and hussars followed him. It was at that moment that the soldiers of the left wing, with shouts of " Hurra ! " clamoured for the order of advance.

Charles, Duke of Lorraine, stood on a hillock with the generals of the left wing and surveyed the situation. He asked the assembled officers whether, in their opinion, the relieving army ought to consider itself satisfied with the present victory—in accordance with the agreement made with Sobieski—or whether at least a war council should be held. But the general, Field-Marshal Goltz, answered that now was not the time for councils—now was the time to fight. God had already pointed the way to victory, and they must strike the iron while it was hot. As a " quiet " man, and with God's help, he cherished hopes on this very evening of sleeping in " good quarters " in Vienna !

His words were received with general rejoicing. " Let us march, then," shouted Charles of Lorraine, and the left wing of the relieving army set itself in motion.

The Turks still made an effort to defend themselves. But, as the Christians approached, they lost their positions, and the Imperial troops took Döbling, the Turkish bulwark. Here also scarcely an attempt was made to put up a defence.

The engineer Dupont gives an account of it : " Suddenly, while both armies were stationary in their positions, a small red tent made its appearance from the place where it had been set up behind the centre of the Turkish battle-array ; and next to the tent was the Ottoman flag which is brought every year with great piety from Mecca. The Turks always observed this custom at such critical moments. By this sign the commander-in-chief reminds his troops that under this flag they must be victorious, or die in the attempt."

But this final rally lasted only a few minutes. While the Imperial troops, in closed columns, pressed their way into the Turkish camp, the Poles hurled themselves into the frightful turmoil round the flag of the Prophet.

The assault made by the Polish cavalry was so violent that the Turks were completely overthrown. Flag and tent lay at the feet of the King of Poland.

It was at the twilight hour—between six and seven in the evening—when the Duke of Lorraine ordered the Margrave of Baden to press forward to the walls of the town and, in conjunction with Starhemberg, to drive off the Turks who were still fiercely bombarding the town from their batteries. The Margrave Ludwig hastily collected two dragoon regiments together and, with Prince Eugène at his side, proceeded, to the joyous " sound of trumpets and drums," in the direction of the city, to the Schottentor, *fasste posto*, and informed the commandant of his arrival, so that with his men and the soldiers who could be spared from the city they might " make a sally and attack on the enemy, and cut down everything that was still to be found in the Turkish trenches !—But, while Count Starhemberg made the necessary preparations, and in the evening, in company with the

Margrave, himself went ahead into the trenches, the Turks had in the meantime evacuated the camp so completely that no one was to be found there ! "

With persistent endurance Kara Mustapha had led his vacillating troops into battle. When, however, he saw that all was lost, he took to flight. Bareheaded and filthy, he was seen on the following day in the neighbourhood of Raab, mounted on a miserable nag and surrounded by his trusted followers.

The victory was such an unexpected one that at midnight the general, Count Taafe, wrote to his brother from the Turkish encampment, saying : " We have delivered Vienna from the enemy. If the victory is not such a complete one as we could have wished, it must be ascribed to the cowardice of our enemies, whom we drove like herds before us from post to post, and from morning well into the night."

The guns were silent at last, and night descended upon a delivered city. After two anxious, terrible months, it was the first night in which the inhabitants were able to yield themselves to a quiet sleep.

Only the Polish troops plundered the Turkish camp.

The booty which fell into the hands of the victors was prodigious : twenty-five thousand tents, weapons, munitions, and provender of all kinds ; twenty thousand head of buffalo, the same number of oxen, camels, and mules, ten thousand head of sheep, one hundred thousand *malter* of corn, besides great quantities of coffee, sugar, honey, rice, and grease. Now there was an end to the hunger and want !

King Johann Sobieski spent the night in the Grand Vizier's tent, which, as he wrote to his wife, was the equal in circumference of towns like Lemberg or Warsaw. The interior was luxurious to a degree that was, in those days, quite unknown to Europeans. There were gardens with fountains, bathrooms with scented waters and soaps, sumptuous beds, shining lamps and chandeliers, carpets worked in silver and gold and all manner of other costly objects. In special tents there were small cabinets so successfully hidden that only on the third day after the battle was one of the Grand Vizier's wives discovered in one of them. Beside her lay another, who had been beheaded. The survivor explained that the Grand Vizier had not wished this " Pearl of Loveliness " to fall into the hands of the Christian dogs ! Besides richly chased weapons and embroidered clothing, this tent contained rabbits, dolphins, and every kind of bird ; there was even an ostrich, which had been decapitated by the Grand Vizier so that it should not fall into the hands of the despised enemy !

The victorious Princes and army commanders spent the night in the tents. For the troops, quarters were found inside the walls of the city, in the houses of the citizens, who thought themselves lucky in being able to house their liberators.

In one of these humble quarters some unknown person sheltered a tired, war-bespattered volunteer—Eugène of Savoy.

This was Prince Eugène's first night in Vienna—but no marble tablet marks the dwelling of his first host in the city that was now to be his home.

PART III

"Austria Holds the Trumps—If She Would Only Play Them"

CHAPTER I

THE YEAR 1683, the year of the deliverance of Vienna from the Turks, does not yet mark the dividing-line which separated two epochs—that of the Great Power, laboriously pasted together, consisting of the Imperial Crown and the exploited Habsburg dominions, on the one hand, and the powerful united State which Prince Eugène aspired to create out of Austria on the other.

As an immediate result of his first night in Vienna, even Eugène himself ceased to believe in the success of his fantastic plan. It seemed to him quite impossible that he should remain in Austria for a lifetime. How could he serve an Emperor whose only idea of influencing the destiny of his Empire was by means of prayers and devotions? How could he ever feel at home in this barbaric land? The events that he saw taking place around him reacted upon Eugène like a bad dream. In the first place, there had been the disorderly march before the battle ; and now, outside the walls of the half-destroyed city, the Poles were plundering the Turkish camp ! The dead were still lying about, unburied, yet undisciplined crowds marched yodling through the streets, and at every street corner and in every square a lively trade in booty had been established. It was a hideous market. Eugène wondered whether defeat could be more revolting than victory !

The French Army had evoked in Eugène his war enthusiasm and the desire to serve under a nation's flag. A well-know historian says, not without reason : " Every people carries with it, under the helmet, the characteristics it has acquired—in other words, its history." The remark is particularly apposite for the case of the French Army, inasmuch as it was built up from a single people—a people speaking a single language and recognising but a single will, the will of the Bourbons, to which it had been submissive for hundreds of years, and which was so typically represented in the person of Louis XIV.

But what were the characteristics and of what nature was the history of the Imperial army as it had shown itself to Eugène in the battle of Vienna? He had to admit that it consisted of a motley army of auxiliary troops who had great difficulty in understanding one another. One soldier spoke the Croat language, another spoke Polish, a third German, a fourth Italian, a fifth the Magyar tongue, and so on. Each of these nations had its separate tradition and its individual history. The Cross was the only symbol which held them together. This army could be no more reduced to a common denominator than a collection of heterogeneous objects can be added together to make a sum. It was not a national army, or in any way the self-expression of a people : the many different uniforms and the varied weapons alone showed clearly enough that the unity was merely arbitrary. The troops had been welded together into an army by accidental diplomatic soldering. Was Eugène to serve in an army like this ? Now that the war of deliverance was over, what was the point of further warfare ? To increase the power of the House of Habsburg ? What did the Habsburgs matter to him ? Eugène was sobered. He was in need of a confidant, of someone to whom he could confess that with his whole heart, soul, and body he belonged to France, and that he was homesick for Paris. He was lost in the Babel of languages whose syllables jarred on his ears. He tried to think of a way out. If only he could get to Savoy, since France was barred to him ! He wanted to talk the matter over with Tarini, but Tarini wasted no words in telling him that in Turin there were no prospects for him.

This declaration was equivalent to an official rejection,

KING JOHN SOBIESKI, DURING THE BATTLE

for Tarini must have had official instructions before he expressed himself so definitely. The Duke of Savoy did not desire his cousin's services. . . . " Not yet," was Eugène's comment. He clung to the little word " yet." Did they wish to see whether he would prove himself to be worth anything, and if so, what ? But where could he demonstrate his capabilities ? It was obvious that he could only do so in the Emperor's army. Besides, he was without means of subsistence : he must become a soldier in order to be able to live. His decision was made, forced upon him by circumstances. In spite of everything, he must serve in this army that was so distasteful to him. But under whom should he serve ? Who commanded the army ? Here the generals were all of equal status and each refused to subordinate himself. Sobieski, as independent King of Poland, insisted that his was the prior right to the supreme command ; the Duke of Lorraine was the official Field Marshal of the Holy Roman Empire, and Max Emmanuel, the Elector of Bavaria, as Prince of the Empire, with an auxiliary army at his back, had an equal claim. At any moment any one of these gentlemen, if he were so minded, could send his soldiers home and retire to one of his pleasure palaces to recuperate after the exertions of the campaign. It was entirely a question of goodwill when the King of Poland, after the battle of deliverance, started off with his troops in pursuit of the Turks ; and equally a matter of goodwill when the Elector of Bavaria besieged the mountain fort of Ofen. If the Emperor had ordered him to do it in a firm and autocratic manner such as Louis XIV was accustomed to use in distributing his commands, then Max Emmanuel would most certainly have returned to Munich.

The Imperial dignity was not a power ; it was a concept ; and the powerlessness of this concept had shown itself during the Thirty Years War. In spite of his attempts at a show of dignity the Emperor was obliged to humble himself. Which piece of territory on the map could he really claim for his own ? What revenues did he draw from it ? He possessed the Austrian hereditary lands, which consisted of part of the territory of the Austria of to-day, together with Bohemia. For Hungary, of which the part not occupied by the Turks was in constant rebellion, could hardly count as a dominion.

Was that a Power comparable with the might of Louis XIV?

The Imperial treasury was empty, burnt out like the towns and villages through which the Turks had passed. The Emperor was dependent upon subsidies and upon the Peter's pence which he received from the Pope, and for which he had to pay with his good conduct. He was dependent upon the feeling of duty or, better said, upon the favours of the reigning Princes of the Empire, or perhaps even more upon their business instinct, which extracted profits from every service rendered for as much as could be extorted by taxation.

The need and distress were only very scantily hidden by the paltry screen of princely pomp. The Spanish etiquette had been transferred from Madrid to Vienna, and the ceremonial was stricter than at the French Court. But while in Paris it played its part in satiated pomp between marble walls, and in mirrored galleries, amidst brocade and damask, Gobelins and porcelain, in Vienna the Imperial Hofburg was a shabby grey building that looked more like a barrack than the residence of the greatest ruler of Christendom. How poor Vienna looked in comparison with Paris, that gay city at the height of its bloom, with its numberless palaces, wide squares, and flower-gardens! Vienna seemed to be a city of corners and alleys, and for the first few years after the Turkish siege continued to look seared and demolished. The houses in the narrow streets were like a patchwork that was only very slowly restored. Why did everything happen so slowly? Eugène discovered the reason only too soon: Vienna lacked a single all-powerful will to spur on slow hands and lagging feet. No one attempted to accelerate the slow trot of the official mule, which, instead of choosing the direct path to attain an objective, pursued the most complicated serpentines.

Austria Holds the Trumps if She would Only Play Them was the title of a pamphlet that appeared at the time, to the contents of which Tarini drew Eugène's attention. If the data quoted were correct, then the Imperial hereditary dominions, together with Hungary and Bohemia, were capable of raising, arming, and equipping an army of two hundred thousand men. The effect of that would be to spread well-being in the dominions; but first it would be necessary to establish order and a new system of finance administration, such as Mazarin had created in France during the minority of Louis XIV.

Austria holds the trumps if she would only play them! Would she be capable, then, of overcoming the power of Louis XIV? Eugène's whole being was obsessed by that idea. It was the only justification for his remaining in the country; but in order to realise that project he would have to transfer himself, body and soul, to the service of the House of Habsburg. He drew parallels between Austria and France, which all led to the same conclusion : the Emperor must will it. If he did not, then Eugène would force him to it ! That was a fantastic resolution on the part of a young man, hardly more than a child, who had come uninvited to Austria, and whose access to the Emperor could only be gained by fighting for it step by step.

The historical narrative of the period immediately following the death of Leopold bestowed upon him the lofty title of " the Great." A hundred years later it was recognised that the title was not appropriate to Leopold, but rather to his period—or, even better expressed, to the half-century during which the volunteer, Eugène of Savoy, had been the servant of Austria.

Eugène was an unwilling volunteer. He had hoped that, after the battle of Vienna, he would be promoted to a colonel's rank. His cousin, Ludwig of Baden, had promised it him. But Eugène had still to learn that in Austria nothing was accomplished quickly—not even with the aid of patronage from the highest quarters !

How could he, as a stranger and immigrant, hope to attain office and dignity at the Court of Vienna when in the ante-chambers of the Hofburg hundreds of indigenous cavaliers were waiting to come into His Majesty's field of vision, in order to beg for the meanest office? Eugène mingled with those who were waiting; but he was at a disadvantage compared with them, inasmuch as he did not understand the languages of the various countries, and in order to obtain information was obliged to invoke Tarini's assistance. But his questions were not confined to matters about which he wanted definite information. They always overlapped, and usually satirised the Emperor and the conventions of the Court. It was bitter self-torture (of which he was himself well aware) when he asked why the Emperor always dressed himself in sackcloth and ashes, while the Ministers' cloaks even were lined with the *drap d'or* and the *drap d'argent*. The Emperor lived in poverty, and the beggared Prince of Savoy must compete with the plutocratic nobility of the country in soliciting a menial post of an apparently impoverished monarch! The contrasts were perpetually thrust before Eugène's eyes. On gala days, for instance, the liveries of the noble servitors shone and glittered, while the Imperial Guard, the Hatschiere, wore, over their shabby everyday livery, miserable *kasaken*, bound with plain braid. The gilded coaches of the nobles paraded the streets, while the Emperor drove in a plain black coach, devoid of any precious metal. To make up for that, however, the Emperor sat erect, like an idol, and not even the Empress might sit beside him. Her place was facing him, and the seat was placed an inch lower, according to the dictates of Court ceremonial. Of Imperial pomp, only the stiff gestures remained; the glamour was lacking.

The unapproachableness of Their Majesties remained unchanged, however, although the Emperor's Court could only be maintained on money borrowed with the greatest difficulty. Yet the immense salaries of the Court dignitaries and officials were not reduced—as, for instance, that of the Lord Chamberlain with his staff, the 414 aristocratic

chamberlains, and the thousand Court servants, creditors of
the Emperor, to whom his indebtedness increased daily. For
the service of Their Majesties' table, ninety-nine cooks, head-
cooks, under-cooks, master-cooks, scullions, and baker-boys
were maintained. But the table itself lacked even the bare
necessities. The Emperor and Empress were reduced to the
meanest diet. Their palates and the exchequer were similar
cases ! The dishes passed through so many hands that, at
the end, nothing was left over. His Apostolic Majesty,
Leopold I, would grant audience with his pale, hollow-
cheeked countenance bent slightly forward, his sponge-like
underlip hanging down almost to his chin—fatigued almost
immediately with the effort of sitting on his Throne. No one
ever heard him utter " Yes " or " No "; his expression never
changed, and his mournful eyes, with their blue-black
crêpe halo, never moved. Only the sound of church
bells caused the Emperor to relax his stiff demeanour.
His only friend was the all-powerful High Steward,
Count Bonaventura von Harrach, as weighty, immovable, and uncompromisingly given over to tradition as
the Emperor himself. One anecdote recounts how the
two men would sit opposite one another for hours without uttering a word, only moving now and then to cross
themselves. Any kind of innovation appalled them ; everything must remain as it was—as " God willed it " ; above
all, no reforms and no new faces ! They always avoided looking at Eugène's peculiarly ugly face, which ever and again
made its appearance in the *salons* : they evaded his eager,
ambitious glance. They intended to take as little notice of
Prince Eugène of Savoy as of the numberless other adventurers who had come to Vienna to take part in the battle
against the Turks. But Eugène saw them, and that was
enough for him to guarantee their future. He observed their
lives, confirmed the relationship of the individual Court
dignitaries to one another, and investigated the thick net of
connections so as to find the mesh through which he could
work his way. He was lying in wait. In a very short time
he would force the Emperor to take account of his existence !

The youth of twenty was full of self-confidence. Although very remote from dignity and office—not even entitled to solicit an unimportant command—yet he surveyed the situation at the Austrian Court with such clarity of vision that he wrote with a supreme self-confidence to Savoy : " I see myself in a position here to obtain all offices which are appropriate to my capabilities."

That again was an entirely unfounded prophecy, based solely on Eugène's own estimate of the capabilities which he as yet had no opportunity of putting to the test. Up to now he had been nothing more than a hanger-on—a plain horseman, an unpaid and casual soldier attached to the Margrave of Baden's corps during the pursuit of the Turks. During the battle of Parkan he had had the opportunity of distinguishing himself by proving that he was unafraid ! But, if he was really honest with himself, Eugène must have admitted that the number of soldiers courageous and unafraid like himself ran into thousands, and that only his noble birth and his connection with the army leaders could avail him anything. He possessed theoretical knowledge, it was true, but of what use was that in the hand-to-hand fighting that confused his brain ? He knew Vauban's system of taking forts ; but when galloping in pursuit of enemy cavalry, charging the movable wall of armed human beings, all his knowledge abandoned him. . . . He only saw faces—at the side of him and in front of him—which seemed suddenly to emerge from nothingness like some wild vision . . . he saw snorting, champing horses, heard the clash of weapons all about him. His pistol, which he had discharged, fell out of his hand, and over there a man fell from his horse. A flashing noise whistled past his ears ; his arm lifted itself in defence and, at once, his sword sank unresisted into a man's breast. Hardly had he time to draw it out, still steaming from the warm blood, when his horse plunged forward again. Unconsciously he gave it the spur. Beside him and in front of him the cavalry were pressing forward. He was almost unconscious—it was intoxication. Forward—forward—ever forward—on—on—until a wide field stretched before him or a forest loomed up in front of him, which swallowed the Turks into its gloom ! He came to himself and heard cries of victory ; but he was as exhausted as though he had spent a night on sentry duty. Now what about strategy and his resolutions to look and to learn ? Only afterwards, in the headquarters tent, did he hear what the object of the attack had been in which he had taken part. He tried again and again to maintain a cold-blooded attitude ; but each time, in every skirmish, his self-control gave way ! He was born to be a soldier certainly, but—a leader ?

Doubts on that score tormented Eugène to such a degree that finally he begged his cousin to allow him to remain with the staff on the occasion of the next battle. He had already proved himself to be beyond suspicion, so that this request could not be misunderstood for cowardice. It was granted him all the more readily as on more than one occasion Ludwig had had to exhort him to be cautious.

The staff watched the advance march of the troops from a mound. In that moment Eugène saw the landscape in the form of a map, and all at once theory became reality for him. The men, crowded together into regimental units, were the elements : on the right, one element more ; on the left, one less. With a sure instinct he recognised where a regiment needed to be inserted ; he felt the ratio of strength in his bones. There was the enemy's weak point : he felt it before he knew it. He listened to the reasons for this and for that move from the lips of the experienced Margrave ; he was able to raise objections now, and the Margrave consulted with him and kept him with the staff instead of sending him back to the troops. In a few weeks Eugène had learnt the application of strategy. But when would he have the opportunity of using his knowledge ?

The campaign for that year had come to an end, and the army went into winter quarters. The generals departed into the hinterland, and Eugène saw himself threatened by the lack of money, which had been the worst enemy of his youth.

For him the war had been an escape from want. How, without money and without resources, was he going to live through the winter until the next campaign in the spring? The Court was now in residence in Linz. But the Court household was very different from that of Versailles, where anyone could live as a courtier on credit, and where anyone who had the entrée could eat, drink, sleep, and live generally, without paying for all the necessities of daily life. Now, after the privations of the campaign, Eugène saw himself faced with the fate of an unemployed soldier at the end of a war; and what made the situation all the more oppressive was the fact that, in order not to discredit himself for ever, he must live in a manner that became his princely rank. He could not, as in Paris, just disappear from the picture; he must remain in touch with the generals and force himself on the notice of the Emperor!

In despair he wrote to Victor Amadeus, the young head of his House. This letter was a contrast to the last, in which, full of hope and confidence, he had declared that no roads were closed to him. This letter was a release of his pent-up feeling of despair, thoroughly foreign to his consciously superior nature, and an expression of humility which he can only have permitted himself in the extremity of need, or for diplomatic reasons. "I hope," he wrote to the Duke of Savoy, " that Your Highness will honour me with the same favours as my brother, and render me assistance. I am forsaken on all sides."

This call for help was hardly made before it was modified. Hardly had Eugène expressed his need of assistance, and confessed his desperate position, than he ceased to write in the spirit of a petitioner; he promised something at the same time. He was aware of his worth. " Your Royal Highness will surely approve of my taking the opportunity of learning something in order that I may serve him." He put in a limitation, " if Your Royal Highness should need me," in order to render a refusal difficult. Eugène begged—but he offered at the same time. He knew very well that it would be quite important for the Duke of Savoy to have as a representative of his interests at the Imperial Court someone who could, without arousing suspicion, write harmless letters and reports to the head of his family. ... Even the avaricious Duke would not refuse a modest allowance to one who could play this part. And at the moment Eugène believed that his whole life and future depended upon that allowance.

The Prince of Savoy still maintained himself on an equal footing with the Elector of Bavaria, and waited every day for the money to arrive. He accepted an invitation to take part in the carnival at Munich. He knew that if he were to combine the protection of the Elector and the recommendation of the Margrave of Baden he would succeed in attaining his goal. But would he be able to hold on so long without money?

Eugène was at this period a desperado, and for many a long year afterwards he still retained the feeling in his blood of belonging nowhere. He was not a Frenchman, in spite of having been born in France and of knowing no other than the French language; he was not a Savoyard, although he belonged to the House of Savoy; not an Austrian, and not a German, in spite of having served with distinction in the Emperor's army. He belonged to no nation and to no State. When he analysed his position in the world, he discovered it to be that of an adventurer without means and without a home, who had no one to depend upon but himself. He looked at himself in the mirror and saw a wasted figure, weakened by the hardships of the campaigns, dressed in shabby civil clothes. This hollow, unattractive countenance was all that he possessed. A very weak support for life! His ego, which he could only cling to like a Münchhausen, and his prospects, whose ratio to his ambition were so small that as a mathematician it must have appalled him, were the sum total of his possessions. He must redouble his efforts with his fellow-men, or rather multiply them many times, without their becoming aware of his intentions!

He managed to remain in their midst as an amusing companion whose eager eyes were able to bring humour into their glances, whose irony stimulated and whose intelligence and Parisian sophistication diverted them. For their amusement he recited all the amusing anecdotes that he had ever heard, and adapted himself to the different temperaments of the Princes, particularly to that of the Elector, whose character he had thoroughly analysed. Max Emmanuel pursued warfare in a dilettante fashion, in order to kill time. It represented for him exactly the same sort of diversion that the chase is for the huntsman. In a word, it amused him.

The Elector was vain, and did not tolerate delay in the reward for his efforts. Max Emmanuel arranged a meeting therefore between the Emperor and Eugène. Again these two men, Leopold and Eugène, who in the future were to be indispensable to one another, met face to face. Once again ensued the mutual depreciatory, mistrustful consideration. There seemed to be no good reason why Leopold should appoint the thin little Eugène to a colonel's command, but, because his son-in-law made the request, he did not say " No." But neither did he say " Yes " ; he only inclined his head. His melancholy eyes fixed themselves on Eugène's mask-like face. The audience was not a success ; but, on the other hand, it was not a failure ; and, in any case, Eugène made capital out of it. The money from Savoy had still not arrived, nor had the Duke as yet answered his letter ; but Eugène used his unproductive audience with the Emperor as a pretext for writing another self-confident letter from Linz. He wrote : " The Emperor was gracious enough to promise me, with his own lips, the command of the first available regiment."

He still needed the money, otherwise he would not have written the letter. He wished to force the hand of his unwilling patron. As commander of an Imperial regiment he was worth so many hundred ducats more to the House of Savoy. If he did not receive the money, then the Duke of Savoy would have nothing to hope for from him ! Secretly Eugène felt himself to be the future protector of his family. But whoever left him in the lurch would equally be left in the lurch by him !

He was overcome with despair when the Elector of Bavaria left Linz—without him. Once again he was abandoned entirely without means, like a fish out of water. As long as Max Emmanuel was in Linz, Eugène had nonchalantly made himself a member of his princely household. He stayed in the Elector's house as a matter of course, and now the obeisance with which he made his adieux cast him on to the pavement. He could not admit to the Elector that he was unable to travel to Munich because he was not in a position to provide himself with suitable clothing. By such an admission he would have depreciated the value of the protection from which he hoped to gain the most. At the best he would have been given a regiment as a charity offering. But for his ambition the title of colonel was nothing. He would surmount his difficulties somehow, rather than risk losing the friendship of the Elector, from whom he hoped to receive more than mere maintenance.

Eugène considered : he had, as yet, made no use of the letter of introduction to the Spanish Ambassador, the Marchese de Borgomaniero, which his mother had sent to Passau a few days before the battle of deliverance. Perhaps it would prove to be a paper anchor. Eugène cast it—and discovered in the person of the Marchese a friendly old gentleman who anticipated his confession of his miserable position, and offered him hospitality.

Then Ludwig of Baden came to Linz. He had been the first to receive the news of the death of the colonel of dragoons, the Count von Kufstein. The Margrave asked the Emperor to appoint Eugène in his place. Another protector : this was the second captain who had asked for a command for this Prince of Savoy ? Leopold hated decisions, it was true, but he hated still more to be pressed. In order to hear nothing more of the affair, he left the decision to the Margrave ; and two days later Eugène became colonel of an Imperial regiment.

At last he had arrived at dignity and office ! But a colonel ; only a colonel ? That was no career for a Prince of a reigning House ! He was ironical at his own expense ! He knew that the appointment had been due entirely to his cousin's insistence; and his cousin had insisted chiefly so that an income might be secured for the impecunious Eugène.

In the army the bestowal of appointments proceeded in the same manner as in the Church. The command of an Imperial regiment counted as a profitable occupation. The Venetian Ambassador reported to the signoria that the commander of a regiment received the same income as the owner of a marquisate, and that an Austrian generalship yielded more than an Italian dukedom. A colonel's income was estimated at a yearly sum of between ten and twelve thousand gulden. But as it proceeded from dues paid to the colonel by officers for their commissions, it was paid in irregularly, and did not protect Eugène from monetary cares.

But, now that at least some kind of an income was assured him, Eugène laid the embarrassment of the impecunious aside and wrote to the Elector saying that he would have had great pleasure in coming to Munich, but that, unfortunately, his money from Savoy had not been forwarded, and with only the income of an Imperial regimental commander he did not care to take part in the carnival. Almost immediately one thousand Hungarian gold gulden arrived !

The dragoon regiment remained in Hungary without a colonel, for the new commander—who, it must be said, ought to have hurried to his regiment first—arrived in Munich in Max Emmanuel's palace most elegantly turned out. He had the honour of finding in readiness for him the private apartments nearest to those of the Elector.

Now that Eugène stood upon his own feet, he was for the first time treated as a Prince. Gentlemen of the bedchamber were placed at his disposal, and asked after his state of health. The craftsmen of Munich had a profitable time: Eugène understood the rôle of a *grand seigneur*. He ordered clothes, shoes, stockings, buckles, a sword, and lace collars. In a very few weeks after his arrival, and in spite of not having to pay for the necessities of life, the small income which the Elector had sent him was reduced to not more than twenty gold pieces. He was again without money. He had been extravagant : now the care-free time was over, but he accepted the consequences. He explained to the Elector that he had neglected his duty long enough : now he must return to his regiment. Although he enjoyed the life of a man of the world, yet he preferred that of a soldier. A man of the world ? The other cavaliers courted beautiful women ; there were anecdotes about all the renowned generals and Princes ; their love affairs were the sensation of the curious crowd. But there is no record of a love adventure in Prince Eugène's youth, and no romantic or frivolous occurrence was ever authenticated. His name was never mentioned in connection with a woman of any kind. There was only one report received in connection with his visit to Munich at the time of the carnival. In an inn, amongst a typically boisterous Bavarian crowd, a "four-leaved clover" had disguised themselves as servants, and behaved, to say the least of it, in a very hilarious manner. They were said to have been the Elector of Bavaria with his mistress, the Countess Kaunitz, wife of the Imperial Ambassador in Munich, and the Bishop of Passau with Prince Eugène.

A few days before his departure from Munich, a nobleman from Savoy brought Eugène a fairly large sum of money. He did not come from the reigning Duke. Apparently the young Victor had not yet decided whether he would acknowledge Eugène or not. By this single donation of money he would have felt himself obliged to provide Eugène with a permanent appanage ; and, wishing to evade this obligation, he insisted that the Prince de Carignan should be the official donor. But Eugène saw through the manœuvre : he had already himself acquired the courtier's sleekness. He took the money, but refused to recognise the diplomatic move, and thanked the Duke with excessive politeness for the assistance which he had rendered him " in a foreign land." He wrote the letter with a cold and superior smile. He knew that he must continue to consider himself a Savoyard, however the Duke behaved towards him, and was determined to do so, even against Victor Amadeus's will, until his position in Austria had made an Austrian of him.

Through a remittance of money he had become a recognised Prince of Savoy and then an Imperial commander. Things were improving! And now came a letter of maternal encouragement from Olympia. The ambassador Borgomaniero had proposed that he should try his luck in the Spanish service. Why did he not agree to that? The appointment to a Spanish generalship in the Netherlands might lead to a governorship. Here was a possibility of leaving this Austria which he decided was now no longer so distasteful to him. He would make no hasty decisions!

Before taking leave of him, Eugène discussed his chances with Max Emmanuel. "A Spanish general in the King's service; what does Your Highness think of that?" he asked.

The Elector, who would have missed an amusing friend, promised to arrange that in a short time Eugène should be promoted to the rank of major-general of the Imperial army. Max Emmanuel confirmed and strengthened his promise by presenting him with three magnificent horses. Now Eugène was able, with a gesture, to offer Count Tarini and another cavalier a horse each out of his own stables —on the condition that they accompanied him to his regiment!

The little cavalcade set out for Prague, where the Kufstein regiment of dragoons—henceforth called the Savoyard Regiment—was preparing for the new campaign.

Up to now Eugène's military practice had been confined to a few rides, one or two battle skirmishes, and the observation of strategic events. Now he was faced for the first time with the task of administration. He must care for the commissariat, for the pay, and for the munitioning of his regiment.

Before he arrived in Prague he did not even know how to obtain uniforms for his soldiers. He let the regiment parade in white coats worn over red, tightly fitting tunics, with white trousers and low boots. The dragoons counted in the Imperial army as mounted infantry, and carried powder-horns on their body-belts like the foot soldiers. They wore the same red hats, with the only difference that theirs were decorated with golden galloon. They had no helmets, and wore leather collars like the cuirassiers.

Later, when Eugène became Field Marshal of the Holy Roman Empire, he wrapped himself for the most part in a plain grey or brown cloak, which covered the signs of rank on his uniform. But now, when for the first time he appeared before his regiment as its colonel, he wore the white cloak without sleeves, which left the gold stitched collar free ; underneath, the colonel's uniform of fine pearl-grey cloth, richly bordered in gold, and breeches of scarlet cloth.

The thin little man in this many-coloured uniform did not make the best impression on his soldiers, any more than he did in the campaign of the year 1684, when he led his regiment for the first time. The order for the gallop was given—that famous *Marsch-Marsch* of the Austrian cavalry—in order to save the Imperial General Hallwyl from the superior Turkish cavalry. But the Savoy dragoons came too late.

A few days later, on the occasion of the siege of Ofen, it was proved—according to an autographed letter from the Duke of Lorraine—that the dragoon regiment had acquired a leader who was not only cold-bloodedly brave, but exceeded his orders, and on his own initiative pursued the enemy at the head of his troops, returning with a captured gun. For the first time the Emperor was forced to recognise an achievement on the part of the Prince of Savoy. That the Emperor had taken account of this Eugène knew ; and he knew also that the Elector would have no difficulty in procuring a generalship for him.

The campaign of that year was not a very fortunate one for the army, but Eugène sent his regiment into winter quarters in Silesia, and himself, as a very esteemed officer, returned to Vienna. He was the guest of the Margrave Ludwig, with whom his friendship became so intimate that a Savoyard agent reported : " The two cousins love one another with more than brotherly tenderness."

CHAPTER II

SIX DAYS before the siege of Vienna was raised, Jean Colbert died in Paris. During the last few years of his life he had fallen from grace in the eyes of his sovereign. But the master, also, had fallen into disfavour with his servant. The colossal building schemes, and the unceasing war preparations, threatened to wreck his finance system. Colbert warned and protested: his life's work, as well as the well-being of the country, was at stake. He offered to hand in his resignation, but it was refused. He was obliged to continue in the King's service, to levy new taxes, to discover fresh sources of revenue, and to act against both his better judgment and his conscience until the end of his life. But on his deathbed he refused to receive the King.

Louis thought that he could disregard the testamentary protest of his most able Minister, who had embodied Mazarin's last will and testament. He was at the height of his power, which seemed unshakable. On the far-extended frontiers the Frenchman reaped the harvest from the seed that Colbert had sown. The army exceeded in numbers the combined forces of Europe, and in equipment was unequalled in the whole world. Louis's actual strength was unbroken: only his diplomatic prestige was suffering from the diminishing possibility of vanquishing the ruler of the Holy Roman Empire. Indeed, the Emperor's fame was in danger of becoming as brilliant as Louis's own; for the power of the Turks—the Habsburgs' worst enemies, and France's most dangerous confederates—was shaken, and they had been forced back into their own territory, pursued by the victorious Imperial troops.

The maps of Hungary and the States of the German

Empire were now more often to be seen on Louis's writing-table, and on that of his Foreign Minister, than those which marked his own frontiers. Every month, and now and then weekly, a letter arrived from the barbaric east, sometimes bearing the postmark Esseg, sometimes Waitze, sometimes Gran—all small towns and forts which were only visible on the map with the aid of a magnifying glass. The letters described in full detail events in the Hungarian theatre of war, and they were signed " Marquis de Villars."

Who was the Marquis de Villars ? At the time when Madame la Comtesse as Olympia played the leading part at Court his family was in the background. But they were descended of ancient French lineage, and for this reason the King could not without a very good cause refuse them smaller offices and dignities. The father of the young Marquis had been a diplomat, an able official in the foreign service. His son had the good fortune to become a page at the Royal Court. One day, as the boy heard his father and mother complaining of their humble status, he said, " I shall make a great career ! "

It was a prophecy which, just as unfounded as Prince Eugène's, was to be as brilliantly fulfilled. Several episodes conducted with energy and purpose forced the Court to take account of the young Villars. First, he attracted attention by acts of disobedience so arranged that their consequences were bound to justify them ; and then, when the King granted the young Marquis the company that he had coveted—the same favour which had been refused to the Little Abbé—he attracted attention to himself on the battlefield by clever and opportune suggestions. He proved his acuteness so satisfactorily that after one battle a Marshal of France remarked to his generals, " This young Villars sees clearer than the rest of us."

" Career ! Career ! "—was the inner echo which resounded night and day in Villars's ears. He knew that the patronage at his disposal was too insignificant to accelerate his promotion. In order to achieve something extraordinary he must do something extraordinary. In his imagination the concept of a career was linked with that of achievement. This distinguished him from the parade officers and Court generals whom he afterwards superseded.

After the Vienna episode, Villars asked for an audience with the King. It was granted him, and the most amazing thing happened : the insignificant Marquis, the little officer, remained for one hour, for two hours, closeted with His Majesty in his private cabinet. What had he said to the King ? What intrigue had he disclosed ? In what relation did he stand to the widow Scarron, Madame de Maintenon, whom Louis now honoured with his affection ? Two hours in the private cabinet—two hours *tête-à-tête* with His Majesty?

A rise in rank was expected : the appointment to Marshal of France ; the grant of a Peerage ; the promotion to a Dukedom ! But none of these things happened. The humble Marquis de Villars left the Royal presence just as modest in his bearing towards the courtiers, just as smooth and humble in his demeanour as he had been before he entered the cabinet. The only apparent consequence of the long-drawn-out audience was a bill of discharge for a miserable six thousand thalers which the treasurer paid out to him.

The episode was forgotten, and the Marquis de Villars also. He was no more to be seen either at Court, or in the Army, and his name did not appear in the diplomatic list. The ambitious Villars disappeared from the picture.

Four weeks later, there appeared in Vienna an elegant young man, meticulously turned out, with a modest, even-tempered, undistinguished face, and introductions which enabled him to be presented at Court. Everyone asked what he was doing there, and the nature of his purpose. He answered that he was travelling in order to see the world ; if it were possible, he would be honoured to increase the strength of the Emperor's glorious arms by the contribution of his unworthy sword. He wished to join in the war against the Turks, and wished to serve as a volunteer. He coveted no office, and no command ; it was enough for him if he might fight for the good cause.

Soon the attractive young man was a guest in all the great

Viennese houses, had become the friend of Princes, and a welcome comrade-in-arms in the advancing Imperial army.

He was roughly of the same age, as pleasure-loving, and as brave—in a word, hewn out of the same block—as the Bavarian sovereign. The Elector who commanded the army at that time was Francophile in his private life. He received Villars all the more enthusiastically, as now, besides Eugène, he had found in him a second French friend.

Eugène had shown no interest in the female sex, and had not participated in Max Emmanuel's orgies, or only to such a limited extent as did not satisfy the Elector. Villars was a woman's man, a Gascon nature, the terror of all married men, as was the Elector himself. But, while Max Emmanuel gave himself up to a life of debauchery out of conviction, Villars only did so in order to further his political mission.

If, later, as Marshal of France and commandant of the French armies, he had unmasked such a fellow as he himself was at that time, he would have had him hanged as a spy and criminal purloiner of military and diplomatic secrets.

Men of Villars's stamp only acquire scruples when they have something to lose : as long as they have only their own person to set at stake for the sake of their career, they must be unscrupulous. At least, Villars possessed one advantage over ordinary spies : when the rope was round his neck, he had the possibility of withdrawing his threatened head. He had arranged with Louis that he might at any time legitimise his position by saying that he was there in the capacity of military attaché or envoy extraordinary. And one who did not wish to ruin his chances with the King of France must manage to extricate himself from his difficulties.

Villars had divided his task into two parts. The first was concerned with the technique, the strength, and leadership of the Imperial army. The second aimed at winning over the Elector of Bavaria gradually, by means of promises and proffered bait, from his alliance with the Emperor's House. He must make it clear to him that an Elector of Bavaria was not born in order to hold the stirrup for an Emperor of the House of Habsburg. He must explain to him that he was not merely a German potentate : by his marriage with the daughter of Leopold I, who was first married to a Spanish Princess, the sister of Louis XIV's wife, his was the right of succession when the Spanish King, Charles II, died. Max Emmanuel objected that his mother-in-law had renounced her hereditary rights.

"Yes, but she did not renounce them on behalf of her daughter," was Villars's reply. He explained to the Elector that after the death of Charles which could not be long delayed, his monarch had envisaged such a division of the Spanish monarchy as would give his heirs the Spanish peninsula, but would allow the Elector to acquire the Spanish Netherlands for himself. For this purpose, and in order to avoid a war, the Elector should waste no time in signalising his agreement with Louis's plan. Villars said that Louis, who had engaged in nearly all the wars of his epoch, did not go to war willingly ; and there would be no question of war if Bavaria were to unite with France. The Emperor would not attempt to combat against such superiority of strength.

Against the Emperor—against the Empire ? The Elector refused such an imputation. It seemed to be a hopeless undertaking to win over Leopold's spoilt, much endowed, and honoured son-in-law as Louis's confederate.

The adventurer Villars refused to recognise the word "impossible." He had a plan ready. A man of Max Emmanuel's type was only to be ensnared by the aid of women, but Max Emmanuel had one mistress already. Here Villars laid the emphasis on the adjective. "One mistress ? " he asked. One only, and she the wife of the Imperial Ambassador in Munich, whom he could not hope to influence. Yet he made no mention of this limitation. On the contrary he announced all the more loudly that he intended to find a new object for the Elector's passions—a second one. Naturally, not a French woman. That would have been too transparent. But he did not mention that either. A short while previously, during his stay in Vienna, Villars had begun a connection with a young lady in waiting to the Empress, the Countess von Wählen. The Countess was younger and more attractive than Frau von Kaunitz, and, besides this, she had for the Elector an enhanced charm in that he could win her from his friend Villars. But the little Countess found so much pleasure in the love of the Elector that she did not covet Villars's interest. Apart from that, he was sick of Austrian women—at any rate for the time being. All at once he held himself mysteriously aloof from the Elector, disappeared into his own apartments, until at length Max Emmanuel divined that this devil of a fellow had a new mistress whom he was keeping from him: an Italian by the name of Signorina Canossa—she had naturally diverted his affections.

Count Kaunitz cried murder, and reported to Vienna that the Countess von Wählen had driven the Elector from his wife's bed ! The roundabout way through the Canossa to a Fräulein von Sinzendorf, whom Villars thought even more suitable for the Elector, inasmuch as she was entirely submissive to him, remained unsuspected by that old *intrigante*, the Countess von Paar, who had come to Munich by order of the Viennese Court in order to bring about a reconciliation between the Elector and Frau von Kaunitz. To be sure she had been the mediator in all the Elector's love-affairs at the Court of Vienna, but the old *intrigante* had not grasped the *tempo* of Versailles. Villars bought her silence with a hundred thousand thalers, and Max Emmanuel was left in peace with the Sinzendorf, to the complete satisfaction of his French friend.

For Villars the game of love intrigues was over ; now began the serious business. He could report to his King that the Elector of Bavaria was as good as won over to the French cause. The question of the Spanish succession could now be viewed from another angle.

In Vienna no one suspected the connection. It was merely thought strange that the Emperor's son-in-law should defend France at the Reichstag of Regensburg, and express his disgust that the German Princes and people of quality should contribute one mite after another to increase the power of the Austrian dynasty when the Emperor himself contributed nothing.

Leopold wondered also, but his initiative did not carry him beyond the point of wondering.

Villars's personality, and the circumspection with which he fulfilled his mission at the Imperial Court, can be most easily appreciated by reading the letters and characterisations of leading men which he sent to Versailles. Louis had now a very definite picture of the Emperor's Court, and, in addition, he had the pleasure of laughing over the witty remarks and comments of his emissary. " The Elector is, naturally, of great value," he wrote of his friend Max Emmanuel, for instance. " He would never be bored in a war as long as there were daily combats. The skirmishes divert him. Even if they are not the correct thing for a general, yet he would very reluctantly abandon them in order to give the necessary orders at some other place where there was no shooting. . . . Yes, he has courage and understanding, and could become a great man if he wished. But one is forced to doubt his strength of will ! "

Each one of the personal descriptions was garnished with wit and irony : not every one was correct. The oddest might be expected of Prince Eugène, whose appearance at the time that Villars wrote his reports belied his real character. Villars's description is indicative of Eugène's simulated attitude : " The Prince of Savoy is courageous. He has more goodwill than understanding. All the same, he is cultivated, and endeavours to be an efficient officer. He is very suited to become one some day. He is ambitious, and actuated by all the motives of a pious man."

This portrait is the best characterisation of Prince Eugène's attitude at that moment. Of course it may have been painted in such modest colours so that Louis should not hear anything too flattering of the Little Abbé. No frown should sully the brow of the Roi Soleil in consequence of a report of

Villars's. Louis must be served, and at the same time enlivened. With that object in view, a late subject, and one who had been a disloyal subject, of the Most Christian Monarch's must under no circumstances be praised.

However that may be, it is quite certain that Eugène's impenetrable expression and reserved demeanour did not permit of Villars's painting a true portrait of him. Besides, Eugène was brought up in much the same diplomatic atmosphere as Villars himself, saw through him, and knew that he must on no account lift the veil of mediocrity in his presence. Again, Villars never saw Eugène except in the company of the Margrave, where he remained humbly in the background. He could not divine that the ugly little man who appeared to be content to play the part of an attendant had an object in so doing. Alone, Eugène would have attained the proximity of the Emperor only on special pretexts. But in company with the Margrave he could be present at Court daily. It was essential that the Emperor should become accustomed to seeing him. He must get into conversation with him, and then he would tell the Emperor how he also, in his childhood, like His Majesty, had been destined for the Church, and how he also, like His Majesty, had been instructed in theology; and would assure him that now, as a soldier, he intended to lead a blameless life!

Common interests were there to bind the two men. He must make the Emperor aware of them, and somehow cause that melancholy glance to fall upon him with pleasure and sympathy!

Eugène began to be a cold and deliberate careerist. He had arrived at a generalship by his methods. Major-General Prince Eugène of Savoy, Marquis de Saluzzo and Piedmont —that sounded good. Eugène used all his hereditary titles in order to counterbalance his apparent humility. He liked to believe that his quick promotion was due rather to his skill in Court etiquette than to his achievements, forgetting that at Court he thought over every action beforehand in order to avoid making an unpleasant impression, but that on the battlefield, his rash, incautious, courageous acts were just those that had more than once made a pleasant impression. He had certainly achieved something ! But when he saw the mediocrity that played first fiddle at the Emperor's Court, and when he read the letters that his mother wrote him, he wondered whether that something was worth while !

Eugène's career hitherto had been too modest to suit Olympia's ambition. She bombarded him with questions. Did he wish to bury himself in Vienna as an insignificant general ? Had he forgotten his political plans ? He must go to Spain, or, at least, to the Spanish Netherlands, where there were prospects, and where she could work something for him. Everything was prepared for him. Every day that he spent in Vienna now was a day lost. What did he expect to achieve in Austria ? She urged and promised. Immediately on his arrival in Spain he would be promoted to be Governor-General of the Spanish Netherlands, or to Spanish Viceroy !

But all that Olympia wrote and promised was pure phantasy. Spain was, for her, the land of promise. She saw, at last, that the return to France was denied her for ever, and she now sought a new field of activity. Charles II of Spain was married to the Princesse d'Orléans, the daughter of Henriette, the friend of her youth. That in itself made an opening. She must renew her relationship with the young Queen, so that in Madrid she might maintain the rank that she had been forced to renounce in Paris. How could she stay on in Brussels ? How could she, with her energy and at her age, grow crabbèd in a provincial town ? Was it to this purpose that she had learned statesmanship and the handling of men from her uncle Mazarin ?

She was determined to set off, but did not wish to travel alone to a foreign land and arrive alone in a foreign city. Her son Eugène, the only one of her sons who represented anything, must go with her. But he should not go with her merely as her son. She wrote to him and suggested that he should go to Madrid as the Emperor's unofficial ambassador, in which capacity new fields would be opened up for him. He must sound the Spanish Court on behalf of the Emperor. He must open the eyes of the people in Vienna to the fact that Spain was the corner-stone of politics. One must make early provision for eventualities. The Succession was in the scales. After all, the greatest inheritance that the world had ever known was at stake. Why had Louis XIV married his niece to the King of Spain ? Charles was so frail that every day his death must be reckoned with. Who would then be responsible for the guardianship of the widowed Queen ? Louis, of course—as his niece's uncle. Who would raise on the Iberian Peninsula as unjustified a claim for his wife as that which had been raised previously in the Netherlands ? Louis, of course. That must be prevented. Eugène must come. Even if the Emperor refused to make him his official ambassador, Eugène could still serve him, and appear officially as his mother's travelling companion. He could go with her on the pretext that she was seeking an official position in Spain for him. Had not the Duke of Savoy already suggested it ?

The Spanish Camera Major comprised the rights and duties of three French Court officials : of the Surintendante, of the Dame d'Honneur, and of the Dame d'Atours. This office was usually relegated to an elderly widowed lady, who lived in the Queen's palace, had permanent access to Her Majesty, followed her wherever she went, and actually dominated the unfortunate Queen, who was overpowered by Court ceremonial. Olympia wished to become the successor to the Duchess of Terranova, who fulfilled her duties so strictly that the Queen's state was one of greater slavery than even etiquette demanded. The Queen longed to have a more sympathetic companion than the Duchess, who forbade every pleasure and every recreation, who never laughed, and who suppressed everything that did not please her. Charles could not withstand his wife's supplications. The Camera Major had to resign. In the meantime, Olympia had offered herself to the Queen, naturally with reservations ! " The gay Cousine Olympia ! " the witty, lively Comtesse de

Soissons to be Camera Major ? All at once Olympia's hopes were expressed in the heartfelt wish of the Queen, who was oppressed by the boredom of the Spanish Court life.

Louis was informed in detail of the smallest occurrence in Madrid, and heard of Olympia's candidature. The Queen's wishes were not compatible with his intentions. If Madame la Comtesse once became Camera Major, then his prospects were doomed. Without Olympia, the Royal pair would remain childless, for, according to all secret reports, the marriage had never been consummated. But Louis was acquainted with Olympia's talent for intrigue, knew that suddenly, no matter from whose loins it was begotten, an heir to the throne would appear in the cradle, and thereby his hopes of the Spanish Crown destroyed ! While he was still ruminating on how he could hinder Olympia's journey, he received news that Madame la Comtesse had already arrived in Madrid accompanied by her son Eugène. He demanded an immediate report, and by return a secret agent sent a reply which has been preserved in the archives of the French Ministry of Foreign Affairs :

" With respect to the journey of the Comtesse de Soissons, it appears to have been chiefly inspired by the little courtesy shown towards her on the part of the Spaniards in the Netherlands, and the complete lack of it shown towards her son, Prince Eugène. She is going to Madrid to make a complaint, and to demand that she be given the title of Highness. All this has created unrest here in Madrid. She may have the additional purpose of seeking a post for her son. She is in intimate relationship with the Queen of Spain, from whom I have seen her receive several letters."

An appointment for the Little Abbé ? If that were her only purpose, Louis was almost inclined to leave the matter at that. His opinion of Prince Eugène was so very poor that he did not consider him worth troubling about. He had heard no more of him than Villars's report, and had not asked for any further data. After all, of what importance was a courageous officer, especially when, according to Villars's report, he possessed more good will than intelligence ?

Olympia need foster no illusions about her sons. But had she really only gone to Madrid for the sake of this misshapen son of hers? Louis was mistrustful. Where Olympia was concerned he was always mistrustful. In the end she would become Camera Major! He must not allow the matter to develop further! He wrote a letter with his own hand to the Comte de Rebenac, his ambassador in Spain, to ask for a report on Olympia's life and prospects.

An interchange of letters began. The Master of the World was disquieted. The past rose before his eyes. Olympia's house in Madrid resembled in no way the Palais Soissons; but perhaps the Comte de Rebenac only described it disparagingly because he knew how little it would please his master if he were to describe Olympia's life in more favourable terms? The report was certainly not favourable to Olympia. Could he—Louis of France, Louis the Great—have anything to fear from such a woman? He read the letter once again. " Her main occupation consists in receiving all people who wish to visit her, from five o'clock in the evening until two or three o'clock in the morning. Every day she has the table laid for between ten and twelve guests, and five or six of these places are claimed by as many gourmands of repute. They appear unfailingly in the evening, and neither take part in the conversation nor play cards. They do nothing but fill their stomachs. In no other country in the world are the people so moderate at home, and so greedy abroad. That is an experience that one may verify every day in this country. The rest of the company consists of about twenty persons of insignificant standing, who behave with such a lack of respect that they appear with hair bound tightly back, without ruffles, and lay aside neither their swords nor their daggers. Sire, in my opinion such behaviour in the house of a lady is carrying familiarity and contempt too far. Your Majesty will pardon the circumstantiality, which I have only permitted myself because I think I owe Your Majesty as exact a description as possible of the life here of the Comtesse de Soissons. Moreover, it is certain that Madame la Comtesse, if she were to give herself the trouble, could get to the bottom of many things. I will observe her very closely, and do my best to prevent her from renewing the old intimate relationships."

For a short time Louis was pacified. His diplomatic service seemed to be functioning ! But he was not satisfied for long. Monsieur de Rebenac's efforts did not avail him much. He had, after all, only been trained in the school of Louis XIV, and Olympia had been trained by Mazarin himself. In a despatch dated a few days later Rebenac confessed his failure : " Madame la Comtesse de Soissons has again entered into friendly relations with the Queen." He had to admit it. But he adds : " Since I have been in Madrid, I have avoided meeting her anywhere."

Or was it that Olympia did not wish to meet the French Ambassador ?

In any case Louis replied : " I approve of your resolution to enter into no sort of relationship with the Comtesse de Soissons." He continued : " It looks very much as though her life and habits will not secure for her any great respect or authority in the place where she is ! " But, in spite of Olympia's small amount of authority, Louis was very troubled, and very much on his guard. He enjoined his ambassador to be cautious : " See that you are well and exactly informed of her intrigues, in order that the Queen's interests may be protected." Louis, evidently, was afraid of Olympia, however much he tried to conceal it from himself.

There is no mention of Eugène in the whole exchange of letters. Nor was anything definite decided for him in Madrid. He did not wish to let the Habsburg Ambassador, Count Mannsfeld, know of his intention to leave the Emperor's service ; and, to all outward appearances, he was only his mother's travelling companion, so that he could not negotiate directly with the Spanish authorities. Only Count Mannsfeld knew that his mission was to discover all he could about the question of the Spanish Succession. His mission was similar to that of Villars in Vienna : but Eugène remained in the background. His mother learned all that he desired to know. He watched her, and soon saw through her position.

He knew exactly the value of her protection for his admission into the Spanish Army ! She spoke no more of a cavalry command in the Spanish Netherlands, and still less of his future appointment to Governor-General. She suggested that he should become a Knight of Malta, on the strength of which he would immediately be appointed Grand-Prior of Castile. Was this another offer based on nothing more solid than phantasy and goodwill ? Eugène smiled : he had no thoughts of marriage and had previously written to the Duke of Savoy to say that he would like to receive the Cross of the Knights of Malta. Why should his mother not attempt it ? But even that project came to nothing in Madrid. The negotiations lasted too long for Eugène : he preferred not to miss the beginning of the campaign in Hungary, and departed prematurely.

When he decided to leave Madrid, and to say farewell once and for all to the life of an adventurer, he was not disappointed with his fruitless journey. It only made him think more than ever about Vienna. Now he had the material for making a definite report to the Emperor. He would be able to discuss the Spanish Succession as no other could, and demonstrate his knowledge of diplomatic questions.

The only thing that depressed him was the parting with Olympia. But even she agreed that it was best for him to go. With an enchanting gesture, she begged him to stay on one day more, two days more. He obeyed, and observed how she was perpetually going out, now in State dress in a gilded coach, and now as a plainly clad citizen. She was even more busy than usual. Then other strange phenomena made their appearance ; monks in brown sackcloth, cavaliers, political agents, crowded her reception-rooms, sometimes announced with great pomp, and at other times conducted with great secrecy up a back stairway ! On the last day, a coach with the Royal arms of the King of Spain drove up, a gentleman of the bedchamber descended from it : Eugène had been made a Grandee of the first class, and a Knight of the Golden Fleece ! His visit to Madrid had not been in vain. It was Olympia's farewell gift !

Up to the moment when Eugène found a firm footing in Austria, his whole life had been guided by his mother. He had been dependent upon her in a manner that contradicted his otherwise decided character. Her every wish found its echo in him; every plan that she made excited his phantasy. She was—until much later, when another woman entered his life—the only female being to whom he was attached. He had educated himself to be a specialist, he was a self-educated authority on strategy, on military science, and was well on the way to becoming a self-educated authority on diplomacy. His was already an independent mind, a controlled nature, and yet he responded to his mother's every mood like a small iron splinter which her magnetic personality drew towards her. Because he was the only one of her sons whose future still appeared in a rosy light, she had firmly decided to do something for him. For her ambition, the order of the Golden Fleece was an absurdly little thing to have attained. She had not abandoned her idea of the Governor-Generalship of the Netherlands. Oh, no! But, because she had been taught in Mazarin's school, she did not merely devise diplomatic means and intrigues by which she could realise her plans; she decided to naturalise Eugène in Spain, as Mazarin had naturalised both herself and her sisters in France. Hardly had he left Madrid than she denied ever having suggested his becoming a celibate and a Knight of Malta. That was a mistake! On the contrary, Eugène must marry! After all, his was a dynastic family, and as a Prince of Savoy he was related to all the Princely Houses; as a very young man, and entirely by his own efforts, he had succeeded in becoming a general in the Imperial army; his reputation was of the best, and his income secured. No Spanish heiress should refuse him! Whatever he, personally, thought about the matter, Olympia had made up her mind to get him married!

She decided that at first Eugène should not be consulted; he must be faced with the accomplished fact. If a suitable marriage were to satisfy his ambitions, then he would agree to it ; and, above all, he would do it for her sake.

Olympia was not unlike the mother-in-law whom in her youth she had twice affronted by a refusal. Eugène should marry—yes. But he must marry a rich maiden, a very rich maiden, and one of such an influential family that by the marriage alone his career was assured for ever.

She chose the only daughter and heiress of the Viceroy of Naples, the Marquese del Carpio ; and, in order to have a second string to her bow, the daughter of the Connétable of Castile as well—the wealthiest heiress in Spain. The historiographer Sourches relates that each of the maidens possessed an income that ran into millions, besides magnificent furniture, jewels, and plate. Prince Eugène is said to have been given the choice between the two. Sourches adds maliciously : " The little snub-nosed man would have looked around him with astonishment in the midst of such prodigious estates. He was happy to have left France, where he was hardly given water to drink ; and content to remain in the service of the Emperor where he had found his good fortune."

Madame la Comtesse had chosen well. The Ducal House of Savoy supported her efforts. Eugène was formally urged to marry.

From every point of view it was important for Victor Amadeus to have a kinsman settled in Spain ; apart from the fact that, by such a marriage, Eugène would be freed for ever from money troubles. Olympia persuaded him to introduce the subject in Turin. This did not happen without reservations, however, for Eugène was not elated at the idea of having to live with a woman. He wrote to Victor Amadeus : " The marriage presents a favourable opportunity of transplanting a branch of our family to this country ; that is my only reason for requesting your Royal Highness's consent."

Victor Amadeus said, " Yes." But Eugène, when it turned out that he must travel to Madrid again, into the arms of his bride as it were, sent a friend, the Chevalier de Roccavione, instead !

It is not known how this trusted friend fulfilled his mission, nor in what it consisted. Only the fact is certain that nothing came of either of these marriage projects.

Perhaps Eugène personally was not responsible. Perhaps his mother's excessive zeal, which made her as unpopular in Madrid as she had been in Paris, was at fault. The Spanish Court was at that time a rendezvous for intriguers and political agents of every description ; so much so, that the good could not be separated from the bad. The fate of the world depended on the fact of whether Charles II, the weakly Spanish King, was, in the true sense of the word, a man !

The official *communiqués* of the diplomatic representatives of all the European Princes are full of details concerned with the probability or improbability of the King of Spain's procreative powers. On one occasion, the Comte de Rebenac —as he communicated to Louis XIV—had the good fortune to appropriate the King's trousers, which he had examined by two surgeons ! He wrote to His Most Christian Majesty that His Catholic Majesty the King of Spain wore shirts which only reached as far as his belt, and those of coarse linen, that scratched him considerably. One surgeon was of the opinion that procreation was possible ; the other said not ! In a postscript, Rebenac adds that His Majesty must pardon the *lèse-majesté* represented by the mention of the trousers of His Majesty's colleague on the Throne.

At other times still more indiscreet reports found their way to Sweden, to England, and to Holland, but none were sent to the Emperor !

The direction world politics was to take depended upon the receptiveness of the young Spanish Queen, and the capacity of Charles to prove his manhood !

Nothing succeeded with the young couple : all efforts failed, and, as it might not be assumed that they were at fault, then a culprit had to be found.

The cunning of the French Ambassador pointed to Madame la Comtesse. The suspicion alone should be enough to ruin, once and for all, her chance of becoming Camera

LE

Major. Where the question of the potency of the King was concerned, His Majesty was vulnerable. Rebenac declared that Madame la Comtesse was responsible for the fact that the Royal pair were unable to unite in marriage. She had bewitched the Queen, and the King could have no children as long as the Comtesse de Soissons remained in Spain.

Charles decided first this way and then that way. Her reputation had been damaged already by the poisoning case of La Voisin, and by the ugly rumours that Louvois had circulated. There might be some truth in it! When his next effort with the Queen failed also, he decided that Rebenac was right; the Comtesse de Soissons must go. It was suggested to Olympia, on behalf of the King, that she must leave Madrid.

Olympia had fled from Paris in a panic, before a decree of banishment had been issued. But in Madrid she remained even after she had been threatened with an order of banishment. She could not go. She must hold on to the last chance that life offered her. She assured the King that she had not bewitched him; on the contrary, her presence gave him his only chance of having children. Only her departure could bewitch him, and thereafter he would never be potent!

The King trusted her.

This unbelievable episode is supported by a letter from the French Ambassador, in which he writes hypocritically: " A Dominican monk, a friend of the King's confessor, had a vision which revealed to him that the King and Queen were both bewitched. I remark, by the way, Sire, that the King of Spain had thought for a long while that he was bewitched, and, moreover, by the Comtesse de Soissons. It was suggested that the spell be lifted. The ceremony of exorcism was terrible. The King and Queen were stripped naked. The monk, dressed in sackcloth, had to undertake the exorcisms, but in a vile way, whereby, in the presence of the same monk, one was forced to test whether the spell had been lifted or not!"

Olympia remained in Madrid, and even became Camera Major. She was not to be defeated by a simple diplomat of Louis's school ! Oh, no ! She was Mazarin's niece. The King was convinced that only her presence could bestow upon him the power to beget a child. But then the Queen inopportunely died !

Her death brought Olympia's career in Spain to an end together with the marriage projects for her son. She returned to Brussels, and Eugène remained in Austria.

CHAPTER III

THE IMPERIAL general, Prince Eugène of Savoy, was in the small town of Vukovar, on the Danube, when he received the command to gallop to Belgrade with a troop of five hundred horsemen.

Five years had passed since Eugène first drew his sword from its scabbard, gripped his pistol, and received his baptism of fire. Five years is a long time in the life of a man who turns each moment to account and deliberately avails himself of every opportunity, however small.

Eugène, who was scarcely twenty-five years old, and who, not so long ago, had been refused every military appointment both in France and Austria, was now in a very responsible position. He was the leader of a storm troop chosen to prevent the Turkish Army from setting fire to the suburbs of Belgrade. He was commandant of a handful of horsemen to whom the task had been allotted of intimidating thirty thousand men ! The misshapen little abbé was now an experienced general who had proved his ability, both at the siege of Ofen and on all battlefields. He had been wounded, and sent to Vienna to bring the news of victory to the Emperor ; and already his voice had been heard in the War Council. True, it was still a humble, quiet voice, which only occasionally ventured to make itself heard in the discussions. But, although he played second fiddle in the Margrave Ludwig's orchestra, yet his cousin consulted with him on all military and strategic questions. Eugène could afford to remain in the background, for he knew that the Margrave had expressed an opinion of him to the Emperor which predicted the fulfilment of the wildest dreams of his childhood. " In time, this young Savoyard will equal in excellence

those whom the world regards as its greatest commanders."
In his outward appearance there was nothing reminiscent
of the starveling of former times whose ambition had looked
out of despairing eyes. Certainly Eugène was still dressed as
plainly as his rank would permit. He was quite conscious of
his ugliness, and knew that in multi-coloured uniform or in
the magnificent costume of a cavalier he produced a repellent
effect. Simplicity was his rôle, and the clothes he wore
must not contrast rudely with his controlled and reserved
nature.

His movements were sedate, as became the stiff Spanish
ceremonial of the Court. He avoided hasty gestures and swift
glances in favour of a dignified mien, which he nevertheless
somewhat regretfully adopted. Gone was his youth before
it had begun. He almost regretted the fact that his money
troubles were over, for now and again his mother's adventurous blood still stirred in his veins.

Every family will stand surety for a successful kinsman,
although they may have hitherto despised him. The preferments of the Abbeys of Casa Nova and San Michele, which
were refused to Eugène both at the ages of six and sixteen—
when, as the Little Abbé, he had been predestined for the
Church—were granted unasked to the Imperial general,
even against the Pope's wish. The House of Savoy decided
to behave generously and to assist this Prince of their House
towards the maintenance of an appanage. After all, the
Emperor had presented him with his own portrait set in
diamonds!

The contributions which Eugène received from Savoy
increased with his rank. Turin was convinced that not
merely fame, but practical advantages as well, were to be
gained for the House of Savoy from the achievements of this
young Prince. Victor Amadeus admittedly preferred the
practical advantages to the fame, and looked upon this
cousin of his, who was honoured by the Margrave of Baden's
friendship, as an investment which might be expected to pay
interest. He advanced capital in the hope of obtaining
usurious interest. Eugène's material existence was secured,

but to *him* the fame was more important than the money. His was the fate of all backward, crippled, or disfigured human beings who try to compensate for their natural disadvantages by some extraordinary achievement. At first their ambition is limited to the effort of competing with those more favoured by nature than themselves : afterwards the wish carries them beyond their goal. It was with an extraordinary feeling of satisfaction that Eugène tasted the joys of knowing that he, the youngest and most ridiculed member of his family, was yet the only one of the brothers who could boast of achievement. But now he was beyond that stage. Only his ambition remained fierce in its determination to make himself of account to the great man in Versailles. The French King should regret having despised him ! Eugène knew that he would not have long to wait for that moment.

His mother was in Brussels again, and Eugène had been to visit her. This time he was given the title of Highness, and this time it was the Governor-General of the Netherlands who paid his respects to Eugène—by no means the reverse. Madame la Comtesse was content, for she now believed in Eugène as her instrument of revenge against Louis XIV.

His mother was the one person to whom Eugène could unburden himself ; she was the only being whom he trusted. He explained to her the reasons for his certainty of attaining the highest post in the Imperial army and becoming in consequence Louis's most powerful opponent. He was a theorist through and through. No detail of the arts of fortification and strategy was unknown to him ; and as a practician he had helped the greatest commanders of his time to sketch and carry out plans of campaign. But his quality of unshakable self-confidence distinguished him from those generals who for the most part derived their enthusiasm from the flag. His self-confidence communicated itself both to the army and to the masses, as well as to individuals. He had had occasion to verify this fact over and over again. While the other commanders made their plans with a great expenditure of effort, he felt the plans within him. He felt himself endowed with a quality which he could only divulge to Olympia. On the battlefield, when the encounter was at its fiercest and most confusing, he was possessed by an inner certainty which enabled him to survey the situation and feel automatically drawn to attack at the right moment. That it had been the right moment he only learned afterwards. How it happened he did not know!

During his unconstrained conversation with his mother, he confessed his knowledge of the real cause of his unfailing success. He had the unconscious certainty of genius, which without forethought or deliberation, makes the right decision at the right moment, and only after the accomplished fact searches and discovers the logical sequence which had been forestalled by intuition.

When Eugène received the command of his friend, the Elector of Bavaria, to proceed with his five hundred horsemen to the defence—on strategic grounds—of the suburbs of the town of Belgrade, which was already occupied by the Turks, he did not obey the order in the spirit of a young Hotspur. The general, Prince Eugène of Savoy, never committed himself to a success that he did not already hold in his hand. This quality was one of his greatest assets. He never disappointed. He never promised where he was not certain of being able to fulfil. He never guaranteed that he would arrive in time. He would do what he could : and it was well known that he would leave no stone unturned to carry out his mission. This quality gave him the reputation of complete dependability.

No one had the slightest idea that Eugène's outward reserve was merely the demeanour that he affected. He longed to be able to speak without forethought, to express himself openly, and to give the lie to the reputation of unapproachableness. His high birth, which need cause him no further shame, since he now had the means to live in conformity with it, and his descent, which was no longer in disproportion to his station, put him, in private life, on a level with the army commanders. The nobility was always divided into strata, and Eugène belonged to the highest, to the sovereign stratum. But in the hierarchy of the army the gradation of rank was observed, and the more familiarly Eugène was able to associate with the commanders in civil life, the more strictly he adhered to his rank in the service. He preserved his distance with the other generals. He wished to distinguish himself from them, so as to lay emphasis upon his exceptional position.

When, a few years later, he himself became a commander, he altered his system. He had achieved his goal, and could afford to unbend. He made an effort to win the friendship of the other commanders, but it was too late : he had cleared a respectful space around him, and no one dared to trespass upon it.

Instead, therefore, of seeking consolation in the society of human beings, Eugène took refuge in books. They were chiefly political writings, geographical works, and the history of the world. Even now, just as in former times, he wanted to learn and experience all new things in order to be able to make comparisons. It still cost him an effort to accustom himself to this foreign country. His first glance had not misled him ; he had had occasion to experience and to suffer from the fact that Austria was not a nation but, by means of clever diplomacy and marriage contracts rather than by military superiority, an arbitrary unity, a mosaic of States and territories whose frontiers were elastic in accordance with the momentary condition or strength of the individual rulers. To repeat, Vienna was not the centre of this mosaic, but an eastern frontier town.

Inspired by a writing of the philosopher Leibnitz, to whom, later on, he owed many an inspiration, Eugène made Hungary the centre of his activities. Leibnitz had said that Hungary would be the source of the Emperor's wealth. Eugène shared his opinion. But such plans were for the future. In Leopold's time, Hungary was in constant rebellion. During his whole reign the Emperor had never enjoyed his dominion undisturbed. Hungary was the inflammatory spot in the body of the State, the sore place which needed constant attention. It was a devastated territory which Leopold was continually winning and losing again, although, admittedly, after the deliverance of Vienna step by step and kilometre by kilometre it was more and more forcibly cleared of Turks and rebels, until the Elector of Bavaria finally decided to banish the Turks for all time from Hungary by the conquest of their most important frontier fort of Belgrade.

As Eugène, with his horsemen, approached Belgrade, he saw that his raid was useless. Columns of fire rose on the horizon and fire sheaves shot out of the thatched roofs of the houses in the suburbs which Eugène had come to defend. Far and wide, no Turk was to be seen.

Eugène gave the order to dismount, and himself led the patrol which approached Belgrade to within firing-range.

Here, alongside the fort, the Danube was very wide, and on the right was joined by the silver band of the Save. The line which marked the uniting of the two streams was recognisable from its colour. Eugène sounded the terrain. Was it possible to capture Belgrade from this point? He knew that here the bridge for the passage of the troops must be made. He began to tremble. In a mysterious mirage he saw the army which, twenty years later, he was to lead across the river from this very place. Pontoon after pontoon stretched across the stream in rows. The bridge was made. Now—forward! Eugène looked round : his men cowered beside him, on the damp marshy land. On the opposite shore the fortress rose like a mountain, surmounted by red brick walls in the form of steps.

Eugène kept his opinion to himself. He was not even second in command. He was an executive organ who could only allow himself independent action when the moment irrevocably demanded it. He decided to wait quietly for the arrival of the Elector. Whatever measures Max Emmanuel took to capture Belgrade, he would remain in the background. Eugène did not believe in the permanence of the triumph of the Emperor's arms until the unity of command was guaranteed by a single man. A State like Austria, consisting of so many different constituent parts, could only be victorious when a single person with a single aim remoulded them into unity ; and when a predominant influence opposed and controlled the many other heterogeneous influences. Max Emmanuel would capture Belgrade—and then ? Eugène had already experienced the inadequacy of the resources of the country. Would it be possible to hold Belgrade even with an Imperial garrison ? The Elector would return to Munich for the carnival and would take his troops with him. Eugène knew him well enough to know that he only made war for the sake of the sport, and treated it as a sensational diversion. After the conquest of Belgrade, Austria would feel insured against the Turkish menace, and in consequence the next invasion would be even more serious. Austria had not yet arrived at the stage where she could overcome the East before she was secured in the West.

Eugène's principle of considering himself, to a certain extent, as an employée of the Emperor's forced him, despite his pessimistic outlook, not to be idle during the four weeks' continuous siege of Belgrade. He intended not to do more than his bounden duty, but the close fighting fascinated him in spite of himself. In the fiercest tumult, a sword split his helmet. He heard the cry of a janizary and thrust. The man lay on the ground, but Eugène also staggered and reeled.

From that day on Eugène felt unsure of himself. Death had passed very close. Moments of weakness overcame him which reminded him of his childhood's days, when he had run races against his brothers. Thenceforth it was only by summoning all his forces that he took part in the encounters. He was oppressed by premonitions, and felt a sense of relief when, a few days later, a bullet hit him in the knee. He collapsed and lost consciousness.

Eugène came to himself in Vukovar. The pain unmanned him. He lay strapped down upon a stretcher. A surgeon opened the wound in order to remove the bullet, which could be found neither in the flesh nor in the bones. Could the leg be saved? Eugène saw the surgeon's grave face. A cavalry officer with only one leg? If the bullet could not be found, then the wound would begin to fester. The voice asked, " Shall I amputate ? " Eugène answered that he would rather die. The surgeon continued to search for the bullet with his bloody instruments. The death mask, with teeth clenched, remained unmoved. " In place of health, peace of mind." Eugène, accustomed to a life of constant ill-health, had preached that doctrine to himself. But this time the pain was greater than his will-power. He was unconscious during the whole of the long journey, and in this state was brought to Vienna.

It was soon evident that Eugène's tranquillity and courageous bearing in face of all bodily exertions had only been attained by the exercise of the utmost effort of will. The weakness from which he had suffered in his childhood demonstrated itself anew. Or was it the *morbus viennensis*, the chest trouble which all Southerners suffered from who came to Vienna ? He was ill for months. The wound had to be kept open, as splinters were for ever separating themselves from the bone. The doctors feared for his life. He raved in delirium. All his efforts had been fruitless and were in vain ! He would lose his leg, and there was no hope for him. He was ill and already forgotten. He opened his eyes and saw a strange face. " Who is that man ? " he shrieked. " The surgeon to His Highness the Duke of Savoy," was the reply. Eugène fell back on his pillows, overcome with relief. Then Victor Amadeus believed in him, and had sent a doctor from Turin ! After all, he was not forgotten !

His mother's letters were read aloud to him. But Olympia was not alone in her anxiety about her son. He was not only *her* son now : he had become the child of his period, and the period needed him. Letters came frequently from the Duke of Savoy to the sick-bed, which was visited every day by the

Emperor's physician-in-ordinary; and in the visitors' book in the new house in the Himmelpfortegasse were inscribed the names of the members of the highest nobility, as well as those of diplomats and officers of the army, who came to inquire after Eugène's condition.

The house in the Himmelpfortegasse was not the palace whose magnificence was to contribute to its owner's fame. It was a modest house with very little comfort, and was Eugène's first possession of any description, as well as being his first property in Austria. In this house he was visited by Count Tarini, who had at length left the official service of the House of Savoy and transferred himself to the service of the Prince of Savoy; Prince Lichtenstein; and the Princes Commercy and Vaudemont, who were of French upbringing like Eugène himself and now served under the Emperor's flag.

As he lay in bed, furnished with all the news, Eugène could devote himself to the survey of the political and military situation. This he did with voracious interest. His political activity began during this time of his enforced rest. It began by guessing, by groping after connections, and by putting out feelers to the ambassadors of the German States; less in order to interfere with the course of events than to perfect his conception of the state of the world.

Belgrade fell. Eugène was not surprised: what concerned him most was the fact that his cousin, Ludwig of Baden, had defeated the Turks without him! Was his career really at an end?

Hungary was subject to the Emperor once more, and it seemed as though his rule would now remain undisputed. In Constantinople a revolution had broken out, and rebellions and insurrections shook the Ottoman Empire. Leopold now fulfilled his dearest wish: his son Joseph was crowned King of Hungary. But hardly was the country freed from the rebellious floods of Hungarian nobility than the Emperor embarked upon a "religious liquidation." Catholic Austria would no longer tolerate Protestants within her frontiers. General Caraffa established a tribunal in Eperies, at which the executioner's axe obeyed the will of the Jesuits rather than the dictates of justice. This gave rise to a subterranean revolution, while all the time the House of Habsburg was congratulating itself on having attained peace at last! Peace? Peace was spoken of when the match was already set to the fire!

Eugène cautioned and admonished. He had had news from France. He held before the eyes of all who came to visit him the warning example of the French Protestant persecutions. But in vain! It was always the same story. After every success, the Austrians felt themselves secure and gave themselves up to the enjoyment of the present. The vineyards around Vienna bore once more the bitter *Heurigen Wein* (wine of the year), and in the newly built suburbs of Vienna every house put out the sign of a tavern. Freed from their dire need, the Viennese gave themselves up to their love of wine. During the daily drives which the doctors allowed him, Eugène learned to know the peculiar temperament of the Austrians. As long as it was possible, they refused to admit difficulties. Forethought and foresight were unknown to them. If it was in any way possible, they gave themselves up to a life of enjoyment. God would take care of the future!

In his oppressed mood Eugène wrote: "They are of an extraordinarily easy-going nature, and let everything run its own course." Now that the Turks were vanquished, he would have liked the Emperor to begin to arm against the possibility of an invasion on the part of Louis XIV. Why did Leopold refuse to make peace with the Porte? The position of the French King at home was so critical that at any moment he was likely to search for a pretext to begin an offensive action in order to divert the attention of the French to a new war theatre. Would Austria be capable of the double offensive—against both the Turks and the French? Eugène concentrated all his attention on watching France. The smallest scrap of news from Versailles was important. He must verify its accuracy and then . . . warn!

At this period, plans for the mutual reconciliation and understanding of the two Churches, the Catholic and the Reformed, were being discussed everywhere. The unbeliever had been driven out of the Christian territories, and it was now urged that only the settlement of religious differences was needed in order to attain peace in Europe.

These plans were naturally not approved of either by the Pope or by Louis XIV. Even during the lifetime of Colbert, Louis had issued edicts which were directed against the Protestants. But Colbert had been largely supported by members of the Reformed Church in establishing his mercantile system, so that he opposed the persecution of the " most useful members of the State body." He was unpopular on this account, for the greater part of the French population was anti-Protestant, even at that time—largely in consequence of the propaganda against Holland and the Protestant traders. The wealthy state attained by the industrious and intelligent Huguenots called forth a movement which differed only slightly from the anti-Semitism of the present day. Trade rivalry and an incited fanaticism brought matters to such a head that, for instance, the guilds of sempstresses and embroideresses of white wares issued an interdiction forbidding the employment of heretics in their corporations. At Court also, the *numerus clausus* for Protestants was carried through according to a fixed plan. No Huguenot received either a sign of favour or any profitable employment from the hands of the King.

Louis only decided upon a final plan of extermination after the death of Colbert and after he had legitimised his relations with Madame de Maintenon, the widow of the satirist poet Scarron. Madame was the principal champion of the religious war. To begin with, Protestants were deprived of all honours, offices, pensions, and the like. The right to practise a craft was confined to members of the Catholic faith. Then began the Dragonades. Soldiers were quartered in the houses of the Huguenots until such time as the heretics confessed their belief in the Catholic faith or left the country. That was only the prelude. The Parliament of Paris registered a Royal edict whereby profession of the Reformed faith became a punishable offence. The churches were to be destroyed and religious gatherings, even in private houses, were forbidden. All preachers were banished, with threats of corporal punishment or on pain of death, but the remaining Huguenots were not permitted to leave the country. They were not to be allowed to depart in comfort and spread their erroneous beliefs abroad. They were to become Catholics. A permanent St. Bartholomew's Eve was declared. Every Protestant house was the scene of a desperate struggle. The Huguenots were beaten, pierced, and roasted on a slow fire ; whole families were literally driven naked through the streets ; and, finally, all children between the ages of five and sixteen were taken from their Protestant parents. Convents were founded for girls who had been converted, and any opposition on the part of the children was punished with imprisonment or public thrashing. Nearly two hundred thousand Huguenots, the flower of the French Protestants, escaped from these atrocities by taking to flight.

Louis's diplomats could negotiate as they would abroad, the acts of violence in his country turned all the Protestant Princes against him. Eugène heard this from the German envoys. Every pulpit in Protestant Europe preached against France, and hatred of the *grand monarque* penetrated every village.

At this moment the last Elector of the Palatinate died. At last Louis had a pretext to terminate the untenable situation by an act of violence. Eugène had predicted correctly. In the name of his sister-in-law, Liselotte of the ready pen, the sister of the last Elector, Louis raised a claim on her behalf— much against the will of the Germanophile Princess—to a considerable part of the Rhine Palatinate.

This new pretension gave rise to the greatest protest in Germany. The atmosphere in the Empire, stimulated by the recent victory over the Turks, was now one of confidence and exaltation. Should yet another piece of Germany territory be allowed to fall into the hands of France ? Was no frontier, and no Imperial territory, to be secure from the greed of the French ? This arbitrariness must come to an end ! Since the German Army had succeeded in beating the Turks, it would be able to vanquish the French also. Even Bavaria, whom Villars had won over to the French side, did not withdraw herself from the general current of opinion.

In spite of all this, Louvois urged war. A large French army crossed the frontiers of the Palatinate. Mainz fell ; Trier fell ; and the French pressed forward, burning and levying contributions, right into German territory. Within a few weeks the four Rhine Electorates became the spoil of the French arms.

No one in Paris thought any more about the Huguenots. At least Louis had succeeded in attaining his first objective. But his other calculation—namely, that the German Empire would be terrorised into concluding a peace—was not fulfilled. On the contrary, the Empire declared war on France !

Another Imperial war ! Louis smiled. His couriers galloped over the whole of Europe. His first success was in London. England became his ally. The great King was triumphant. But his triumph was not long-lived. For this alliance gave William of Orange a pretext for landing on English soil a few weeks later. He overthrew the Stuarts, Louis's only allies, and England and Holland declared war on France. As the English Parliament granted the necessary funds for the war against France, William of Orange, otherwise so cool, controlled, and silent to the point of dumbness, exclaimed in a state of ecstasy : " This is the first day of my reign." The great object of his life was attained : for now Louis XIV had to match himself against more than a single State at a time. This time the whole of Europe was armed against him.

That had been Eugène's aim also. The greatest man of the outgoing seventeenth century was united in purpose with the greatest man of the incoming eighteenth century. But Prince Eugène was not triumphant. He had made use of his time in Vienna in strengthening his position at Court. He was now no longer merely the courageous general who had led an expedition to the defence of Belgrade. He was now a statesman. He had quite recovered from his illness, and, owing to careful nursing and attention, was stronger than he had ever been. The war did not alarm him personally : he could only gain by it, for he would be promoted. But he saw the almost insuperable difficulties ahead.

The Emperor was between two enemies : on the one side, the Turks who, although they had been many times vanquished, yet were ever raising new armies ; and, on the other, Louis, possessor of the strongest armed force in Europe. " For heaven's sake," Eugène cried, " no war with France until peace with the Turks is concluded ! Then yes ! Then, with united forces, let us march against the Roi Soleil."

A letter written at this time by Prince Eugène to his cousin, the Duke of Savoy, expresses his opposition to the double war. " Everyone is in favour of conducting two wars at the same time, although the wise and sagacious are beside themselves ; for they realise that such a project can only be fostered by the monks."

This was the first occasion on which Prince Eugène took a definite standpoint against the overwhelming influence of the priesthood at the Court of Vienna. But the Pope and the clerical party were stronger, and prevailed upon the Emperor to continue with the war against the Turks, and at the same time to engage in a struggle against the Most Christian King !

Eugène warned them once again. He represented to them that, without the *nervus belli* of money, a successful campaign was impossible. It would be better to make concessions to the Turks rather than to sacrifice the whole of the vanquished territory. His temperament forced him to prophesy defeat. He was told that a general was not capable of judgment on questions of *haute politique* ; and intrigues against him were

ME

started. The Emperor's favour, which he had won with so much labour, was at stake. At first Eugène was silent, having determined to keep his opinions and his advice to himself. But he could not withhold them for long. He had adopted Austria as his country, and he feared for Austria. Did he feel a patriot in this strange country? Once more he repeated his advice to submit: on no account war on two fronts. His objection was ruled out by the reply that the alliances with Spain, with England, with Holland, and with Denmark guaranteed enough auxiliary troops to defeat the French!

" On the Rhine—yes, certainly; but what about Italy? " he objected. That was it: Eugène surprised himself. Was that the reason for his persistence in stating his opinion? Did he aspire to the supreme command against the French in the Italian theatre of war? His thoughts went a step further. To that end he must win Savoy over to an alliance with the Emperor. The Duke was his cousin. He pulled himself together. There he sat in the War Council, and all those present were watching his face! Yes! Savoy would turn the scales. He insisted again on this point. He represented to the Council that Vauban's chain of forts made the north of France impregnable, but if Savoy were to declare herself for Austria, then Louis would have to send troops to the frontiers of Savoy in the south, thus disburdening the Imperial troops on the Rhine, and at the same time protecting the Spanish possessions in northern Italy.

This was a new point of view. The Council began to debate the matter, and Eugène was entrusted with the negotiations with his cousin Victor Amadeus. No sooner were the papers of authorisation in his pocket than he casually announced that he still lacked his promotion to the leadership of the Imperial army in Italy. He avoided the word " command." The Duke of Savoy would be the commander-in-chief: he demanded this promotion for his cousin, as a condition for the latter's support of Austria.

It was agreed; at last Eugène had achieved that much! He would command an army in the struggle against France

—and Louis XIV. Allied with Spain and Savoy, he would be able to keep the promise he had made to himself and to his mother. He would see France once again—and this time from the head of an army!

He wrote to his cousin : " I am quite recovered. The wound has closed. I await your news with impatience so that I may set forth."

Eugène set out for Savoy in the certainty of success ; and, after very brief negotiations, gained his point, and won Victor Amadeus over to the Austrian cause. But, when he took over the command of the Imperial forces placed at his disposal, he realised that he would win no laurels with them. To this young man of twenty-seven the road to his goal seemed interminably long ! " We are still here," he wrote, " we are still here, and it seems as though we should continue to remain here for the rest of our lives. We have been about to start for fourteen days now, and still we do not move out of this hole. At every moment new difficulties arise."

There lay the Po basin, that mighty tract of land divided by the tributaries of the Po into strategic divisions. Eugène knew every elevation. He had sent out spies to report on the water level of every single river, and he knew all the places from which the French were to be most advantageously attacked. But he saw no possibility of moving. He sketched out plans, and put them before the War Council. His cousin Victor Amadeus presided over the Allied generals. A smile spread over his narrow face. Why was his cousin Eugène so impatient ? Why was he so anxious for an encounter at all costs ? Would it not be better to wait for the situation on the other battle fronts to take shape ?

Victor Amadeus vacillated during the whole war. Ought he not to make peace with Louis ? Would not an alliance with France be more to his advantage than one with Austria ? He adopted an attitude of passive resistance.

Eugène was in despair. His opponent, the French Marshal Catinat, commanded forces that were far superior to his, and gained one advantage after another, while Eugène was scarcely capable of making the smallest raids. Moreover, behind his back, whenever he gave an order, the friendly, crafty Victor Amadeus patted him on the shoulder in feigned familiarity, and answered his every question with an indefinable smile.

When Eugène turned to the other generals, they shrugged their shoulders indifferently. " No sooner is something decided at the War Council and the generals are agreed," he complained to Tarini, " than in an hour's time they are making so many difficulties again that nothing is achieved. If they had as much understanding and enthusiasm for the general welfare as they have acuteness and dexterity for the furtherance of their own ends—in a word, for doing nothing at all—then all would be well. Do not think that this is merely the opinion of fiery youth and prejudice. What I am saying is pure truth, and I only express what the army and the whole country know as well as I do."

Eugène was incapable of that kind of diplomacy, and intolerant of that sort of indolence. When in the evening he gave an order, by the morning it had either been shelved or had not been carried out. He fought a battle against windmills, while, in the meantime, the army was badly quartered and in want. Eugène wrote letters to Vienna begging for money for equipment, but, instead of the money, the War Council sent the Field Marshal Caraffa as commissary to the army; and Caraffa was superior in rank to Eugène.

The two men—the " bloodhound of Epereis," whose reputation for cruelty preceded him everywhere, and Eugène who had won the increased esteem of his soldiers the more they realised that he put their welfare before everything—were hostile to one another from the very first day. To establish this enmity once and for all, Caraffa caused a Savoy dragoon to be put to death for some quite trivial reason. He wished to force Eugène, the illustrious Prince, out of his apparent tranquillity. What did it matter to Caraffa that this was an insult to the rights of a regimental commander and to a colonel's privilege of jurisdiction?

Eugène, in a rage, would try to put his superior officer in the wrong. And then : away with His Highness the General ! He would be cashiered.

Caraffa's calculation was correct. Eugène was beside himself, and used threats. Caraffa replied that he intended to exact obedience from Prince Eugène, however nobly born he might be. At the same time, as general commissary in charge of the army funds, he stopped the payment of Eugène's allowance.

A few days after this Eugène arrived in Vienna to hand in his resignation from the Army. It was a choice between Caraffa and himself. He was tired of the Austrian service.

The situation at the Imperial Court increased his irritation. He had the feeling that nothing that happened had any point. " What disturbs me most," he said, " is the fact that, however bad the news is, the people here are too detached to concern themselves about it or to attempt to think of a remedy. They are all too easy-going and are content to let things take their own course."

He asked for an audience with the Emperor, which was granted him at once. He found Leopold oppressed by the war on two fronts, which Eugène had so fiercely combated. The Emperor was always mild and conciliatory towards anyone present. Eugène found a willing ear as he described to him Caraffa's behaviour. Yet another who complained of Caraffa ? The effect of the blood tribunal was painfully apparent in the form of unceasing disturbances in Hungary and fresh conspiracies between the nobility and the Ottoman Porte. The conquered territory was again at stake, and the position was all the more menacing in that the Turks had succeeded in taking possession of Belgrade once again.

Was it true what this young Savoyard said ? That war on French territory was an easy possibility ? If it were true, then perhaps he, the Emperor, would attain peace at last ? But Eugène wished to be commander-in-chief ? Not only Caraffa, but the Duke of Savoy also, was to be dismissed ? Leopold was evasive. " Patience, patience," was his cry ; and then he took refuge with his father confessor, to whom he spoke in his beloved Italian tongue, " *O padre mio, come detesto il dovere prendere delle rissoluzione!* " Yes ; it was difficult for the Emperor to make decisions, but nevertheless Eugène succeeded in accomplishing Caraffa's overthrow, although he did not get the command for himself. The Duke of Savoy remained commander-in-chief.

Eugène was beside himself. He was so near victory, and yet it had slipped out of his grasp. He had held himself long enough in the background, and had hidden his commander's talent under the uniform of a general who was only a subordinate. It was time that he came forward. He stormed the Emperor and importuned him with entreaties. But in vain ; Leopold only crossed himself and was silent.

Eugène swore in irony. " There is nothing new at Court," he wrote to the Margrave of Baden. " No one thinks of anything but eating, drinking, and gambling ; they trouble themselves about nothing else. . . . " " The tragic circumstances in the Empire certainly disturbed the Emperor for the space of an hour. But, luckily, on that same day there was a procession, and he forgot everything again. I noticed that the sentiments of the various Ministers differed considerably. Some were pleased, others were troubled, according to their own personal interests. But the majority did not trouble themselves at all. But they are all united in the opinion that, however the circumstances may be, and whatever happens, they are not going to miss a single moment of enjoyment. That is the only matter about which they are in agreement. You will probably think it misplaced that I should make a jest of it all at this moment, when you have at least fifty thousand French troops hanging round your neck. But, if you think it over, you must agree that the behaviour of these gentlemen is so absurd that it is impossible to take them seriously."

It is a cold and malicious irony. Eugène felt that he had it in him to find a remedy, and that he could create a unity out of this Power whose constituent elements had been pasted together, if he were given the chance of becoming the head of this unity ! But although he knew that now, at last, the chance had come to overthrow the might of France, he was bound hand and foot.

Ludwig of Baden suggested that Eugène should join him on the Rhine ; but he refused. The chain of French forts in the north was too dense, and the power of the Coalition too small to destroy them. Oh, if only he had the supreme command !

As second in command, as a subordinate division commander, he returned to the seat of war in Savoy. His first act was the siege of the fortress of Pignerol, the fort to which Mazarin owed his career in France. But Mazarin had won it through clever diplomacy : Eugène found the Imperial forces too weak to take it !

He formed a plan for advancing into French territory, and his suggestion was accepted. He was astounded. He looked around the War Council in astonishment. After three years of thankless effort, were the generals really coming round to his way of thinking ? He did not know whether to laugh or to cry. He took over the command of the vanguard. The way led across the mountains. Eugène shunned no hardships. He was a cavalry officer, unused to marching, but he experienced no fatigue. At last things were advancing—at last the moment had arrived when he would tread French soil at the head of an army.

As the news of the invasion of French territory reached Versailles, Louis was enraged with his cousin, the Duke of Savoy. But when he heard that the commander of the vanguard was not Victor Amadeus, but the Little Abbé, he shut himself up in his private cabinet and issued orders that Catinat was to leave his entrenchments, to abandon the method of wearing out the enemy, and to force a decisive action.

But Louis's command came too late. The south of France, at the place where Eugène had penetrated, was unprotected.

The abandoned town of Gap took him in ; wine and food were there in abundance. His intoxication at having proved the power of his personality to Louis XIV was celebrated by the soldiers without his assistance !

The army came up with the vanguard. " Nothing hinders us now from pressing forward to Grenoble," declared Eugène to the War Council. There were neither patrols nor forts which could hinder his advance. He had *said* Grenoble ; but he meant Paris ! But already, during the march to Gap, the Duke of Savoy had fallen ill of fever. A rash broke out, and Victor Amadeus's life was in danger. The army's progress depended upon the outcome of the illness. Victor Amadeus had no male heir. The deaf mute Prince Emmanuel Philibert de Carignan, Eugène's uncle, was next in the line of succession. But it was thought that, on account of his disability, his succession would be out of the question, and that his seven-year-old son would succeed to the dukedom. The Emperor wished to make Eugène regent. Eugène received this communication in Gap. He was to become Master of Savoy—master of the land whose name he bore ; and the neighbour of Louis XIV, to whom he had demonstrated his ability to cross frontiers !

The dream was a short-lived one, for the Duke recovered and commanded the retreat of the Savoyard troops. Was it possible that the chamberlain of his enemy Louis, who came to express the good wishes of his master, in reality brought more than mere good wishes ? Eugène opposed the retreat, but his opposition was useless. He knew that the matter was not above board ; of that he was convinced. But without the Savoyard troops further advance was impossible. With clenched fists Eugène was forced to retreat.

He went to Vienna. On the day of his arrival he craved an audience with the Emperor, and begged for a Minister to be relegated to him to whom he could vindicate his proposals for the future conduct of the war in Italy. Leopold answered that he himself would fill the rôle. Eugène worked out a detailed plan, but he did not achieve anything more by it than his own promotion to Field Marshal. He remained

VICTOR AMADEUS, DUKE OF SAVOY, HUMBLES HIMSELF
BEFORE LOUIS XIV. A CONTEMPORARY CARICATURE.

subordinate to the Duke of Savoy, whose actions corresponded to the swing of the political pendulum until the magnetic needle of his disposition drew him ever further in the direction of France.

Already, before Eugène's return to Savoy, Victor Amadeus had concluded a secret agreement with France which culminated in the promise to break his alliance with Leopold gradually, and in the meantime to obstruct the plans of operation of the Imperial army.

How punctiliously this promise was kept is shown in Marshal Catinat's report : " In agreement with the Duke or with one of his Ministers, we are kept supplied with news which is always corroborated and which gives us previous information of every movement of the enemy."

Eugène's genius had to fight a battle against dissemblers. He felt that a strange force crippled his arm, and that, whenever he undertook any action, the counter-movement was already planned with absolute precision. Once his impatience overcame him, and, without betraying his plan to the Duke, and with the aid of three thousand troops only, he captured the very important Fort of San Giorgio.

It was the most difficult year for Eugène. He began to see through his cousin's game. But he had no proofs. He heard that Victor Amadeus had agreed to go over to France in order to keep the small number of Imperial troops united with his little army, so as to release the French army for the war on the Rhine. The marriage of his daughter with the Duke of Bourgogne, Louis XIV's eldest grandson and future King of France, was to seal the alliance. It was a secret agreement, and Eugène had no proof of its existence. He could only guess, and arrange accordingly. He separated his troops from those of Savoy, observed all he could, reported everything to Vienna, and, above all, emphasised his own loyalty, to prove that he had already chosen between his cousin and the Emperor. From the very first moment it was clear to Eugène that he could not remain on his cousin's side, because that would be equivalent to the transfer of his loyalty to Louis XIV, and therefore equivalent to the denial of his life's plan and to the end of his career. He knew now that he could no longer look upon himself as a Prince of Savoy, but that he must become an Austrian through and through. No other possibility was open to him.

Once, as he availed himself of his right as a kinsman to enter his cousin's presence unannounced, he found him poring over maps, in lively conversation with the French General Tesse. He asked his cousin for an explanation. But Victor Amadeus smiled, as usual. Would Eugène renounce the revenues of Casa Nova and San Michele by betraying him?

Eugène reported the incident to Vienna. His conduct consolidated his position at the Viennese Court for ever. He lost the income from the abbeys, but the incident gained him more capital.

In Vienna, the plan of moving him to some other theatre of war was discussed. The Duke of Savoy had finally abandoned the Emperor's cause and had subjected himself to Louis XIV. Could his cousin Eugène be allowed to assume the command against him? The result of these deliberations were expressed thus : " In consequence of the trust in Eugène's well-known experience, of his oft-proven valour, of his reasoning powers, and of his good conduct on all occasions, the Emperor appointed him commander-in-chief of the army in Italy." But the command was not one which would enable him either to prove his ability or to become famous ! The war in Italy was no war ! The Emperor had been too late in deciding in his favour. With his small army, Eugène could only hold the enemy in check. He achieved no more and no less than his cousin and teacher, Ludwig of Baden, had been able to achieve with the great Imperial army on the Rhine.

But his time in Italy was not spent uselessly. He knew every stone of one of the future theatres of war.

The world was tired. Leopold concluded a treaty of

neutrality with Savoy, and, soon afterwards, peace with Louis XIV.

The power of France was unbroken—of that Eugène was well aware. But, in the next war with France, the Imperial Field-Marshal, Prince Eugène of Savoy, would lead the Imperial armies against the Grand Monarque!

CHAPTER IV

AMONGST thousands of documents, testimonials, and letters written on the subject of Prince Eugène, the young research worker, Stelling-Michaud, found, not long ago in a castle in Switzerland, amongst the Prince's own letters, a writing of the Count St. Saphorin's, in which he congratulates His Highness most heartily and devotedly on his great achievement : the Elector of Saxony had become King of Poland !

But why should the Count congratulate Prince Eugène on this event ? The gilded letters on the parchment state the reason : " In consequence of the great excitement caused in the world by this unexpected choice, the new King is never spoken of without Your Highness being mentioned in the same breath."

St. Saphorin was one of the numberless adventurers who came to Vienna after the Turkish war, and had been a rival of Eugène's in his candidature for the smallest position in the Imperial army or administration. He was a fortune-hunter whose efforts were eventually crowned with success. In his youth he had been a political agent, was now commandant and organiser of the Danube flotilla, and Eugène's trusted servant and diplomatic agent. When he congratulated the patron whose favours he wished to retain, he knew that he had good reasons for so doing. His indiscreet felicitations were intended to flatter the Prince, but, also, at the same time, to let him know that the Count St. Saphorin was well informed, inasmuch as no intrigue in which the great man was involved was unknown to him.

St. Saphorin knew the circumstances of the mysterious choice. He also knew the previous history of the affair. During the war against Louis XIV, a new organisation had established itself in Constantinople, and an energetic régime had succeeded in raising new troops in the Ottoman Empire. Belgrade had fallen into the hands of the Turks once more, and they had extended the theatre of war fairly far into Hungary. That was the unhappy consequence of the war on two fronts ! The War Council had no troops at its disposal. The Emperor turned for help to the Empire. The Elector August of Saxony offered eight thousand men of his own troops, but only on the condition that he was made commander-in-chief in the campaign against the Turks. In his desperate position what could the Emperor do but support the nomination ? He knew that the Elector was inefficient and devoid of talent. Physically he was the strongest man in the world, and had ridden from Vienna to Wiener Neustadt in an hour and three-quarters ; but as a commander he was incapable of making a decision. The military were nervous, and the uncertain behaviour on the part of the Saxon Elector increased the discontent of the peasants, who felt themselves unprotected by the Imperial troops. From all sides came urgent demands that the danger threatened by the rapid unhindered advance of the Turks should be checked. A second in command was sought, a general staff officer in a position of authority. The previous defender of Vienna, Count Rüdiger von Starhemberg, had the highest military position in Austria : he was President of the War Council. Asked whom he would recommend as subordinate to the Elector, he replied that he could think of no one who had " more understanding, experience, and energy in the Emperor's service, or whose generous, unselfish nature possessed the affection and loyalty of the soldiers in a greater measure than Eugène."

A short time elapsed before the appointment was finally made. Eugène was not sure of his willingness to risk expending his energy a second time, as a subordinate in a difficult situation in the service of a faithless or untalented commander. He hesitated in signalling his agreement.

At this point, the observations of St. Saphorin began : Why, the Count asked himself, did the Prince of Savoy not lay hold of his opportunity ? Was it not, in spite of the Elector, the very chance for Eugène to prove his genius as a commander ? Eugène hesitated ! Hesitated, and yet, despite everything, accepted the position offered him ? The Count further observed that Eugène, although accompanied only by his staff, betook himself to Hungary by very slow daily marches. In the meantime, one courier after another left his nightly halting places to proceed to Poland, to Vienna, to Brandenburg, and to Hanover. A very few days after Eugène had reported himself as second in command to the Elector, came the news of the election of Frederick Augustus as King of Poland. The supreme command fell to Eugène. Hence his efforts towards the choice of the Elector ! St. Saphorin understood and congratulated !

Up to now Eugène had always been in a subordinate position. For the brief command in Italy, which was doomed to failure from the outset, did not count. He had been forced to obey the orders of strangers—orders which he had often considered misjudged, and as often despised. Now, for the first time, he was independent. He had no command over him—no superior officer who might equally well be a friend or an enemy. He was thrown back upon his own resources, and was dependent upon his own genius. The moment had come for him to prove his military capacities and his genius as a commander—or to deny them.

In the first moment, Eugène beheld once again the vision which had passed before his eyes as leader of the cavalry corps at Belgrade. The walls of the town rose before his eyes : the Danube and the Save flowing together, and the place from which he had thought of attacking Belgrade. There was the Danube flotilla, one ship ranged alongside the other, and lying across them the bridge of planks over which the army must pass. But then he came to himself. He could not march straight to Belgrade. He must reckon with the circumstances.

The time of year was too advanced. The army was denuded of everything, the discipline too lax. First, an insurrection in Hungary, caused by excessive want in the garrisons, must be suppressed by his friend and subordinate the Prince Vaudemont. The army which Guido von Starhemberg was assembling near Esseg was in such a miserable condition that Eugène, immediately on his arrival, sent a messenger to Vienna to obtain remedies and to ask for a free hand in introducing energetic measures.

Instead of the desired assistance, a letter arrived. Eugène did not even open it. A letter ! They thought they could put him off with phrases ! There was nothing to hope for from the Emperor. Eugène decided that he would have to help himself.

It is necessary to study the map in order to get an accurate idea of Eugène's actions during this swift campaign.

The Turkish army had arrived in the neighbourhood of Belgrade, and the universal supposition was that it would cross the Save and attack Peterwardein. But the Turks wandered further towards the east, and only sent their ships to the mouth of the Theiss. Eugène assembled his army around Peterwardein. He wished to wait and see which course the enemy would take. A deserter from the Turks brought the news that in the Turkish camp it had been decided to march along the Theiss as far as Szegedin, to conquer the town, which was only very sparsely garrisoned, and then to turn aside and invade Siebenburgen. Siebenburgen threatened ? Eugène hesitated not a moment, but staked everything in defeating this plan. He ordered the camp to be struck, and set himself at the head of the army, which then marched in quick time towards the north-east.

On the way, Eugène was surprised by the message that the Turks had remained in the neighbourhood of Zenta, a small town on the Theiss. He sent out patrols. Several horsemen returned with the news that, actually, the Sultan was in camp near Zenta. They had seen the guards' fires with their own eyes. And then a patrol arrived bringing in a pasha as a prisoner.

During the uninterrupted march, with threats of the loss of his head if he did not speak, the prisoner was put on trial and coerced into making statements. He said that as soon as the Sultan heard that Eugène was following on his heels, and that the garrison of Szegedin was strong enough to withstand the Turks until the arrival of the Imperial army, he had decided to abandon the attack on Szegedin, to cross the Theiss near Zenta instead, and to march direct to Siebenburgen. Eugène listened with unusual excitement, and made the interpreter repeat his statements twice. " Near Zenta ? " " Near Zenta," the interpreter repeated. Already, on the previous day, the pasha continued, the Sultan had crossed the river with part of the cavalry.

There must be no delay. Eugène continued the march without a halt, and at an increased speed. Were he to stop, and thus fail to overtake the Turks, then Siebenburgen would be lost. Everything cofirmed the news that the enemy was still occupied with the process of crossing the river. Eugène, with the cavalry and a few guns, hurried ahead, and approached the Turkish encampment. He was now only a very few kilometres away. He would like to have started the battle just with the cavalry and artillery alone—after all, every Turk who crossed the bridge had escaped and was a menace to Siebenburgen !

But he must be certain of all details. He must risk nothing. This would be the first great battle which he himself directed. With teeth clenched he waited for the arrival of the army, to give the order for the attack. For several hours his messengers rode to and fro to bring the generals of the approaching army the *ordre de bataille*, so that they might arrange their battle formation beforehand.

Eugène surveyed the landscape. The Theiss is a wide stream across which the Turks had thrown a bridge mounted on sixty ships, over which the troops passed unceasingly. The Sultan was already on the other side, and his tent was plainly visible in the clear atmosphere of the September day. The bridge had been made where the ruins of an Imperial magazine provided cover, and round this ruin, although

PRINCE EUGÈNE'S PALACE IN THE HIMMELPFORTEGASSE

they did not expect an attack, the Turks had set up waggons in a wide ring as a precautionary measure. In addition, they had constructed provisionary, unfinished ramparts. The land was flat, and exposed to the sun. Only a few isolated trees interrupted the view. So long as only Eugène and his vanguard were to be seen, the Turks took no notice of him. But as soon as the column of dust thrown up by the approaching Imperial army made its appearance a furious cannonade from behind the ramparts was directed on the approaching troops. Eugène saw that they were already in battle formation. From the first to the last man, his commands had been obeyed. Now the straight line of the front began to divide into wings. Everything took place according to plan. But suddenly, from behind the earthen ramparts, Turkish cavalry appeared. There was a danger of the battle beginning before the pre-arranged circle had been closed around the Turkish encampment. " Dragoons, forward," was now the watchword. From the curved line, which continued to advance but moved ever more in a circle, the dragoons broke forth in dense squares, " *Marsch, marsch*, on to the Turks."

Eugène's advance was not hindered. The fierce attack on the part of his dragoons drove back the Turkish cavalry. Now the army had reached the Turkish bulwarks. The struggle began.

The river Theiss was very low. Next the bridge was nothing but a sandbank. Eugène, with the *flair* of genius, had decided upon that for the basis of his operations. While the whole Turkish army defended itself in the fortifications, and withstood every attack with persistence, the left wing of the Imperial army, under Guido Starhemberg, marched over the sandbank of the Theiss into the interior of the Turkish camp. At this moment there was great confusion among the Turks, which gave Eugène the opportunity of hurrying his right wing on to their bulwarks. He had placed himself at the head of a regiment, but, when he saw that the terrain was unfavourable for the horses, he dismounted, and, with the cavalry side by side with the infantry, he stormed the first entrenchment, the second, and then the earthen fortifications.

The battle had started two hours before sundown; and now it began to grow dark. The men were engaged in hand-to-hand encounters. They had ceased to make use of shotguns. No one paid any further attention to the word of command, and Eugène's soldiers obeyed the blood lust which had taken possession of them. Their advance was irresistible. In deathly fear, the Turks pressed towards the bridge, which seemed to them the only escape left to them. But here the left wing of Eugène's army stood fast. Starhemberg gave the order to fire. The Theiss was now the only possibility of flight for the Turks. But only a few arrived on the opposite shore. More than ten thousand of them were drowned in the river.

The battle ceased only when night had descended upon the field. As Eugène expressed it, in his report to the Emperor, it was as though " the sun itself had not wished to go down before its shining eye had witnessed the complete triumph."

Helplessly from the other shore, the Sultan watched the defeat of his army. Beset by the fear that the Imperial dragoons would cross the bridge and cut off his retreat, he fled, accompanied by a few horsemen, in such haste that he arrived in Belgrade within a few hours.

The next morning, Eugène led his victorious army across the river into the camp deserted by the Sultan, and realised, for the first time, the incredible losses of the enemy and the significance of his victory. He had not only prevented the march on Siebenburgen; the Turkish army was ground to powder. Twenty thousand Ottomans lay on the battlefield, ten thousand were drowned, and the rest strewn to the winds. Three million piastres, every kind of weapon, all the baggage and munitions, a vast number of horses, camels, oxen, flags, horse-tails, and standards fell into Eugène's hands. But the object of greatest rarity amongst the loot was the seal which the Grand Vizier carried around his neck as the sign of his might, and which had never before fallen into enemy hands.

For days after the battle of Zenta, Eugène was beset by the same inner unrest that he had experienced when, as a young man, he had seen the vision of his victory over the Ottoman Empire. Had he fulfilled his purpose by that battle? Would he at last be able to turn towards the west, and overthrow Louis XIV as he had overthrown the Turks? It was still his dearest wish, and now he felt strong enough to fulfil it. But the Empire and Leopold had made peace with Louis XIV. Now, when at last he had an army at his command, he had no opportunity of making war on the idol of his childhood. Eugène felt empty—deprived of an object, a goal, or a purpose. What satisfaction was there in being, at the age of thirty-four, the commandant of a victorious army, and marvelled at by all about him? What was the satisfaction of having fought his way through all troubles and difficulties? What was all that compared with this emptiness in his heart, this feeling of having no goal ahead of him? What should he do now? This thought obsessed the man who, up till then, had never had the chance of ruminating. The feeling overcame him in the lonely hours which he imposed upon himself almost every day in the forts that he visited. Where—where should he go now?

He could not continue making war on the Turks. The army which owed its impulse to him was too weak. He knew that. Yes, if he were provided with all the necessary means, then he could carry the war right into Turkish territory, and extend the Austrian frontiers as far as the mouth of the Danube.

As a young man he had studied the campaigns of Alexander, and knew the plan, which Leibnitz had suggested to Louis XIV, of an expedition to Egypt (a plan which, later on, Napoleon was actually to carry out). Phantasy took hold of him; but then he began to calculate. Could he possibly, with a couple of thousand weakened soldiers, seek out the enemy in his own country, and, with only a small chance of success, advance into the heart of Turkey, which, since the siege of Vienna, had raised one army after the other, produced new expedients, and had the vast, mysterious East behind it ? There were not even provisions enough for his little army. No oats, no flour, not enough powder, the horses in bad condition, the guns of no further use. All the same, Eugène was determined to attempt it. Day and night he worked out his plans, and then sent them to Prince Vaudemont in Vienna. The War Council rejected his proposals. He was congratulated on his success, but at the same time was asked whether he had received the last communication from the council. Now, Eugène remembered for the first time the letter he had received some days before the battle, and had left unopened. He tore open the envelope, and read : " Command for His Royal Highness, the Prince Eugène of Savoy. That under no circumstances, with his weak army, is he to undertake a decisive action ! " The reminder of the letter was an admonition. Eugène smiled bitterly. Even though he had won a decisive battle, they would still probably subject him to a court-martial for having neither read the commands of his superiors nor obeyed them. He wrote a bitter letter to the Emperor, asking why no attention had been paid to his requests ; preparations for the pursuit of the enemy ought to have been made before the victory—and the pursuit would have been a possibility, even with the aid of quite inconsiderable means.

But what was the use of reproaches ? " Austria holds the trumps if she would only play them." But will-power was needed—and will-power would never be forthcoming !

Eugène did not wait for the Emperor's answer. He had a great desire to know how the Turks lived. Up to the present he had only seen them in the turmoil of close encounters. He had learned their technique in combat. He knew the directions of the Koran, which bind the troops to a triple attack, and the religious instructions for their conduct in case of the attack's failure, in obedience to which they take to flight and throw themselves on the mercy of their fate. The battle of Zenta had not brought the struggle against the Turks to an end. Eugène would come into conflict with them again and again. He must know what kind of men these were with whom he engaged in battle.

With a few thousand cavalry he rode into Bosnia. But in the picturesque landscape Eugène saw only Turkish cavalry squadrons, that would have to be combated, and forts on the road which, in imagination, he stormed and captured. Where was the mysterious East ? At last the town of Serajevo lay before his eyes. From a near-by hill he saw the white minarets of a hundred and twenty mosques. He hoped to be able to attend a service in one of them. But then came mounted messengers to say that the Turks had abandoned the town, and before leaving had plundered and robbed the Christian and Jewish inhabitants. The enterprise had lost its purpose for Eugène.

He turned back, depressed and ill-humoured. A great victory was only effort expended in vain ! Nevertheless, although this young man had been pursued by misfortune for so long, every unintentional action of his was turned to a good purpose. His expedition into Bosnia produced results of military and diplomatic importance which he had not anticipated. The Imperial army had spread terror far and wide into the enemy's country. It was a propagandic success, as no other had ever been. The Eastern peril was over, and in Germany the Turks were feared no longer.

Eugène was soon able to gauge the value of the undertaking. He had kept a diary during the expedition into Bosnia. On the return journey, he wrote the following words : " Amongst the Turks there is terrible confusion. With a little more preparation it would be possible to capture the entire kingdom and keep it."

In the Himmelpfortegasse, a narrow street in the centre of Vienna, stands the modest house—palace it could not have been called at that time—to which the victor of Zenta returned. It was a one-storied house with seven windows. Already certain parts of it showed signs of princely magnificence ; but most of the rooms were uninhabitable. Eugène could only gradually furnish them according to the state of his income. He was not rich, but he was famous. In the reception-room, on a carved console, lay the sword, set with precious stones, which the Emperor had given him in memory of the victorious battle ; and above it, on the wall, hung the medals which had been engraved to commemorate the victory.

Every day, builders, architects, and artists came, all of whom Eugène received with quiet reserve. They came to make suggestions for alterations to the house. Eugène could not make up his mind. He had spent most of his capital in buying the hill which lay opposite the Kahlenberg, the hill which he had seen as he looked on Vienna for the first time. He wanted to build himself a palace there, which should be more magnificent than that of the Count Mannsfeld on the Rennweg, or that of the Lichtensteins at the other end of the town.

Just at this time of indecision, when he had made up his mind to settle down at last, a chamberlain of the Emperor's brought him a deed of gift. The document transferred to him, in recognition of his victory, an enormous territory in vanquished Hungary, and the chamberlain went on to say that whenever Eugène needed ready money the Court exchequer was at his disposal. That day, Eugène decided to rebuild his town house. For a moment he considered whether he would build a second Palais Soissons in Vienna. But the plans of the architect Fischer von Erlach appealed to him so much that, instead, he decided in favour of a new building in the contemporary style. He need not economise. He could choose the ostentatious Italian façade that was in vogue at the time. As Imperial Field Marshal, he possessed revenues that he could never consume. He was the owner of wide stretches of land in Hungary, and worked out a plan of colonisation in order to make them fertile. Even then enough money remained over for him to buy an island in the Danube near Ofen, and to build castles on all his estates. He had become overnight a rich man who needed time to devote to the administration of his fortune.

During the summer months he rode over the fruitful plains in Southern Hungary, where he had introduced

German settlers. A mild wind blew over the fields from which his harvests were reaped. His huntsman had easy game in the richly stocked Baranyer forests. With the passing of the years his wealth increased. Did they know, in Paris, of the rich estate of the erstwhile shabby Prince and Little Abbé ? Eugène often thought of it all : fifteen years had passed since those last days in Paris, when, at the age of twenty, he had raced through the streets in the hot sunshine, and begged for a couple of thalers, as a charity offering, to enable him to start on his journey. He had wished to join the Emperor's army : Vienna was in danger ; the whole of Europe trembled in fear of the Turks. Fragments of the conversation of those days arose in his memory. " Yes, if the weal and the woe of Christendom depended upon him ! " He heard the laughter again, and thought, Who, after all, had vanquished the Turks in the end ?

A few days later a cavalier of Prince Eugène's arrived in Paris. He had come to pay debts for His Highness. He had brought a list of names with him, which Eugène had only recalled with a great effort. Those had been bad days !

The cavalier visited the Palais Soissons, but Eugène's eldest brother was not there, and his grandmother was dead. The great building was deserted. The Comte de Soissons was seeking a position. Louis XIV had banished him. England did not require his services—Venice had refused him. Eugène commissioned someone to search for him. He had spoken to the Emperor, who had agreed to the appointment of the Comte de Soissons as Master of the Ordnance in the Imperial army. If his brother were to bring his wife and children with him, then Eugène would no longer be lonely in his palace in the Himmelpfortegasse ! Why did his mother refuse to come ? Did she wish to remain for ever near Paris and Louis XIV ? How he would love to show her the increasing magnificence of his palaces !

There was peace in Europe, but Eugène knew that the state of exhaustion, in which all armies were equally plunged, was a state of truce rather than of peace. One must look ahead ! In spite of the exhausted condition of his rich country, Louis XIV was still arming. The public credit was drained, and the revenues from taxation decreased from year to year. On the most varied pretexts, money was extorted from corporations and private people ; and all kinds of employment were converted into public appointments.

Traders in cattle, graziers, wine carriers, and all transmitters of goods were converted into Royal officials, who had to credit the Treasury with large sums in payment for their appointments. Forty thousand new offices were created in a few years. But even that was not enough. Artists and handicraftsmen ceased to be commissioned, the Royal pleasures were restricted, and even the Royal hospitality curtailed. The King's Pensions and the salaries of officials were no longer paid out. The whole country was in want. The levies on imports and exports had a disastrous effect on agriculture. Wine and corn could not be exported, because they were burdened with such severe duties. The workers in the luxury industries emigrated. The peasants, who had no custom for their produce, and saw the fruits of their thrift and industry disappearing, limited their activities to their own indispensable needs, on account of the high taxation and the chicanery of the tax collectors. Hunger began to stalk the country. The peasants begging and threatening, thronged the gates of the towns. The stewards hanged some of them in order to intimidate others. But the survivors shrieked that they would rather be hanged than starve. Stories were told, with horror, of parents who killed their children because they could not feed them any longer. In Paris the populace attacked the market folk and the officials. The atmosphere was similar to that which prevailed just before the French Revolution. In Lyons forty thousand hungry workers demanded bread. Charity organisations were established on a basis not unlike that of the dole system of the present day. Louis XIV's sun was setting—but yet he continued to arm !

Eugène received, regularly, news from France. His activities were no longer confined to the military sphere. By his victory at Zenta he had grown in the Emperor's estimation to such an extent that now most political resolutions had to be submitted for his approval. He negotiated with the envoys of the German States, with the Duke of Savoy again, with England, and with Holland. He organised the auxiliary troops that the Empire and the Allies were capable of putting in the field. He must arrive at a state of maximum capacity, so as to be able to compete, on behalf of the Emperor, with the great enemy of the Empire who was his personal enemy as well.

The French armies even now were better armed and equipped than all others. The great King held on. He would soon be sixty years of age, and suffered both from severe fevers and from gout. There were no more celebrations in Versailles. Louis was beset by fears of death and of the Last Judgment—and yet he armed ! He himself saw the change in the times. How different it had all been in his youth ! Now the Court was crowded with nuns, father confessors, bishops, and spies. Where was the past glamour of Versailles and the Trianon ? Instead of the magnificent plays, the gay parties, the gallant cavaliers, and the lovely, frivolous women, now there were moralities, monastic boredom, endless penances ; life had become a contrite, crushed existence. At the same time, Louis knew that, under this surface of piety, societies existed expressly for the practice of debauchery. His beloved France was like a limewashed grave. Where were the happy days with Olympia ? Snow of past years !

From this melancholy France a nobleman in the service of the Most Christian King arrived in Vienna. He had come on a very important mission, the nature of which was only known to Louis XIV's new official ambassador at the Emperor's Court, the Marquis de Villars. This secret mission brought Louis's anonymous messenger, not to the Hofburg, not to Leopold ; instead, he knocked humbly at the door of the palace in the Himmelpfortegasse, and asked to speak to His Highness the Emperor's Field Marshal, Prince Eugène of Savoy.

A messenger from the King of France? Eugène would receive him.

This reception differed from all other receptions in the Prince's house by virtue of the plainness of the clothing which the Prince wore. Eugène wore a simple coat, an old worn garment in which he looked no better off than the princely vagabond of those last days in Paris. He stood slightly bent forward on his thin legs, his feet in plain black shoes without buckles. The dark colour of his long hollow face contrasted with the white flaps of his collar. In what way could he serve the King of France's noble messenger, he asked.

The simplicity intimidated the French cavalier far more than the greatest splendour would have done. His Majesty the King of France, began the cavalier, offers Prince Eugène of Savoy and his family their reinstatement in France. His Majesty the King of France is prepared to restore to His Highness all those dignities and offices which His Highness now enjoys in the service of the Emperor. His Majesty offers the Prince of Savoy the Governorship of Champagne, and a yearly income of twenty thousand louis d'or.

Marshal of France? The words resounded like a trombone. Was the dream of his childhood to be fulfilled at last? Eugène saw in his mind's eye the magnificence of Versailles. He lived over again his arrival there, in company with his friend, Prince Conti. He saw himself again walking up the stairway of honour and through the mirrored galleries. But this time the courtiers cast him no contemptuous glances— this time they bowed before him. And this time the King who received him did not look past him, but thanked him for his greeting and held out open arms. It was an intoxicating vision. Eugène's blood rushed to his head; he gripped behind him with his hand to prevent himself from falling, and came in contact with the sword, set in diamonds, which had been Leopold's gift in commemoration of his victory at Zenta. And then Eugène came to himself again. He was no longer the insignificant Little Abbé. He was the vanquisher of the Turks ! He was known as the greatest commander of his time !

He gave a polite, a very polite, answer, but with such finality that Louis's emissary desisted from making any further efforts.

A few weeks later, Eugène heard that all his family's property in France had been confiscated.

PART IV

"*Genius Wins the Battles—Diplomacy Gains the Territory*"

CHAPTER I

IN A FEW YEARS Eugène, who had been born in France and was a member of an Italian princely House, became a German. To be sure, he still spoke his excellent Parisian French, interspersed, admittedly, with German or Italian words, and preferred French literature to all other. His cuisine was French, and his household, conducted in the manner of a great French nobleman, was not unlike that of the Palais Soissons. But what he dictated to his secretaries in French was directed against France.

His political cogitations were concerned with the frontiers of the Holy Roman Empire, with their defence, and with the organisation of the Imperial army.

Eugène's sphere of interests was not exclusively "Austrian." The prosperity and extension of the Imperial hereditary dominions was only part of his scheme: he cherished in his mind the concept of a great united Germany under Habsburg rule, as the only bulwark against the French policy of extension which France owed to his great-uncle Mazarin. Austria's increase of power in the east would strengthen the Habsburg influence in the west. Austria's civilising activities in Hungary and in the Balkans would create a new Germany which, when placed in the Balance of Power, would so clearly turn the scales to the detriment of the German Princes that it must secure the unity of the Empire. No Prince of the Empire would then set himself up against the House of Habsburg, and no liege-lord or sovereign would be able to conspire with Louis and go unpunished. The might of such a united (hitherto only arbitrarily united) German Empire of Roman nations would be far superior to the national might of France.

Eugène had settled himself as a citizen in Vienna just as naturally as, fifty years earlier, the Italian Cardinal had settled himself as a citizen in Paris. He thought for the Habsburg Emperor and for Germany, just as Mazarin and his predecessor, Richelieu, had thought for the French King and for France. And, like Mazarin, he thought for the future.

Two problems must be solved : the Turkish question—or the extension of the German frontiers towards the east by the method of conquest—was a question to be dealt with later on. An offensive policy against the Porte could only be considered when the Spanish question had been settled. Since the nations had shed their blood in the thirty years' religious war, only disputes of succession could give rise to new wars, and thus to changes in the world distribution of power. These questions of succession, or dynastic conflicts, arose from the family relationships between the individual rulers.

During his stay in Madrid, Eugène had learned the Spanish circumstances. His mother kept him acquainted with all that happened in the Spanish Netherlands and on the Peninsula itself. His aims were twofold : the first was to make the Emperor's second son successor to Charles II of Spain ; and the second—to be fulfilled after the death of Leopold—was to make Joseph, the Roman King, Emperor of a great German Empire extending from the Rhine to the Black Sea, and in the Danube territory, down to the mouth of the river. The second objective was very far from being realised ; Eugène cherished no illusions about it. In the first place, his own position was by no means secure enough for him to take any definite steps towards reaching his goal. He was, after all, only one of the officers of highest rank in the army, a commander preparing for a future war, a councillor unasked ; one who was willingly listened to, it was true, but still, nevertheless, one whose advice was only followed when it was convenient. When his opinions contradicted those of the leaders in diplomacy they were suppressed. In order to disencumber themselves of the victor of Zenta, the Ministers quite graciously reminded him of the Emperor's wish that as little as possible should be altered in the State ! So long as conditions in Austria remained as they were, Eugène knew that the realisation of his plan was not to be attempted.

At the Viennese Court, through the influence of the Emperor's father confessor, the priests ruled. They were of a somewhat different type from the clergy in France who strutted about in the limelight. The priests in the Empire were simple, retiring men, grey shadows who listened behind every tapestried door and knew every secret—an invisible and sinister power. In his youth, while his brother was still alive, Leopold had been, like Eugène, predestined for the Church, and he continued to be attached to the cloistered life. The priests put the lifelong fear of God into him. His was a weak nature which tried to effect a compromise between dynastic action and his faith in God. He allowed himself no amusements : his only pleasure consisted of his devotions in the chapel, conversations with his father confessor who absolved him, and sometimes—but very seldom—the chase. He had been widowed twice : and whether or not it was owing to his repellent ugliness that he had no affairs, it was a fact that he passed his life without the stirrings of passion which might have led to dissipation. A sober, benign tone prevailed in the Favorita, the country place near Vienna which was his favourite residence. The tone was seldom musical, although the Emperor loved music. The priests exhorted Leopold to be modest in all things. " Whoever humbles himself shall be exalted." And so, whenever a care fell from his shoulders, or whenever one of the points of his Crown, which had been dimmed by some misfortune, began to shine once more, they sang hosannas in praise of humility and of the middle way which God had willed. While, in Paris, the rococo age began to make its first dissolute progress, in Vienna, Abraham a Sancta Clara thundered his bitter, vehement sermons from the pulpit. Modesty and humility were his text. He advocated an atmosphere in keeping with the distress caused by the incessant wars. There must be a turning away from joyfulness, in recognition of the gravity of the times. Only then would things improve!

The outgoing seventeenth century seemed to vindicate this severe counsel. In Hungary, which was now secured by the peace with the Turks, a new colonisation had begun, and the fertile plains were bearing fruit, while Vienna, no longer threatened by the Turks, grew and spread outwards in an elegant manner. The suburbs which had been burnt down during the siege were rebuilt, and the small shabby houses pushed ever further outwards, to give place to summer palaces surrounded by magnificent gardens. The manifold rewards, the war booty, and the extravagance of the All Highest Well-wisher had spread wealth amongst hundreds of the most noble families. The rumour that Leopold had rewarded service and attendance at Court by the gifts of rank and fortune induced ever more of the aristocracy to come to Vienna from their far-off castles. Each one wished to live like a cavalier and excel his fellow in pomp and magnificence. In this manner rose the first palaces of the Viennese baroque.

What happened then, was only the beginning. Peace lasted too short a time to allow of the completion of this renaissance. But the beginning was a stimulus which was to lead to fulfilment at the end of the fifteen years of war that followed.

No one thought about the duration of peace, not even the Emperor. But no one was so overcome by cares as Eugène. He was continually to be seen in the chanceries of the War Council, in the barracks, and at the arsenal. The next war was his daily thought. He knew that he would be redeemed by the Spanish Succession question. When he was asked, he replied that there was no possibility of avoiding a war, which, moreover, would have to be conducted on two or three fronts. Wherever there were Spanish possessions they would be disputed. In Italy, in the Netherlands, and on the Spanish

Peninsula itself! Could the armies be equipped, and were there enough troops to supply all the theatres of war? Who would maintain them, equip them, and arrange for reserves? The Supreme War Council, whose business it was to organise preparations, had too often proved its worthlessness in the last war. The Imperial administration was *in extremis*. But even if the members of the Council had been efficient, money was lacking at the Imperial Court just as at Versailles. Eugène proposed the establishment of a war exchequer which should be endowed yearly with twelve millions from the Budget for the upkeep of the Army. His advice was followed, but the greater part of the contribution was on paper only; the money itself, the " nerve of all warlike undertakings," as Eugène expressed it, was lacking in the Imperial exchequer. Often there was such want in the regimental quarters that mutiny ensued in the divisions. An unholy disorder prevailed in the commissariat; the cavalry had no horses, the infantry neither powder nor lead. Yet Eugène knew that enough was there, if it were properly distributed. The Court exchequer ought to have been the head of the finance administration, but, in fact, there were two separate, independent exchequers which were so loosely connected with the central organisation that they could not even make a statement as to the status of the national wealth. In spite of an army of twenty-five thousand men, the administration worked with unbelievable lassitude. All Crown lands, regalia, and revenues were charged with burdens or distrained: one financial crisis followed upon another.

Not content with the empty condition of the State exchequers, everything was done to prevent the influx of wealth from abroad. The hindrances took the form of unsafe roads, innumerable tolls, excises and customs limitations, the fixing of prices by monopolies in spite of superior competition, an intricate and pernicious trade in weights and coins, no less than the clumsiness of an unreliable bureaucracy in the country. Then a movement towards commercialism was attempted, and an attempt was made to hinder, as far as possible legally, the import of foreign industrial goods in order to protect the home industries, and to prevent capital from leaving the country. Yet the high duties encouraged smuggling, and trade did not advance beyond the stage of small industrial production. A world crisis had arisen which was perceptible, at its worst, in Austria.

The burden of debt was enormous, and, what was worse, it was not easily surveyed. It did not arise from a single national debt, but, instead, from individual debts of the most varied origin and purpose which were, for the most part, unconsolidated. The biggest creditor of the State was the Jew, Samuel Oppenheimer. He was the army contractor. He provided for all kinds of troops, clothing, armament, provision, and transport. He supplied horses for the cavalry, mules for the artillery, and furnished field quarters and hospitals. He provided shipbuilding tools and material for bridges, paid advances in pay, gifts of honour, and pensions in advance. He was a merchant on the grand scale. His supplies were distributed over Austria, west and southern Germany, in Hungary, Slavonia, Siebenburgen, and Serbia. He obtained powder from Holland, saltpetre from Bohemia, weapons from Styria, corn and meal from Bamberg, Würzburg, Mainz, and Trier, oxen from Siebenburgen, hay from the Electoral Palatinate, oats from Franconia, groceries from Hamburg, wine from the Rhine; in short, everything that could possibly be needed. But he was not only the army contractor; he was contractor and banker to the Court as well. Amongst the papers of the Court treasury are to be found receipts for jewellery supplied to the Court, for sweetmeats, banquets, theatre properties, and liveries. He supplied the embassies, and was the only man on whom the Imperial Government could depend—he was, in short, an organiser of genius.

Ludwig of Baden, Eugène's cousin, was his patron, and even stood surety for him when Oppenheimer required a guarantee. The two cousins consulted together over ways and means of lightening the Jew's burden and of helping his business. But in vain. Anti-Semitic feeling set one trap after the other for Oppenheimer. He was in danger of losing his life, to say nothing of his fortune. Alone and unaided, he could not carry on his back, which was becoming more and more bent, the whole economic burden of the country. Again and again he was in difficulties about payment, which necessitated the whole Imperial economic organisation to make them good.

It was always the same game. First Oppenheimer's bills had to be met, and then, and not before, the army could count on receiving the barest necessities of equipment.

The difficult position in the country was matched by clumsy diplomacy abroad. The Emperor had approved the appointment of the Elector of Brandenburg to be King of Prussia. Eugène was beside himself. He anticipated that the rivalry between the houses of Hohenzollern and Habsburg would endanger the unity of the Empire, and probably render it unattainable. " The Emperor should have had the Ministers hanged who gave him such advice," he declared loudly.

Political measures were taken again and again without his being consulted. He always endeavoured to foretell the political constellations years beforehand and to tender his counsel in good time. It was useless ; for the most untalented men were confided with ambassadorial posts solely on account of their rank and because they belonged to the Emperor's most intimate circle. Their worst blunder was the appointment of the young Count Harrach to be the successor to his father at the embassy in Spain. But that also Eugène was unable to prevent. He could only ensure to the best of his ability that the Empire was armed against the effects of these blunders, and be on guard to prevent mistakes, or, if that were impossible, at least to attempt to make them good afterwards.

After the death of the young Louise d'Orléans, Charles II's first wife, the King had married a Princess of the Palatinate. But this marriage was equally unfruitful.

At the end of his life the last Habsburg King of Spain saw

himself seated on his throne as though in a box at the theatre, a spectator at the race for the prize of his legacy. Hardly had the Imperial Ambassador left his presence than the French envoy demanded audience. And when the folding doors of the audience chamber closed behind the French Ambassador, the Bavarian agent stood on the threshold, looked at askance by the Savoyard negotiator, who was haggling for the right of succession for his master. And in the antechamber the representatives of the other powers, who were there to support the claims of their Governments, were in perpetual consultation.

None of these aspirants was, *de jure*, entitled to the succession. All these envoys were the emissaries of monarchs who had only come by their doubtful claims on the strength of their renunciation of the rights of inheritance, by marriage alliances to which the condition had been attached that no rights of succession should ensue from them. In the case of the Elector of Bavaria, it was definitely an unjustified claim of the second order. But already, at that time, politicians were concerning themselves with the Balance of Power. England decided that the Houses of Habsburg and Bourbon ought not to attain the ascendancy by a fresh acquisition of power. The prospects of the Elector of Bavaria—not for himself, because he would equally have become too powerful, but for his son Joseph—were the most favoured. His mother was Charles's sister. He was neither Bourbon nor Habsburg. The nation was in his favour. It was said in Madrid that the Crown Prince was still a child and could, therefore, be educated to become a Spaniard. Charles II, in order to demonstrate his preference, appointed Max Emmanuel to be Governor-General of the Spanish Netherlands. But he came so suspiciously near to the throne that he wished to win for his son, that the King broke off his friendship with him.

Eugène threw all his energies into trying to make the Viennese Court fulfil its obligations towards Max Emmanuel, in order that this late confederate should not be lost through ingratitude for the great services which he had rendered the Empire. He was Austria's nearest neighbour. Eugène pointed out the dangers of an invasion from Bavaria if the Elector were to ally himself permanently with the French. But his predictions were not taken seriously enough. Max Emmanuel made an agreement with Louis and separated himself more and more from Leopold—a proceeding which was rendered easier for him by the death of his first wife, the Emperor's daughter. Villars had worked well. Gradually the Elector became entirely French in his sympathies, admittedly with one reservation ! As father of the favoured candidate for the Spanish throne he was Louis XIV's rival, and to that extent anti-French !

Every Foreign Minister of the different candidates had to think in a Janus-like fashion. Friendship and enmity were united in one brain ; the left hand caressed while the right hand felt for the sword. On the tables in every Foreign Ministry lay various treaties, plans, some already signed, some only sketched out by each separate Power, for the exclusion of the others. Nevertheless, Charles II had the feeling that all these efforts and intrigues that went on behind his back, for the purpose of settling a division, would be in vain. In the end it would be his will alone that would decide the issue.

As a matter of fact, this opinion was shared by them all, and constituted one of the pretexts for the race of the ambassadors ! Each wanted to force the King to make a will. Around Charles's throne, amongst his Grandees and Ministers, were clustered as many will-makers for each single great Power as there are competitors for a profitable order ! The French, the Imperial, and the Bavarian parties established themselves in *salons*, while the Duke of Savoy's agent ingratiated himself with all three parties. His claims were of the thinnest. But he wished to benefit in some way by this struggle for the world's greatest inheritance, and gain a small piece of territory for himself. He attached himself most closely to the Imperial Ambassador, for during a fairly long period it had looked as though the House of Habsburg intended to remain faithful to the House of Habsburg, and as though Spain and Austria would be united under one Crown and ruled by the two sons of Leopold. Would the Empire of

Charles V, the Empire upon which the sun never set, cast a shadow upon the kingdom of the Roi Soleil? The first will was made in favour of Austria. But the Imperial Ambassador forgot to pay his homage to the Queen Mother, and, besides that, had not bribed a sufficient number of her counsellors. Although she was an Austrian by birth, the omission was sufficient reason for her to take sides against the Habsburgs in favour of her grandson, the Elector of Bavaria. She did so with so much success that Charles annulled the Habsburg will. While the French emissaries kept in the background, jubilant over the disputes between their two rivals, two parties were established at the Court of Madrid with the watchwords, " Bavaria to the fore," and " The Empire to the fore." They made war on one another with tenacity, and defied the hatred of all the near relations.

At this critical moment Eugène proposed that the young Archduke Charles should go to Spain, escorted by an army, with the purpose of hindering any action that France might take in consequence of Charles II's death. Supported by military power, he would be able to have himself crowned as King of Spain, even if the will had not been made in his favour.

The Austrian party in Spain had already arranged for quarters for the Imperial forces when a messenger arrived from Vienna to announce that the plan had been rejected.

Both troops and money were lacking, and the Imperial treasury was unable to support the Archduke's expenses. The matter was, however, re-discussed, and horses were ridden to death bearing messengers to and fro, until at last Vienna announced that, after all, money and troops would be forthcoming. But then it was too late: not only because the Bavarian party had won in the competition, but also because Louis XIV had waked up from his lethargy. He set an army in motion, not actually in order to wage war, but rather to prove that he was capable of waging war. Instead of giving the order of invasion to the hundred thousand soldiers now armed to the teeth, who were stationed around the

Catalanian frontier, Louis sent a solitary cavalier, the Marquis d'Harcourt, to Spain.

Since the Thirty Years War the whole peninsula had been embittered against France. No Frenchman was welcomed in Spain. But a few months after the arrival of Harcourt both the nobility and the common people were delighted with him. The noble Castilian families were impoverished. In their palaces the contrast between their old magnificence and their present-day shabbiness, and between the claims of their rank and the lack of everything to which their rank was entitled, was very rude. Harcourt flattered their vanity and provided money for their needs. He was a courtier of the pleasantest and most flattering kind, and was a fine judge of human nature. He even adopted the manners and customs of the Spaniards, and thereby together with the help of money won his popularity with the nobility. With the Church he won it by a show of reverence and religiosity, and with the people by his kindness, geniality, and a display which profited the craftsmen of Madrid. In his house the strictest moral customs were observed, and any doubtful *galanterie* was forbidden in the name of his King. His policy was the opposite of Villars's : Harcourt represented France as a morally strict character. He had no mistress with him, but, instead, had brought his wife, whose *salons* were open to the whole aristocracy. The fame of the generosity, charm, and correct behaviour of the Harcourts filled Madrid.

His rival, the rich Count Harrach, was dependent upon his own private fortune, which, although large enough to enable him to buy pictures, was not large enough for him to bribe the Spanish Grandees thoroughly ! For that purpose he was obliged to haggle for every gulden that the Viennese Court gave him. While Harcourt, smooth and agreeable, kept open house, in the Harrach's palace an atmosphere of economy and anxiously preserved ceremonial prevailed.

The little Marquise crept skilfully into the Queen's confidence. Naturally she said nothing of the question of the succession. But when she spoke of Charles's death, which was a topic of general conversation, she mentioned it with a charmingly feigned despair, and said that the Dauphin would think himself honoured if he might marry the Queen after Charles had passed away ! With this prospect in view, the Marquise won the Queen's support. She gave Charles no peace : he must alter his will in favour of France. But Charles was ill and obstinate, and good-humoured persuasion availed nothing. Then Harcourt announced that on the Catalonian frontier a hundred thousand soldiers were prepared to write the name of the heir in blood if the King did not decide in favour of Louis XIV's grandson ! On the same day the Imperial Ambassador asked for an audience. He came in excellent humour. He had had word from Vienna. He brought the news that the Austrian army was in readiness to transfer itself to Spain and to take up its quarters there on behalf of the young Charles, the future Emperor. Everything was in order. All he wanted was an official declaration of succession : but even he went on to say that if the declaration were not forthcoming the Imperial army would not turn back. Another one trying to force his hand ! Charles thought he would go mad with these incessant demands and provocations. France threatened ; the Emperor threatened ? Very well. Neither of them should have their way ! He would make the seven-year-old Prince of Bavaria the sole heir !

His father lived in Brussels as Governor-General of the Netherlands in such luxury that a saying arose in Germany, " In Brussels life is like heaven." But the Germans knew only of Max Emmanuel's vast revenues and nothing of his debts. All his jewels, even those of the Elector's Crown, were pawned with the merchants of Amsterdam. Then came the news that the Elector's son was to be Crown Prince of Spain, and the merchants extended their credit in consequence. Max Emmanuel sent for his son from Munich in order to equip him and despatch him with a suitable entourage to his future kingdom. All Brussels celebrated his arrival, and twenty-four warships lay in the roadstead of Amsterdam to convey him to Spain.

The little Joseph arrived in Brussels in blooming health ; but then suddenly he fell ill. At first, for a few days, it seemed a harmless affair : he just was not well. He merely refused to take his food. The doctors said that the indisposition would pass, but at the end of a fortnight he died in agony. His Lord Chamberlain, Count Tattenbach, had fallen ill with the same symptoms at the same time as the little Prince, and died soon after him. Poison was the first thought. Yet no one examined the corpses, and thus the only method of proof was neglected.

The death of the little Prince gave intrigue a fresh impulse. World politics had to find a new heir to the Spanish Throne. In Vienna everyone was convinced that Charles II would now finally decide in favour of the Imperial family. Leopold attended Mass more often than usual, and recommended the Spanish question to the Mother of God. But if he had paid less attention to his devotions and more to opposing clerical diplomacy, he might have hindered subsequent happenings in Madrid. Harcourt's intrigues, which Charles saw through at last, had strengthened his natural preference for Austria, and his hatred of France and of everything French had increased immeasurably. Even the representations of his father confessor—who had been won over by Harcourt to France—who tortured his suffering penitent in soul and body by telling him that he would be damned for ever if he were not to suppress his family prejudices for the good of his people by naming the grandson of Louis XIV as his heir, were useless. The King remained unmoved. But one thing the father confessor did achieve. His Majesty declared himself ready to make provisions in his will for donations to the Church. The padre gave him a document to sign. The King was tired, and signed the document without reading the contents. He thought that he had only signed away a legacy for a monastery and endowments for several hundred thousand Masses to be read for himself and his parents.

Seven trusted witnesses set their names to His Majesty's signature on the parchment. Apart from these seven persons no one knew anything about the matter—not even the Queen.

Scarcely more than four weeks later Charles refused nourishment. Everything happened in just the same way as with the young Prince of Bavaria. At first the King merely felt unwell, and then he was overtaken by fearful pains. A week later his corpse was cold.

On the day of his death, a Council of State was held. The will was to be read in the presence of the Queen as well as of the Ministers, Cardinals, Bishops, and representatives of the foreign Powers. The throne was gaily decorated; only the gilded seat was empty, waiting for the will to declare who was to occupy it and wear the ermine. The Imperial Ambassador arrived last, clad in gala attire, prepared to accept congratulations on the accession of the Archduke Charles of Austria to the Throne of Spain, and to receive compliments on the victory of his diplomatic talent.

The Cardinal Lord Chancellor read the will in a low voice. Only those standing nearest him heard what he said. Amongst them was the Duc d'Abrantes, who after the will had been read came up to the Imperial Ambassador with open arms.

"I will report your enthusiasm to the Emperor," said Harrach, delighted.

The Duke let his arms sink again. "I came to take leave of the House of Austria," he answered.

Not Charles of Habsburg, but the grandson of Louis XIV, Philippe d'Anjou, had been chosen as heir to the throne according to the will made by Charles II—that is to say, according to the contents of the document which Charles had signed in ignorance of its contents.

As the Spanish Ambassador, in the name of his nation, offered Louis XIV the crown for his grandson, the All-Christian King answered that he must think it over; he was not sure whether he could accept the will. He called a Council of State. His Foreign Minister, Torcy, was delegated to give an exposition of the situation.

Torcy gives an account in his memoirs of the words in which he reported to Louis XIV the state of world affairs at that historic moment.

"The German Emperor," he began, "overcome by old age and misfortune, without an army and without money, is forced to depend entirely on foreign assistance. The Porte requires a short time of repose in which to recover from the enforced peace; after that she will not oppose any enterprise that is to our advantage. The fifteen-year-old Charles of Sweden is preoccupied with the establishment of his own sovereignty. The youth of Frederick IV of Denmark has not yet gathered experience. Peter I of Russia has enough to occupy him with the taming of the Russian mentality. The King of Poland is struggling with the various parties within his country. The King of England is concerned with self-preservation. The Dutch are only inclined to make war when England wills it. The German Princes, as soon as there is a question of war, are hindered by factions from the spirit of unity which can hardly be so much as given that name. The Italian Courts, besides being weak, are not inclined to undertake any enterprise for the sake of others. In Portugal, the King is ruled by his wife's favourite, the Duca de Catalba, who desires only the happy hours of lovers and not war. Spain, which was already in a decline under Charles, has now lost its head as well. Sire, what can hinder us from undertaking an enterprise which the Spaniards themselves, who have long been suffering from an unpleasant destiny, are prepared to help rather than hinder?"

That was an optimistic report. But, on the whole, it represented fairly well the world position. Now, for the sake of form, the Dauphin, father of Philippe d'Anjou, was asked his opinion. This was really nothing but a formality, and the insignificant son of Louis XIV—the "Grand Dauphin," as he was called—declared with a low bow that he had no other wish than to repeat for the rest of his life, "The King, my father, and the King, my son."

But Louis XIV still considered. He was not quite so optimistic as his Foreign Minister. He was naturally cautious, and had been educated in foresight. He wanted a support in the background. A certain time elapsed before he made up his mind—that is to say, before he had found the support!

Then he presented his grandson to the assembled Court with the words, " Gentlemen ! You see here the King of Spain. The nations have chosen him, the Spanish King nominated him, the Spanish nations desire him, and I give my consent. Spain and France must live side by side in mutual peace and contentment, and together secure eternal peace in Europe. From now on, the Pyrénées have ceased to exist ! "

A contemporary reports : " The great King rose to his feet in the throne-room of Versailles. While he spoke, his eyes shone. He felt himself once more Master of the World."

CHAPTER II

THE ACCESSION of Louis XIV's grandson to the throne of Spain completed the execution of a plan of Mazarin's which the Sicilian had sketched out for the House of Bourbon and for France. The Savoyard Eugène, who had been born in France, and was Mazarin's great-nephew, opposed the realisation of this plan on behalf of the House of Habsburg. His life-long struggle against Louis XIV was beginning.

Eugène determined that the Emperor's protest against the accession of the young Philip should be more than a mere protest on paper. Leopold was lacking in courage, but Eugène forced him, before he had secured a single ally, to declare war against France and Spain. He undertook the responsibility for an act of despair which, on the face of it, seemed just as hopeless as his own flight had been from France eighteen years before, together with his plan to make war on the Master of the World. Where Louis XIV was concerned, Eugène's temperament overbore his reason. "Let us march first," he said; "afterwards we shall not fail to obtain allies."

That was easier said than done. Louis's diplomatic preparations had been so thorough that almost the whole of Europe was on his side. The Emperor seemed to be abandoned to his poverty. Allies? The Duke of Savoy had been won over to France, partly by the marriage of his second daughter with the new Spanish King, and partly by an agreement which gave him the supreme command over the Franco-Spanish armies in Italy, secured by the payment of subsidies. The Princes of northern Italy, whose dominions lay outside the territory that was already Spanish, declared themselves for Philip, and in all the Spanish provinces, in Brussels, and in Milan his sovereignty was acknowledged without opposition. A French army had united with the forces of Spain and Savoy which were stationed there and occupied all the key positions. Much the same conditions prevailed in the principalities on the Rhine.

At the same moment Bavaria rose against the Emperor. Leopold ordered a decree of banishment for Max Emmanuel and declared his Imperial fees forfeited. But the Elector looked ahead for consolation. If Leopold wished to effectuate the claims of his son Charles on the Spanish throne, he would have to distribute the Imperial armies on several fronts : he would have to summon all his resources if he wished to prevent peace from being dictated to him in Vienna by Max Emmanuel himself!

"Let us march first," Eugène had said. His cousin, Ludwig of Baden, who had the supreme command in Germany and in the Netherlands, could march. But for Eugène himself, as commander of the Italian army, the possibility was more doubtful.

He had twenty-nine thousand men at his disposal, and their advance into Italy was blocked by Marshal Catinat, who held all the important and accessible passes. The Alpine chain, barricaded by the combined troops of Spain, Savoy, and France, made it impossible for the Imperial army even to arrive on the battlefield.

This news plunged Leopold in despair, and even before the war had begun, the question of the advisability of concluding peace at once was considered seriously in Vienna. But in the south Hungarian plain Eugène had not spent his time solely in the partition and measurement of his property, nor merely studied the plans of his own territory. He had studied the map of Europe again and again— the frontiers of the Empire, and especially the southern frontier, marked in black and white, of the mighty Alpine chain. He had long decided that the Imperial army must, in the event of a war, assemble in Rovereto. In the course of repeated consultations with the Master of the Ordnance, Börner, the "Vauban in the Imperial service," he had arranged that the guns were to be made to take to pieces.

With the assistance of reports from mountain guides, he knew every mule-path by heart. On the 20th of May, when he took over the command in Rovereto, his plan had succeeded. While the French held the ravines, the mountain roads, and all passable routes, he would march across the chain unhindered and unseen, and would appear suddenly on the other side of the mountain wall in the rear of the enemy, who in contemptuous superiority had imagined him to be on this side of the mountains ! When Eugène laid his plan before the War Council, all the generals declared it to be impossible of accomplishment. " What about Hannibal ? " Eugène asked. " Mine will be the second crossing of the Alps ! "

At the end of six days, with the aid of thousands of soldiers, he had already made the road passable. The cannon pieces were pulled up to the heights by means of ropes, and the carriages were taken to pieces. The cavalry dismounted and led their horses along the mule-paths by the bridle. During three days and three nights thirty thousand men marched by smugglers' paths between the watches of the French army, and arrived unnoticed on Italian soil !

To the amazement of the inhabitants—who had never imagined that carts of any description could be transported over the impassable mountain chain—the heavy guns and the carriages in their pieces followed after. Ten to fifteen pair of oxen were harnessed to each cannon. Soldiers walked alongside them, and helped to haul them over the heights with ropes, or held them back when the downward gradient was very steep.

Although the whole territory of Trient and Rovereto witnessed this adventurous progress, and although the country people were well aware of how important the news would be for Catinat, and of how well rewarded they would be for the information, yet no traitor betrayed to the French commander the passage of the Imperial army.

Eugène had studied Hannibal's march across the Alps, and had carried out to perfection the first part of the task.

His army stood on Italian soil, without having suffered the smallest loss, or met with the slightest resistance.

But was he not preparing failure for himself in proposing to march with thirty thousand men against an army of ninety thousand? "Ninety thousand are only ninety thousand when they are all together," he explained. He wanted to force Catinat to distribute his forces so that he might attack the units singly. He made excursions throughout the whole Italian territory, which confused the enemy, who did not know where to station himself for an encounter. It was just as possible that Eugène would make an inroad on Naples and take possession of the kingdom of Sicily as that he would march on Ferrara, Modena, or Milan! Catinat was forced to divide his forces; but hardly was the division accomplished, than Eugène, by seizing single divisions unawares, had taken possession of the whole stretch of territory between Mincio and Etsch.

Was Milan threatened? Or Naples—Ferrara—Modena? Catinat and the Duke of Savoy held a Council of War. They were in constant perplexity and incessant anxiety, due to Eugène's unaccountable actions. Catinat had been a pikesman in his time, had risen from the ranks, and was a rough, rude fellow. He swore that the Duke of Savoy had betrayed him to his cousin. But this time Victor Amadeus was honest. He was himself taken by surprise. Eugène's victory was not in his interests, and he defended himself vigorously against the accusation. His daughter, the Duchess of Bourgogne, heard of the accusation against her father, and accomplished the removal of Catinat from the command of the French troops and the appointment of Villeroy in his place.

Eugène only knew Marshal Catinat as an opponent, but his acquaintance with Villeroy dated back to the days of the Palais Soissons. In various memoirs, Villeroy is described as having been the lover of Madame la Comtesse, and the successor to the Marquis de Vardes in the affections of the King's abandoned favourite. However that may be, it is certain that Villeroy, as well as Louis, was a daily guest in the Palais Soissons, and even after Louis's defection he remained her friend, and even visited her in Brussels, in spite of the contrary orders of his King and master. He was a well-grown, fine-looking man, who understood exactly how to adapt the qualities and weaknesses of Louis to his own ends. He had paid court to all the King's mistresses, one after the other. He was a cavalier with perfect *salon* manners, and a chief of staff of intrigues, who measured his opponent by the manner of his acceptance at Versailles.

Even without the reinforcement of twenty thousand men, he would have felt himself superior to the Little Abbé. He declared that when Eugène had defeated the Turks it was merely due to his having had luck on his side. Catinat had not been capable of the supreme command, he declared, and swore to all the ladies at Court before his departure that he, Villeroy, would have driven Eugène and the Germans out of Italy within three weeks!

Immediately on his arrival, he wrote to Louis XIV that he had far more troops at his disposal than were necessary for the task which the King desired him to accomplish! Did not the advance resemble a walk in the avenues of Versailles?

Villeroy was radiant. Where was Eugène's reputed precision and organising power? Where was the will which he was said to communicate to his troops? Where was his courage? Eugène withdrew, and Villeroy followed him. "The first signs of weakness are there," he reported to the King. Louis was triumphant. On the map it really looked as though the French Army's triumph was complete. But the quality of the Little Abbé's strategy could not be estimated from Louis's private cabinet! During the retreat, Eugène gathered his weak, dispersed troops together without any losses. For this purpose he had allowed Villeroy to advance. Caution was essential in a war of thirty thousand men against a hundred thousand! In the neighbourhood of Chiari he halted and entrenched himself. Here there was no possibility of the French displaying their superior strength. Eugène lay in wait. Would Villeroy fall into the trap? The Marshal marched in magnificent battle-formation against the Imperial entrenchments. The French came nearer and nearer,

PE

and yet no shot was fired ! " They do not even defend themselves," Villeroy thought. From an elevation he watched the unhindered advance of his troops. They were within a few paces of the earthen ramparts before the vanguard observed that the trenches were by no means unguarded, as they had thought. On the contrary, here were rows of helmets, and, in between, the polished barrels of their guns were pointing outwards. Suddenly from the big round holes of the guns shots were fired. Eugène had given the order that the enemy were to be allowed to advance unhindered to within a range that would enable each of the Emperor's soldiers to cover his man with certainty. As the first salvo was fired, and fifty shells distributed death, the French took to their heels in a panic. They ran all the faster when they saw that the emptied guns and cannon were immediately replaced by new ones.

The depression that Villeroy experienced after this encounter matched the exultation he had experienced beforehand. But Eugène underestimated the depression of his opponent. For three days and three nights he held his army in preparation for defence, and expected at any moment an attack on the part of the many times superior forces. Every hour he visited the sentry-posts and encouraged the men who were weary and tired to death. But only after the fourth day did he send news of his success to the Emperor. While Eugène's courier rode to Vienna, a messenger from the French King brought Villeroy the command to act with caution, and under no circumstances to continue to attack Eugène, but, instead, in the hope of a final victorious battle, to lure him out of his entrenchments and to force him to an open encounter. But again that was only green table theory. Just as Eugène's advance at the beginning of the campaign had been impetuous, so the perseverance with which he remained in his positions was immovable. Only now and then a raiding-party descended like a hawk upon a wagon of victuals. Nearly every forage transport was waylaid, and wherever a smaller division of French troops appeared it was attacked and destroyed.

The plan of campaign of both the army leaders was the same : to wait, to stand fast, and to see which would remain the longest in his positions. Eugène's unruffled attitude drove Villeroy to despair. He wanted to win : he had no patience. He had foretold his immediate return to Versailles, to so many friends, both men and women, and now, with his hands in his lap, he was forced to sit and look on while Eugène built wooden barracks and stables ! The Imperial army was furnishing itself a habitation ! How could it be brought out of those entrenchments ? Villeroy was beside himself ! Self-pityingly he wrote to the King : " The feeling of the whole country is on the side of the Germans. Every night the villages send heavily laden carts to the Imperial camp. We, on the contrary, shall in a few days be entirely without victuals. The weather is bad, it rains unceasingly ; the roads are destroyed. Nothing more can be undertaken. If we remain here much longer our cavalry will be completely ruined."

The effect of this jeremiad was that Villeroy obtained the consent of the King to evacuate his positions.

Eight days later, Eugène also set his army in motion, but while Villeroy led his troops into safe winter quarters, Eugène was obliged to secure his winter quarters by raids. He captured the territory of Mantua, he took Guastalla, and then he laid his uniform aside and put on the gala clothes and the wig of a statesman. He visited the Princess di Mirandola and the Duke of Modena. With one gesture, a larger part of north Italy was won for the Emperor.

These military undertakings and diplomatic achievements were only small details in the larger concept of this young statesman, who had demonstrated his efficiency as an experienced general. In his struggle against Mazarin's plan Eugène had proved himself to possess the diplomatic capabilities of his great-uncle. While in the French camp orgies were celebrated—concerning which General Jesse wrote to the Princesse de Bourgogne—and day and night the French amused themselves with cards and women, Eugène pored over acts and documents, despatched couriers, and worked out State treaties and plans of battle. The Emperor was isolated, shut in by the united forces of France, Spain, Savoy, and Bavaria. He needed confederates in order to hold out against the superior power. Eugène succeeded in winning the Elector of Brandenburg for the Austrian cause. The Elector had become King of Prussia. The Emperor had given his consent : that could not be altered now. But the great mistake had brought a small advantage in its train. The Elector might call himself King of Prussia? Why not, if he provided auxiliary troops ? The House of Hanover craved the Ninth Electoral dignity ? Why not, if it paid out subsidies ? With England and Holland Eugène's game was an easier one. The inexorable sequences of historical development came to his assistance. French troops had marched into the Netherlands ; the sea power of England and Holland, with the freedom of the seas for their ships and ocean trade, as well as their trade in the Mediterranean, was threatened by the unity of France and Spain. William of Orange, who had now been King of England for fourteen years, could avail himself of the unanimous feeling of the people to make war upon the enemy of his youth for a last time. James II of England, his banished father-in-law, had died in Paris, and Louis had solemnly greeted his son, the Prince of Wales, as " King James III," while he, William, by the grace of the people, was the rightful King of England ! That made the deepest impression upon the English people. The Parliament set a price on the Pretender's head and named him " Enemy of the English nation." England and Holland declared war on France.

The spring of the year 1702 was to see the whole world in arms !

The winter was given up to the provisioning and re-arming of the troops. All warlike action ceased. Eugène's diplomacy had been successful. Now there remained the half of the winter for him to reorganise his paltry army ; but, instead of reinforcements, instead of the money that he asked for, he received again mere promises from Vienna. He wrote desperate letters complaining of the unholy disorder that prevailed in the finance system. He cursed, but the result was always the same : no horses for the cavalry, no powder, no lead, and no money with which to pay the soldiers. The country in which he had been obliged to set up his winter quarters was exhausted. It was impossible to buy corn of any kind in the surrounding country. " It is indescribable, and no one who had not seen it with his own eyes would believe the misery and want which prevails in the army. From hour to hour the necessity of a change in the conditions becomes more urgent. This state of affairs cannot go on any longer, and at the end of the campaign I shall resign my command. I cannot support any longer the burden of fear, which tortures me night and day, of losing for the Emperor not only the fame of his arms, but his crown, his sceptre, army, land, and people."

At this period Eugène's hair began to grow grey. He tormented his brain with the problem of how to put an end to this enforced inaction. He had envisaged his struggle against Louis XIV in quite different terms. He could not bear this helpless inactivity. Something must happen !

He sent out spies, who located the enemy's quarters for him, and he sent scouts to Cremona, where Villeroy had his headquarters. How would it be to besiege Cremona and capture the town with one blow ? Eugène determined to try. Anything rather than his enforced passivity.

One spy after another came and reported. One day a priest appeared, who remained for more than two hours closeted with Eugène. It was late in the evening when he left the commander, but yet on that very same evening the Master of the Ordnance, Count Guido von Starhemberg, received the order to hold himself in readiness with two thousand infantry !

It was a stormy night of rain. The men marched, invisible in the darkness, on wet roads that had no foundation. At two o'clock in the morning the order for a halt was given. Now for the first time the soldiers learned their destination.

The priest had reported that in Cremona an old deserted sewer, unnoticed by the French garrison, cut through the fortifications and was connected with the cellar of his house.

Eugène divided his troops. One column received the order to creep through the sewer into the priest's house and to remain hidden there until two more regiments had penetrated the city by the same route. The first column was to disable the guard, to open the gates, and to send up three columns of fire from the wall as a signal for the invasion to begin. When the gates were opened, two hundred horsemen were to gallop through the town to the other gateway, through which the remainder of the troops were then to enter.

The Marshal Villeroy was still in bed. It was seven o'clock in the morning when he heard shots in the vicinity of his house. At that moment his servant rushed into the room and announced that the Germans were in the town. Villeroy sprang up and called for his horse. While he was dressing he gave orders for his papers to be burned. Then, accompanied by a page, he hurried to the main guard-house. Suddenly he was surrounded by Germans and torn from his horse. " Ten thousand louis d'or—ten thousand ducats for my freedom ! " he cried. That was a good price. The soldiers fought with each other for Villeroy. They tugged him hither and thither. They all wanted to take him prisoner. If an officer of the Emperor's had not informed Count Starhemberg of the struggle, each one of the excited soldiers would have secured a piece of the Duc de Villeroy so as to earn the ten thousand ducats !

Starhemberg took Villeroy's sword and had the Marshal brought into a house near the city gates, where Eugène at once visited him. It was not a pleasant reunion for Villeroy. But hardly had he complimented Eugène in his Versailles manner—and not at all as though he were a prisoner in Cremona—than the Prince was called away again. His expeditionary force was too weak to defend itself against the superior numbers in the French headquarters. The encounter lasted the whole day. The French occupied nearly all the houses and kept up a well-directed fire on the Emperor's soldiers, who were assembled unprotected in the streets and squares. Eugène decided to leave Cremona again. At five o'clock in the afternoon he retired, taking Villeroy as prisoner with him. " The glow of a barrack going up in flames served him as a gruesome torch to complete the retreat in perfect order."

Villeroy was treated with great consideration during his time of imprisonment, and later during the war Eugène gave him his freedom without ransom. The Imperial Court was astounded. No one in Vienna knew of the earlier relationship of Villeroy and Olympia.

In the *Period of Louis XIV* of Voltaire are some verses relating to the situation and to the person of Villeroy :

> *Français, rendez grâce à Bellone ;*
> *Votre bonheur est sans égal ;*
> *Vous avez conservé Cremone*
> *Et perdu votre Général.*

Voltaire's epigram points out in a humorous manner that Eugène's successful raid on Cremona, and the capture of the French Field Marshal, was, in reality, a failure which became obvious only too soon, inasmuch as the French continued to hold the fortress, and the young Duc de Vendôme became Villeroy's successor.

All the Princes who were fighting one another were nearly related. In fact, their relationship was the chief cause of their disputes. But they, personally, were far removed from the firing, and they lacked the excitement of the front warfare. They received news and distributed orders without their lives being in any way disturbed or endangered. The first occasion on which Eugène was obliged to war against a kinsman was provided by the desertion of the Duke of Savoy. He had no family feeling for Victor Amadeus. The relationship was, so to speak, only on paper, and had never given rise to any friendly intercourse. His pathetic insistence that "neither his honour nor his duty would be affected by any sentiments of blood relationship or the interests of his house" had a propagandic object, which is clearly expressed in an added phrase, "I am determined to let the whole of Europe know this." The world was to believe in Eugène's undeviating sense of duty. He was to be, as it were, a walking monument of devotion to duty. "If the Emperor's service and my own sense of duty were to demand it, I would neglect nothing—even if it meant working against my own father." Big words which were appropriate to the sentimentality of the times; book phrases which in no way corresponded to Eugène's real character; for he was not, fundamentally, of a sentimental or pathetic nature.

The new French commander was a near relation of Eugène's, although not from the dynastic side. Vendôme was the son of one of the Cardinal's nieces, Laura Mancini, the first of the Italian girls who had been married off by Mazarin. Her marriage with the Duc de Mercœur Vendôme had ended the Fronde. Louis Vendôme was a contemporary in age of Eugène's eldest brother, and in the Palais Soissons comments had often been made on the fact that the King had honoured the cousin Vendôme by taking him into the Army, had promoted him, and even when he was quite young had allowed him to take part in campaigns.

Vendôme was a true nephew of Mazarin's. If he had had more disadvantages to overcome he would have become one of the most important personalities of his age. But he had always been healthy, strong, and rich. A contemporary gives the following account of him : " Nature had done much for him, but he had helped himself not at all. He had plenty of intelligence, but had never learned anything. He was handsome and had a good figure ; but he neglected to cultivate a pleasing impression to such a degree that he made a more repellent impression than if he had been actually ugly ! All contrasts seemed to have been united in his person. According to his mood, Vendôme would be, one day full of enterprise, the next so cautious that he visited every sentry in person, on the third day so careless that he neglected to post any sentries at all ! At one moment he could not do enough for his men, and at another time he would abandon them to hunger and cold while he betook himself to some neighbouring château to get warm and to eat a sumptuous meal."

It was inexplicable to the members of the French Court, and to the various families in any way related to the Cardinal's nieces, that Eugène should be commander-in-chief of the Imperial army in Italy, and that he should count as the most celebrated general of his time. Perhaps Vendôme had asked for the command in Italy solely in order to measure his capabilities against those of his cousin. Admittedly, the chances for Eugène were not 1 : 1. He now had only twenty-eight thousand men under him, whereas, in spite of Villeroy's immense losses, Vendôme still had more than eighty thousand at his disposal. The odds were nearly 3 : 1, when the better equipment and provisioning of Vendômes' soldiers was taken into account.

But more oppressive for Eugène than the uneven odds was the memory of his childhood. As soon as he heard of Vendômes' appointment, he was overcome by a tormenting feeling of unrest and of inadequacy reminiscent of his Paris days. He must prove himself a match for this opponent. After all, he was an Imperial Field Marshal, and had by his own efforts acquired a palace, castles, and landed property, and solely by his own exertions had achieved more than Vendôme had inherited ! But his old childhood's feeling of inadequacy and the sensation of inferiority in competition with the healthy, spoilt Vendôme, which had tormented him then, was stronger than his self-confidence. His cousin possessed the King's confidence (Eugène surprised himself by thinking of Louis as " his " King !). Vendôme was a Marshal in the service of the King who had not condescended to glance at Eugène nor thought him worthy of commanding a company !

He must show himself capable of dealing with this opponent !

He expended all his energies in encouraging his troops for the next encounter, and in arranging for their equipment. He wrote letter after letter to the Emperor; but Leopold only handed them on to the War Council, whose President, after the death of Count Starhemberg, the defender of Vienna, was Count Mannsfeld. Mannsfeld was a parade officer whose accomplishment of diplomatic missions had promoted him to his high rank. But these missions had not even been statesmanlike performances. For instance, the late King of Spain had made him Prince de Fondi because, as Imperial Ambassador, he had brought him his second bride. He was not capable of filling the responsible position of President of the War Council; for this post, not in respect of rank, but because of its intrinsic nature, counted as the most important at the Emperor's Court. Not only was the President of the Council responsible in all military matters whatsoever, but in addition, he had the first word in all public affairs; and his authority abroad was so great that, for instance, the Ottoman Porte addressed all its communications and proposals to him. His position, from the Turkish point of view, was equivalent to that of the Grand Vizier of Turkey!

Mannsfeld was aware of his own incapacity, and evaded his responsibility simply by not assuming it. For months Eugène heard nothing from Vienna and received no reply to his demands. When, finally, a letter came, it either ignored all the points which he had emphasised, or only touched upon them in a quite superficial manner. Eugène was convinced that the Emperor, who, during the Turkish campaign, both before and after the battle of Zenta, had always replied in some measure to his reports, was now never shown them. In a confidential letter he urged that a new President of the Council was becoming daily more necessary. " If there be no one to represent military interests at Court with any sort of zeal or enthusiasm, then the armies must go to ruin."

The advisability of appointing the Margrave of Baden was debated, but he was already, as Lieutenant-General, the chief of the Imperial generals, and it was not thought advisable to unite the two most important offices in the person of one man. Eugène was proposed for the appointment, but the Emperor replied that he was too young to be promoted over the heads of so many senior officers.

In vain, Eugène wrote one letter after another. He begged the Roman King Joseph to come to the army, as he knew that reserves, money, and war materials would be forthcoming for the army in which the Emperor's son and heir to his throne was serving. He sent Count Pallfy to Vienna to secure help, but all that Pallfy achieved was the command for Eugène to remain on the defensive until reinforcements could be sent him. "Their Majesties the Emperor and Empress," wrote Pallfy, " have asked me whether it is true that Your Highness has become grey-haired and ill in appearance. I answered that it could not be otherwise when your letters were left unanswered and you were provided neither with money nor with any other necessities."

Eugène did become quite grey during that winter, and his gauntness was so alarming that he looked more and more like a death-mask. He realised that he would just fail to be a match for Vendôme. Day and night he saw the spectre of his downfall. He saw himself as a prisoner in a cage, reviled by the crowd on his way to Paris. He would be forced into the abbé's habit, and would be shown to the public. " Here, ladies and gentlemen, is the Little Abbé who dared to challenge the Lord of the World in battle." The laughter of his brothers and cousins, which had mocked his efforts to compete with them in childish races, now woke him out of his sleep, and the loudest voice was Vendôme's. It rose above all others and sounded like the thunder of the new French cannon which were being tried out in the enemy's camp.

If only Eugène had been able to shut his ears ! If only there had been no spies to report the arrival of more French transports and provisions, while his soldiers were starving in their winter quarters with hardly a rag to their backs !

Eugène ceased to read Pallfy's letters, each one of which

sounded more hopeless than the last. The first signs of spring made their appearance in the plains of the Po, and mists rose from the flat marshy land. The troops began to go down with fever. Now and then, some veteran would venture to approach Eugène and beg him for help. How could he help? In a fever of unrest, he rushed from tent to tent, from house to house, and, although no promises were vouchsafed to *him*, yet he committed himself to promises. He ate nothing so as to give his meagre ration to his men. One night he collapsed, and began to rave. "I will remain an abbé no longer," he cried aloud in the night. The doctors gave up all hope for his life.

The news of his hopeless condition reached Versailles. A courtier, the Marquis de Dangeau, wrote in his diary: "Prince Eugène is very ill. On the 20th of May he was at death's door." Over there, a few kilometres away from Eugène's death-bed, Vendôme's trumpeters practised the bugle-call for the attack. Over there Vendôme reviewed the French regiments with the cavalry mounted on glossy shining, well-groomed horses. Over there Vendôme celebrated the passing of his opponent!

Eugène was dying. The troops crept with bent heads about the encampment. The generals consulted together, and decided to retire and renounce the Italian territory to France. With only twenty-eight thousand men, how could they carry on war against a superior force? Impossible!

On the morning of the 23rd of May the trumpeters of the Imperial army called the troops out of their quarters. The soldiers, thoroughly roused, sprang from their beds and to arms. The regiments were formed, the guns manned, the horses harnessed to the gun-carriages. The whole army stood in readiness. All waited for one of the generals to come forward to announce to the army that its commandant, Prince Eugène of Savoy, had died in the night.

In his brown coat, his face unmoved, Prince Eugène reviewed his troops. He had conquered death and had come to do battle against Vendôme!

But one action after another failed in the struggle against

his cousin. The blood of the Mancinis seemed to have been better preserved in Vendôme's healthy body, than in Eugène's sickly one.

Eugène decided to capture Vendôme in the same manner as he had captured Villeroy. A scout reported that the Duke was living in a house that stood apart from the others. Two hundred men were sent out to take him prisoner. The soldiers crept to a position in front of the house, but a shot which was fired too soon turned the venture into a failure. The next day Vendôme gave the order for a larger number of guns to be set up near Eugène's headquarters and to fire on them. The cannonade was so fierce that the Prince was forced to change his quarters.

For months the two cousins held one another in check, until, finally, Vendôme succeeded in surrounding Eugène's encampment on three sides.

The French Commander's intention was to lure the Prince out of his entrenchment—and it succeeded. Eugène determined to end the untenable situation by an open battle. Either his genius, despite the superior strength of his opponent, would succeed in vanquishing him, or, if he did not succeed, then he would go under !

Vendôme was at Luzzara, a small place in the neighbourhood of the Po. Eugène's decision to force an encounter surprised him. He saw his plan of encirclement defeated. But he set his superior army in battle formation and protected it with strong barricades of trees. The battle began at three o'clock in the afternoon.

Eugène won in the field against a strength three times superior to his own. Vendôme was forced to retire ; the day had demonstrated the shady side of his ability. He had been forced to clear the field for his weaker opponent, for the Little Abbé ! What did it matter ? He shrugged his shoulders and entrenched himself. Now and again cannon-balls passed over the Imperial army, which dug itself in opposite him. Vendôme undertook nothing more, as he heard that over on the other side, in the Imperial camp, horses were dying of pestilence, the men lay ill, and the healthy were deserting. It would only have needed quick action on the part of Vendôme for the remaining small group of Eugène's effective troops to have been swept from Italian soil.

Eugène managed to keep together the men who were neither ill nor had lost their morale. To be sure, he wrote to Vienna that the distress was greater than he could possibly describe and worse than anyone could imagine who had not seen it with his own eyes; but yet, a raiding expedition galloped through the Po territory, laid it under contribution, and broke into Milan. This intrinsically insignificant success strengthened the morale of the little army.

Autumn had come, and winter stood before the door. The little group of men in the camp at Luzzara lost all hope. Eugène wrote to Vienna : " I can no longer witness this misery, and am quite determined to quit, as I cannot serve any longer in such circumstances."

He was determined to cast aside his tabard, to lay down his command, and thenceforth to devote himself to the administration of his property, and to have nothing more to do with war.

Over there in the French quarters the trumpets sounded again, and a fierce cannonade began. Then all was quiet. Everyone expected to see the French advance in close columns, and watched for the artillery to be brought into position. But instead of that, from every elevation it was observed that Vendôme's army was marching towards the west!

Eugène could report to the Emperor that he had " lasted out the enemy " !

CHAPTER III

WHILE Eugène was making a desperate stand in Italy, and Ludwig of Baden held his positions with great difficulty against the superior power of France, young Prince Rakoczy, son of the famous Hungarian rebel, escaped from his strictly guarded palace in the Himmelpfortegasse—the same street where Eugène's palace stood—and fled to Hungary.

His flight raised an alarm, for, since the country had been restored to a peaceful condition, the Emperor and his Ministers had neglected to watch Hungary. Their plan was to reclaim the devastated land, and cultivate it at their leisure. The unsettled horsemen, who were only too easily reminded of their nomadic origin, were to be converted by benevolent laws into contented peasants. But the Hungarians had lived too long under irregular conditions to accustom themselves quickly to a disciplined existence, and every civilised decree provoked a storm of indignation. But the Viennese refused to pay any attention to the disturbance: the Administration and the Court were occupied with wars elsewhere and looked upon the trouble in Hungary as a lesser evil to be remedied later.

Austria's attitude towards Hungary was similar to that of the proverbial cuckold. The whole of the rest of the world knew that revolution would break out; indeed, the Venetian Ambassador, Ruzzini, at the end of the century wrote to the signoria, saying: "In Hungary, the flames of revolution are ready to break out: only a skilful hand is needed to kindle the fire." But at the Viennese Court the danger was unnoticed.

Nor did anyone take account of the fact that the King of France's Ambassador, His Excellency, Monsieur de Villars, had become one of young Rakoczy's most frequent guests. The Marquis had dropped the mask of a harmless French visitor: his accurate knowledge of both Austria and Germany had decided Louis to appoint him official ambassador. He was a statesman first, and an army leader afterwards. His method was the reverse of Eugène's, who had had to make good on the Emperor's behalf the harm that Villars had wrought. When war was declared, the French Ambassador left Vienna in the knowledge that his spirit remained behind. Imbued with Villars's counsels, and provided with Villars's money, Rakoczy collected the Hungarian rebels around him and unfolded the flag of insurrection.

All the victories which Eugène had won for the Emperor were at stake. Diplomats in Constantinople reported new war preparations at the Porte, for the purpose of supporting the Hungarian rebellion. One fort after another in Hungarian territory capitulated. Manifestos were distributed throughout the country, and messengers rode from farmhouse to farmhouse. The horsemen, on whom the Imperial government had expended so much labour in converting them into peasants, left the plough and took to the saddle once again. The Hungarian nobility, who had chosen and marked out the sites for their palaces in Vienna, flocked to Rakoczy's flag. Hussars raided the country and attacked the Imperial troops wherever they made an appearance. Of what use was it to take possession of Rakoczy's palace in the Himmelpfortegasse? The Hungarian rebels entered Mähren, and marked their passage with incendiaries and ravages. The distress became frightful; there were no troops available anywhere, and, even if any had been forthcoming, there was no artillery to support them, no munitions and no provisions. Ofen lay in ruins, the remaining Hungarian forts were in a state of devastation, quite unfit to put up a defence, and no money contributions of the smallest kind were forthcoming.

At this moment Eugène returned to Vienna from the Italian battlefields. He had not been in his palace for over two years. For two whole years he had led the desperate struggle against the French; and this journey of his to Vienna was made for the purpose of obtaining assistance for his army. If he did not succeed, then he would retire from service and withdraw to his estates for the rest of his life.

But Eugène was greeted in Vienna as a saviour in time of need.

The staircase of the palace in the Himmelpfortegasse is supported on the shoulders of Herculean men carved in stone. They are mighty figures from the world of myth and fable ; giants supporting the burden of the magnificent balustrade. Every day the infirm, little, prematurely aged man could compare his own frail figure with these colossi. He had come to take leave of military service, and of the burdens which had bowed him and which he felt he could no longer support. But, instead of taking his leave, he took office.

Two years before, Eugène would have felt gratified at having achieved the highest rank and the highest position in the army. But, in these days, the office of President of the War Council, which was now willingly offered him, involved sleepless nights, interminable days, unceasing conferences, a daily exchange of hundreds of letters, interviews with generals and contractors—in fact, a titanic battle with a thousand-armed bureaucracy, and with the complicated system of Austrian officialdom, of which the innumerable threads lay over Eugène's body like a net. To become President of the War Council involved a declaration of bankruptcy, for the President was responsible for the pay of troops, as well as the cost of provision and armaments. Meanwhile the exchequers were so empty that such requisites had to remain unpaid. So desperate was the position that no couriers could be despatched as the treasury could not raise money for their travelling expenses. The majority of the provinces which constituted the Emperor's territory were devastated, uncultivated, and only capable of the smallest returns. Trade was ruined. Only the most energetic measures could effect a remedy. But, despite everything, the Emperor still baulked at radical changes!

Eugène was well aware of the condition of Austria. He had had enough personal experience of the desperate state of affairs, and had no illusions when he took over the Presidency of the War Council. " To-morrow I shall be appointed President of the War Council," he wrote on the previous day. " I am conscious of all the duties entailed, and have little hope of being able to better the conditions which these gentlemen have allowed to develop. I am quite aware of my inadequate ability for this position, but, unless I were a traitor to the Emperor and to the army, I could not leave it any longer in the hands of such inefficient persons. I have therefore begged His Majesty to support my suggestions for the benefit of his service and of the army, and I have insisted that, unless he does so, I shall irrevocably refuse the appointment. For I can only serve those who submit themselves for the sake of more important problems."

The stranger, in a strange land, the homeless Eugène, had naturalised himself within the frontiers of the Holy Roman Empire (of German nations), and had adopted the Empire as his native land. He identified himself with the Emperor and with the army. He was no longer the egoist, the cold and calculating careerist who had no thoughts outside his own advancement. The transformation of his character was completed. He was once more full of ideals, and at the present moment was imbued with the detached idealism of the human being who cannot live without ideals. What more could the house of Habsburg offer him? His personal ambition was satisfied. The possibility of carrying on his life's struggle to the end, perhaps? But at that moment Eugène believed no longer in the success of his plan to bring about the downfall of Louis XIV. To cherish such thoughts was to indulge in irony directed against himself. At the best, it might be possible to conclude a peace under conditions that were not too unfavourable, to effect a kind of truce which would, perhaps, give Austria, under his leadership, the chance of arming successfully for another war. But to hope for an overwhelming victory was vanity. Eugène had abandoned his phantasies! He felt himself no longer young enough to give rein to his optimism. His youthful dreams had vanished, to give place to the considered calculations of fact. In the course of years of hardship he had lost his suppleness. Field Marshal Prince Eugène, President of the War Council, was, at the age of forty, a stiff, irritable, elderly man, who had no use for exaggerated politeness or superfluous courtesy. He expressed his opinions abruptly, and concisely and, wherever possible, avoided unnecessary phrases. The Emperor, who was accustomed to submissiveness, had no easy time with Eugène. He was obliged to listen to plain truths, and to ignore figurative rudeness, if he wished Eugène to retain his office. Sometimes Leopold protested, but when Eugène's stern glance met his unsteady eyes his opposition melted. The old man was helpless. His features had already lost all firmness. His was the lined, hollow face of an old man, the mask of an incessantly weeping Niobe. "To subordinate himself in the performance of higher duties." What did the Savoyard want of him? Was it not enough for him to sacrifice the peace of his country, and his own personal peace of mind, in order to secure the Crown of Spain for his second son, to whom it rightly belonged? Was it not enough to live in the fear of God—to the satisfaction of the Holy Father? The Prince was adamant: to subordinate yourself in the interest of more important problems did not mean to protect either the interests of your own family or those of a dynasty! The monarchy was not an object in itself—neither was the war. They must be so conducted that they contributed to the common welfare. "The success of an enterprise depends upon the common effort and endeavour, solely in the interest of the general welfare."

That was Eugène's confession of faith. That also gave him the strength to maintain the struggle to the end against the windmills of Austrian inadequacy and futility. The stranger felt himself at one with his chosen country, and with every individual of that country, including the Emperor, whose person represented the community just as much as the plain man in the street was also a part of the community. In his intercourse with the Emperor, and in the society of the Ministers, Eugène adopted an unamiable manner, but when he conversed with his soldiers and subordinates the old elastic cadence and persuasive tone was heard in his voice. He did not seek a cheap popularity; on the contrary, he declared: "One should never take the praise and abuse of the crowd as the standard of one's conduct." But he felt intuitively (and this divination was as much the basis of his philosophy as it was the reason of the people's endearment to him) that a new era had begun, that no one was put in the world for himself alone, but rather in order to work for the benefit of his neighbour and for the good of the greatest number!

Eugène had not yet transferred this feeling into the sphere of knowledge. He only knew that both his inspirations in time of war and his richness of comprehension would have been useless had it not been that the man of the people, as well as the peasant at the plough, knew that the Prince of Savoy never commanded him to do anything that would not be as much for his ultimate benefit as for that of the Emperor. When the war came to an end most of the soldiers became peasants again, as were the people on whose land they camped and over whose fields they rode in time of war. They felt that *their* interests were concerned when the Field Marshal ordered that "special care must be taken that no field produce is damaged in any way, so that there be no cause for complaint on that score, and the peasant, even when he is surrounded by troops, must be able to bring in his harvest undisturbed. There must be no interference with husbandry, trade, or barter of any kind." The soldiers knew that Eugène thought of them, and it came to their ears also, when he said: "I think that in military life there would be more enthusiasm if duty were enforced rather by the methods of friendliness and humour than by severity."

But in Austria Eugène was forced to introduce the concept of duty more frequently than that of loving-kindness. The little man himself understood its meaning, but the gentlemen at Court were singularly deficient in it !

Although Eugène had left the army of Italy in a helpless condition, yet he did not forget his men. " I have spoken with the Emperor to-day, and have begged him urgently not to allow the remainder of his army to go to pieces," he wrote to Guido Starhemberg, who had taken over the command. " The Emperor has promised me definite help, as on many previous occasions, and, up to the present time, without fulfilment." His contempt was very apparent. " One might as well speak to the wind as talk to his Ministers. If one complains, they sympathise and complain with one. When one has talked for a long while, and explained that the country is going to ruin, they agree. If, however, one goes on to urge that remedies must be forthcoming, they just refrain from answering at all. Here, at Court, an unbelievable state of indolence or of ignorance prevails (perhaps of both !). . . ."

The battle against the enemy outside the frontiers was not nearly as bitter as the struggle against the enemies of indolence and lethargy inside the walls. Only when Eugène firmly declared that he would resign for ever if a new régime were not introduced did he succeed in effecting changes. He proposed Count Gundacker von Starhemberg for the appointment of President of the Court Exchequer, and Starhemberg, who by exemplary administration of his estates had become the richest man in the State, was elected.

Now Eugène could begin to work, which meant finding money, raising troops, provisioning them, and arming them. But how ? He used the methods that were customary at the French Court. In order to raise the first earnest money, he sold the post of Head Burgrave of Bohemia to Count Czernin, and thereby gained one hundred thousand gulden for war expenses. The sum was, admittedly, only like a drop of water upon a hot stone, but, nevertheless, it was the first liquid money that had been available for a long time.

Eugène sent out an appeal for contributions of horses for

the army. His popular name conjured patriots from the hitherto indifferent population, and the University of Vienna alone produced not less than eighty horses. With a dry humour, Eugène begged the donors to provide harness and a pair of serviceable pistols each, so that the horses might be put into immediate use ! In this manner he recruited a new cavalry division, which although it consisted of only one hundred horsemen strong yet made a beginning.

Count Gundacker von Starhemberg succeeded in raising the sum of six hundred thousand gulden on his own credit, which meant that the campaign against the Hungarian rebels was already financed. Naturally, Eugène could only muster a very weak defence organisation against the insurrection, and, at the most, could only hope to prevent the rebels from invading Austrian territory. In order to avoid any mistakes being made, he went in person to Hungary to organise the defence. He found the country in a desperate condition, and, in addition, received news that the whole State mechanism in Vienna had threatened to come to a standstill. He could control himself no longer ; he became abusive. " When war is conducted on paper, and by means of word battles only, this is the result," he wrote to the Roman King Joseph, the Crown Prince. " The time has come when I can no longer desist from vindicating myself. I hope to appear before you personally in order to prevent the worst, and to steer aside from the extreme calamity. Everything now hangs on the thinnest thread."

The Emperor humbled himself, and neither the Roman King nor any of the ministers ventured to oppose Eugène. Without him Austria was lost. That they knew. For, as he returned to Vienna, the pressure of circumstances reached a crisis. The greatest danger threatened from Bavaria, for Upper Austria and Bohemia were quite unprotected against attacks from the neighbouring country. By the loss of these provinces, the Emperor would be deprived of the only remaining sources from which he supplied his army with the minimum of its needs and would be forced to agree to outrageous peace conditions.

The last man was recruited and the last gulden released, but what was that against France's superiority?

Louis XIV returned to life, and experienced a revival of potency. He felt himself young and strong. The whole world was against him, but he had won Spain for his grandson, and possessed sufficient military power to hold it for the Bourbons. Let the Austrian Prince call himself King of Spain! Where was the Archduke's kingdom? A chimera in the Emperor's brain, or a phantom realm existing only on the parchment of the map, while his grandson actually governed the peninsula! Let the world protest! Louis walked in the clipped avenues of Versailles, where even the growth of the foliage was controlled in accordance with his wishes! So the Duke of Savoy was coquetting once again with that damned Little Abbé? Louis refused to be duped. He sent a " command to the Minister of War "? " For the sake of security—the army of Savoy which is allied with France, shall be disarmed, and [bloody irony!] since Savoy is in any case allied with France, the Duke can have no objection to his subjects serving under the French flag—but they must be separated and distributed amongst the most reliable regiments of the French army.... France's frontiers will be extended at the expense of Savoy." Thus, not only Spain, that vast Spanish territory with all its colonies and provinces, but little Savoy as well was won for the Bourbons! Paris had raised a monument to Louis, and called it " Louis le Grand." He was pleased with it: he had certainly won the title!

At all the tailors' new uniforms were cut out for France's new subjects. The King's couriers galloped to Turin with the order for disarming; but the walls of Louis's private cabinet were not thick enough. At the same moment spies set out at high speed on the way to Vienna to take the news to Eugène. Now was the moment to win over Savoy for Austria—quickly, before the army of Savoy had been forced into French uniforms.

Eugène sent a secret agent to Turin, but Victor Amadeus hesitated. He did not believe Eugène. Surely Louis XIV would not reduce to powerlessness the father-in-law of both the King of Spain and the future King of France? Eugène simply wished to dupe him!

Victor Amadeus did not trust his cousin, but neither did he trust Louis. He came to no decision, but he withdrew the larger part of his troops from the encirclement of the French army. Only when the remainder were actually disarmed and clad in the new uniforms did Eugène succeed in effecting Victor Amadeus's desertion from France.

In his childhood Eugène had dreamed that the right side of his head was adorned with the wig of an officer, and his left with that of a diplomat. That symbolic apparition became reality. He concluded a State treaty with Victor Amadeus, and simultaneously made the Archduke Charles, the Pretender to the Spanish Throne, go to Spain to encourage with his presence the English and the Spanish supporters of the Habsburgs, who were fighting in his cause.

Amid the difficulties and dangers of the times, the original cause of the war had almost been forgotten. Spain was to be won for the House of Habsburg, and, instead of the forged will and testament of Charles II, the fulfilment of his real will and testament was to be achieved by God's judgment of arms! The danger and distress had caused everyone to forget that Austria had won confederates, that the Imperial army commanded by Ludwig of Baden held the French in check, and would continue to hold them in check so long as Max Emmanuel were prevented from attacking the Emperor's forces from Bavaria in the rear.

"I can go on no longer," was Eugène's last thought every night as he went to bed worn out with his exertions. "I must go on," was his first thought as he awoke in the morning. Then he entered his magnificent conference chamber and read the reports. Every hour of his day was planned beforehand. "I would rather work on a galley than work here either as President of the War Council or as a general," was his oft repeated remark, which to this day can be read in black and white. What was a galley compared with the servitude which was Eugène's portion? He had hardly

THE BATTLE OF HÖCHSTADT (BLENHEIM). IN THE FOREGROUND, TO THE RIGHT: PRINCE EUGÈNE AND MARLBOROUGH.

time to take a meal. He had no private life, and had not a single friend. His eldest brother, who had been Master of Ordnance, was killed in the field at Landau. Prince Commercy was dead. It was a good thing that Eugène had no free time. Then the news came that his sister in Lausanne had fallen into a decline and was dying. Amongst his daily visitors was the Count St. Saphorin, whose family place was near Lausanne. He was looking after Jeanne de Soissons. Olympia wrote despairing letters—all her children were dying ! She was so lonely. She lived forlorn and in exile in Brussels. Louis XIV was winning, and she was for ever exiled from Paris !

" One must live on with clenched fists—and not lose courage ! Work—work—work was the only consolation ! " Now and then Eugène sent for his eldest brother's children so as to have some youth around him. But nothing succeeded in lighting up his features with pleasure. He had been too long in the theatre of war, had shared the misery of his soldiers in the field too long, not to suffer in sympathy with them when he read the reports of their distress. He saw again the wasted, starving men, wearing their ragged Imperial tabards, in the feverish swamps of the Po basin. Despairing letters came from Ludwig of Baden. The army on the Rhine could hold out no longer unless provisions, munitions, reserves, and guns were forthcoming. Eugène wrote to the Margrave : " I am working night and day to refurnish the neglected equipment on all fronts. Patience, patience—only have patience ! " Beside himself, he added, " but I cannot hope to repair in one day the damage of years of neglect and disorder."

During these desperate days Eugène had news from England. " One of the handsomest men that can be imagined," wrote Liselotte of the Palatinate of the man who now informed Eugène of his imminent arrival in Germany and begged him to name a place at which he and the Prince might meet. The man was the Duke of Marlborough.

The fame of the great English general was enshrined in the popular song, "Malbrough s'en va-t-en guerre," which was sung for some years afterwards in France, where everyone hoped that events would correspond to the text of the song: "Malbrough ne revient pas!" In Versailles it was hoped that he would never come back, that he had fallen in the war, and that his wife waited in vain for his return! For, next to and alongside Eugène, Marlborough was the most famous and popular commander of his time—he was the symbol of victory for the Allies, and of downfall for the French.

But, at the time when Eugène received the news of his arrival, he was not yet famous. He was commandant of an English auxiliary corps in the Netherlands, where his actions had been purely defensive. Less, in fact, was known about him than about the offences of his sister and his wife.

Miss Churchill, his sister, was the mistress of James II, and slander related of his wife that she was the lover and best friend of Anne, who after the death of her husband, William of Orange, reigned over England. The Queen was anti-French, and consequently the Duchess of Marlborough was hostile to Louis XIV, and her husband became commander of an army.

Eugène knew no more of him than these facts. But he was fascinated—here was a confederate, and a possible source of funds. Here at last was a possibility of preventing the Elector of Bavaria from marching boldly across the Brenner Pass and joining up with the French army in Piedmont, or from attacking the unprotected Western frontiers of the Habsburg hereditary dominions. Eugène breathed again. Bavaria must be subjugated! With the war areas reduced to two, there might be some chance of making an offensive instead of continuing with this desperate war of defence! With this idea, Eugène had written to the Imperial Ambassador in London exhorting him to obtain the consent of the English Government to the transfer of General Marlborough and his troops from the Netherlands into Bavaria.

Marlborough's name worked marvels in advance. No one

knew why, but, nevertheless, the whole of Vienna rejoiced. A hand-written paper announced that Prince Eugène (already at that time he was called familiarly by his first name) was going to meet the Duke of Marlborough in Bavaria. Perhaps their misfortunes would come to an end now?

For the first time for a long while Eugène was confident. On the day before his departure he wrote to the Duke of Savoy that the enterprise would be crowned with success within two months. "Naturally everyone must do their utmost." Eugène did not rely upon his luck even when he felt that it would not fail him. " Success must be won by achievement, and must be earned beforehand." He remained humbly superstitious in his presentiments of success.

Eugène left his magnificent palace, and his high position as President of the War Council, ready, if necessity demanded it, to subordinate himself to another's command " for the common good," as he called it.

As the news of the little man's departure penetrated into the enemy's encampment, the Elector of Bavaria wrote to the King of France, " It is certain that the Prince of Savoy can only have come to the seat of war to carry out some great project."

A mighty army sent to the assistance of the Margrave could not have made more impression!

The Imperial army on the Rhine had fallen into such a state of inaction and idleness that Ludwig of Baden was no longer trusted in Vienna. So much so, that a messenger followed Eugène, and exhorted him to watch the steps of the lieutenant-general with great attention, and to report the least signs of suspicious activities on his part.

For answer the Emperor received a reproof from the President of the War Council. Eugène wrote that certainly for a long time there had been such rumours in currency, without anyone being able to produce a proof of their veracity. It was a well-known fact that insults were never more frequent than when people were met with reverses of fortune. He had personally observed the Margrave's behaviour very carefully, and had not seen the least sign of anything that could give rise to suspicion!

It was a strange experience for Eugène to have to defend his first leader and instructor, the man who had protected him at the Viennese Court, and who had been responsible for the beginnings of his career. Eugène defended him energetically. He was curt and impolite to the Emperor, but he tried to please the Margrave just as at the time when he had been a volunteer. This grey-headed man with the lined face and leathery skin tried to be agreeable and friendly and to a certain extent to hide his own light under a bushel so that his own cousin, who was senior to him in years, should not feel his superiority. Eugène listened to reason but, at the same time, he was determined to lead the army to victory; and, in spite of his fatigue and exhaustion, he was certain that he would succeed.

Count Wratislaw reported that Marlborough had written to London that he would be victorious or die in the attempt. Marlborough too? What a glamour there was in the very name—in spite of its being unknown! Ordnance officers reported that Marlborough had already set out on the march to Germany! " Malbrough s'en va-t-en guerre! "

Seven days later the two commanders met. Eugène had set a very high standard of courtesy, but Marlborough surpassed him. " I have heard much of the English cavalry," said Eugène, " but now that I have seen it, I realise that it is the finest and best trained that I have ever set eyes upon. The quality of these stout warriors cannot be bought and is a sure warrant for victory." To which remark Marlborough replied, with a winning smile, " My men are ever endowed with zeal, but to-day the fact of your presence has given them enthusiasm, and you, alone, are responsible for the spirit which you admire in them."

After that the two commanders ceased to pay one another compliments. The understanding was accomplished! Neither did they continue to discuss their respective troops: each knew that the other would care for them——! They now only exchanged their experiences of their respective opponents.

Marshal Tallard commanded the French army in Bavaria. He was one of the many generals who were products of the France where social talent had been essential to promotion. They had proved their value in the diplomatic service, and thereafter received promotion in the army. The second commander, the Elector of Bavaria, lacked even the sporting impulse to wage war on his own territory.

Marlborough and Eugène did not think there would be any great difficulty in defeating these two leaders. They soon agreed to a plan. Their plan was to " let the enemy think himself wise, and then profit by his mistakes." They arranged the disposal of their armies. Eugène's intention to leave the supreme command to Marlborough, if he wished it, proved itself to be unnecessary; on the contrary, half in earnest and half in jest, each general volunteered to take over the command for the other! Smilingly they agreed that they were " one heart and one soul," and therefore both could take the leadership.

Count of the Empire von Schulenburg wrote in his diary: " Prince Eugène converses sometimes for two or three hours on war affairs. . . ." "But the days which Eugène and Marlborough spent together were taken up with the discussion and annotation of strategic possibilities which the coming battle would bring in its train. The map was spread out before him on the table like a chess-board, and Eugène studied the moves. He was all fire and flame. At last he had found a being who understood him, who appreciated the circumspection of his plans and who thought in the same way as he did. Marlborough's handsome face glowed! But he listened with the cool ardour of the Englishman, and was amazed at all Eugène's precautionary measures. Why did the Prince consider so many possibilities when one was enough for victory?" Later he recounted: " It is part of Eugène's character to see difficulties and obstacles before beginning a task. When the moment for action arrives, then he is all strength and activity."

" This morning at two o'clock the enemy sounded the

reveille," wrote Tallard, on the day of the decisive battle, to the War Minister. " He is arrayed in battle order before his encampment, and gives every appearance of marching off this very day. By doing so he leaves the Danube between us, and it will hardly be possible for him to defend his magazines in Bavaria."

Marlborough had estimated the enemy correctly. " Let him think himself wise and then profit by his mistakes." While the French thought that they were marching away, in reality the Allied armies advanced in the direction of Hochstàdt. They had an easy game. The Franco-Bavarian army was completely destroyed.

For six days Louis XIV had known that his army was beaten. He had received the message, but knew no details. Versailles was in a turmoil ; the Little Abbé again ! When the report came, Louis tore the parchment in fragments. Bavaria lost ! Marshal Tallard taken prisoner ! The German war-theatre in danger ! Had the time arrived when he must protect his own frontiers ?

In Vienna, at the Court, the victory was not celebrated to any great extent. Marlborough was praised, but of Eugène it was said that he made war *à la hussarde*, and left the *raison de guerre* too much out of account. What would have happened if the battle had been lost ? It was questioned whether he ought to have risked it at all. Thus it came about that after the victory an exaggerated caution was practised.

What now ? What did Eugène want ? Did he wish to conquer the whole world for Austria ? Bavaria had been conquered, and in consequence an enormous new territory lay under contribution. But the Savoyard raised objections. Did he assume the protectorship of the Bavarian Elector ?

No one ventured to reprove Eugène ; his authority was too great for that. But he knew what was said behind his back. However, he had his principles : " Whoever does his duty is above the criticism to which all are exposed." But this time he felt the need for making his standpoint clear. " Whoever knows me, knows that always, on every occasion, I endeavour to act without passion and without prejudice. I have always considered the well being of the Most Noble House and of the people, and do not allow myself to be deterred by intrigues and cabals." Eugène had not forgotten that to Ludwig of Baden as much as to Max Emmanuel he owed the beginnings of his career. He had always been opposed to the enmity to Bavaria, chiefly because he was convinced that a final victory over France could only be attained if Germany were united internally throughout.

The situation became less strained. The Hungarian rebels had been repulsed, reforms had repaired the lack of money, the position of President of the Council lay no longer so heavily on Eugène's shoulders ; he could now turn his attention to the battlefields. At this time Leopold died. His successor, Joseph, was young. He differed from his father and his brother in the possession of a lively temperament. He was thought generous, was known to be full of enterprise, and was on friendly terms with Prince Eugène. This fact alone counted for much in the army.

Eugène received the news in Italy. His position was too oppressive for him to grieve much. The Emperor is dead —long live the Emperor ! He had never cared about Leopold. Would he be able to realise his plans under Joseph ? He wrote him a curt letter. He would be willing to serve the new Emperor only on the condition that His Majesty remove all the evil conditions. He would not submit to the fact of his army going to ruin, and, with it, to the loss of the Emperor's hereditary dominions. That was not the letter of a subject ! Instead of waiting for a proclamation on the part of the new Emperor, Eugène had himself issued a proclamation which was the conditional communication of an equal power !

Eugène was in a bad humour. Hardly had he arrived in Italy than his cousin, the Duc de Vendôme, once more took over the command of the French troops ! Nevertheless, Eugène succeeded in achieving a few small successes. But the result of every battle went to prove that, against his cousin Vendôme, Eugène had no luck.

The Savoyard troops were obliged to retire on Turin, and camped on the glacis before the town. Every day Victor Amadeus waited for the French to attack his city. If Turin fell, he declared, then the war in Italy was at an end. He would prostrate himself before Louis. He could not go on, no matter what happened to him and to Savoy ! That Turin would fall, the Duc de Vendôme had guaranteed the King of France, and his second in command, the Duc de Lafeuillade, wanted to stake his head on his ability to capture the town in the shortest possible time. Eugène sent promises of assistance. From within the besieged city, the English Ambassador Hill wrote : " We sleep with the feeling of certainty that Prince Eugène will do everything that lies in his power to save us."

A promise against a promise ! Admittedly the distress in Eugène's army had reached a point which equalled that of the worst days in his first Italian campaign. The troops suffered so terribly that Eugène feared a mutiny more than he feared the enemy. " It has gone so far," he wrote to the new Emperor in bitter irony, " so far that the men are not ashamed of saying that they cannot live without bread and without money." He continued : " Each one from the first to the last, is desperate. The common soldier laughs at every interdiction, fears no threats, and defends himself whenever his wantonness is punished. The army does not belong to me, but to Your Majesty. It is the last pillar supporting the Crown, the sceptre, and the monarchy. The consequence of the loss of these is easy to foresee. I, however, shall not be responsible either in the eyes of God, Your Majesty, or the world, if everything is smashed in fragments, as from day to day seems more likely."

The state of affairs was worse than it had been heretofore.

Again Eugène was driven into a corner by Vendôme. He was so discouraged, and so hopeless, that he defended himself from every reproach even before it was made. "To be sure I owe Your Majesty the sacrifice of my life, my blood, and my possessions, and I would willingly sacrifice them all if by so doing the need might be lessened. But Your Majesty must see that to lose my reputation before a world which is ignorant of the state of affairs is harder for me to bear than death itself."

His self-confidence was threatened. The world should not think Eugène's genius inferior to that of his cousin Vendôme! The world should learn that the need and distress were at fault, that the poverty of Austria and the Empire was responsible, and not Prince Eugène! He was obsessed by his fear of a downfall. He considered no method too derogatory to obtain money from the Emperor and assistance from the Empire. He *must* win, and especially against Vendôme! He must hold out for a little longer, effect by every possible means the equipment of the troops, obtain money and reserves, and then victory would be his!

While Eugène was preparing, Turin was besieged. Vendôme was near to capturing it when Marlborough defeated the French army in the north. Once more Marlborough was Eugène's saviour in the hour of need. Louis XIV was forced to recall Vendôme. He needed his best commander to defend France; Marlborough was advancing.

As soon as Vendôme was away, and the Duc d'Orleans had taken his place, Eugène's nightmare was over. The Prince characterised his cousin coolly and deliberately, so as to give Marlborough information about his opponent: "Vendôme is beloved by his soldiers. If he has once made a plan, then he carries it through, and nothing deters him from it. He is excellent at laying fortifications. If, however, it is possible in any way to cross his plans, then he finds the greatest difficulty in adjusting himself to the new state of affairs, even in the middle of a battle. He will then leave all subsequent events to chance."

The Duc d'Orleans was not to be compared with

Vendôme. In the first place he was not adequate for the war in Italy. He conducted the siege of Turin with insufficient means. The town, under Count Daun, held out. Now Eugène could, for the first time, bring up a relieving army. He was full of exalted courage. His plan was thought out, down to the minutest detail, and rehearsed in imagination. Vendôme was not there; it must succeed!

Eugène in person led the troops up to the fortifications. His presence carried them with him. Nothing alarmed him—neither the murderous cannonade nor the thick hail of shots. They crossed the trenches, climbed the ramparts, and strengthened them—Eugène in their midst. A page and a servant were killed at his side. He did not even notice! Then, suddenly, he collapsed. The soldiers fell back in alarm. The French rejoiced: Eugène had fallen! But then he was seen up again! He waved with his hand, and called out that nothing had happened to him; his horse only had been killed!

An hour later victory was won all along the line.

The defeat was so unexpected to the Duc d'Orleans, that, in order to save the rest of the army, he withdrew in the wrong direction.

" Italy is ours ! " shouted Eugène. After twenty years of war, he had achieved his object.

" I cannot tell you how much I rejoiced at this news," the Duke of Marlborough wrote to his wife. " I do not merely admire Prince Eugène, I have a great affection for him as well. His glorious achievement must have the effect of humbling France. If we continue the war, with persistence, for another year, then, with God's blessing, we shall be able to dictate a peace that will ensure us security for the rest of our days."

No more obstacles ! No more Frenchmen on Italian soil. Now the advance must be made to take possession of the conquered territory. Eugène had been made Governor-General of the Duchy of Milan. He rode in ecstasy across the Po valley.

At the Porta Romana, the Burgomaster welcomed the

victor, and gave him the keys of the city. When, in pursuance of an old custom, two vessels of water were brought to His Highness, Prince Eugène spilt water and distributed earth to give proof of his seizin of Milan ! After this symbolic ceremony, the State entry began ; it was Eugène's first triumphant procession. Heralds in ancient costume led the procession. Trumpets sounded ; the streets were carpeted and strewn with flowers, and crowded with jubilant people. Eugène remembered Paris and the triumphal arch which had been erected in commemoration of Louis XIV's passage of the Rhine. He thought, with a little smile : the volunteer Eugène of Savoy had not crossed the Rhine, to be sure, but he had won both Hungary and Italy for the Emperor of the Holy Roman Empire of German nations !

While the nations of Southern Europe disputed the Spanish Succession, the Northern States waged a bitter war. Charles XII of Sweden was fighting Peter of Russia, who, in his turn was allied with Frederick Augustus of Saxony, the King of Poland. In the first year of the war the Swedish King was so favoured by fortune that he succeeded in dethroning Frederick Augustus and in putting Stanislaus Leszczynski in his place.

Nevertheless, Peter the Great continued his alliance with Frederick against Charles XII. But the one-sided conclusion of the Peace of Altranstadt, by which the Elector refused the Polish Throne, embittered the Czar. In a long document, full of the deepest indignation against Frederick Augustus, he wrote to the Emperor, " He who allows himself to be coerced into refusing his Crown, does not deserve that one should make any further efforts to help him to hold it. The Emperor, as Head of the Empire, should condemn the perfidious Elector ! "

The Czar's letter evoked proposals : Peter offered himself as mediator to restore peace in Europe. If his interposition were of no avail, then he would be prepared to send troops to suppress the Hungarian disturbances. Finally, he proposed that, at the next Polish Reichstag, the united influences of the Emperor and of Russia should be directed towards electing as King of Poland the newly promoted generalissimo, who had succeeded to the supreme command on the death of Ludwig of Baden, Prince Eugène of Savoy.

Was the Little Abbé to become King of Poland?

CHAPTER IV

THE THEATRES of war changed like the pictures in a kaleidoscope. Again and again Eugène rode at the head of an army of Imperial soldiers, with auxiliary troops to the right of him, consisting sometimes of Hanoverians, sometimes of Prussians, and to the left of him the English army, with Marlborough at its head. Here the broad band of the Rhine flowed, there the Danube, and even when Eugène was not actually commanding he was sitting bent over plans sketched out on crumpled parchment covered with writing which came to life under his eyes. The whole of Europe lay spread out before him : he studied Vauban's chain of forts in the north of France ; he studied Spain, the pentagonal peninsula where the young Archduke was fighting for the succession ; and the boot of Italy, ornamented with the Habsburg colours. Hungary was for the most part restored to peace : corn was growing on the rich soil, and the farmers were paying Eugène interest on his capital. The palace in the Himmelpfortegasse was enlarged, and two entrance-gates had appeared. On the hill opposite the Kahlenberg a palace had arisen which would soon be ready to be roofed in. It was to be Eugène's summer residence, with huge *salons* and a garden sloping gently towards the town which was already in bloom.

The enemy in Versailles was now a bowed figure who walked with the help of a stick. His will alone held the ebbing French armies together. For Louis XIV the period of offensive was over : his defence had begun !

The armies of the Allies were stationed on French soil, in spite of the forts set up by the genius of Vauban which were to barricade and shut off France from her enemies. It was springtime, and this year would decide the issue.

The Imperial troops were closing round the town and fortress of Lille, and Eugène was preparing to lay the siege.

In her palace in Brussels, Madame la Comtesse was waiting for her son. He had announced that he was coming to visit her on his way to the army. She had refused his invitations to go to Vienna, not because she was not fit for travel, but because she wished to remain in Brussels, not far from Paris, within two days' journey of Lille, so that she could follow in the train of her son's army when he drove back the last French troops!

Olympia had lost all her children with the exception of Eugène and one daughter, who, however, was no joy or satisfaction to her. The Princess had remained unmarried, and on account of her dissolute nature she had been banished from the court of Versailles. In Turin she was less of a guest than a prisoner. Olympia never asked after her. She thought only of her son! Was there a more famous name in Europe than his—was there a single person alive who had not heard of Prince Eugène?

Olympia's eyes were still vivacious: her personality had not changed. With old age her face had merely become longer and even more pointed. In reviewing her life, she had to admit that since the day when Louis XIV had turned from her, it had been a series of disappointments and useless intrigues. Her only satisfaction had been her son Eugène!

Her pleasure-loving nature had never admitted the hardships of his struggle to fame. She only knew that the deepest respect was shown her, not as the widow of the Comte de Soissons, not as Mazarin's niece, but as the mother of Eugène! He counted for more than Royalty: he had refused the Polish Crown. He never signed his name with all his honours and dignities. His name was enough; it was a symbol of victory to which, even in Versailles, deference was paid. If anyone could be found to bring about a reconciliation between her and Louis, then she, the exile, would be in a position to negotiate peace. Her son would agree for love of her! But Olympia was only conciliatory and forbearing in her sorrowful moments. She could never get over the fact that, whenever she appeared at the receptions of the nobility, the French ladies turned aside. No French man or woman éver played cards at her house, neither Louis's ambassador nor people passing through. Only when Eugène appeared did she become the first lady in Brussels, as in her youth she had been Queen of the French Court. But she would become once more the first lady at the French Court—for her son would vanquish Louis!

The citadel of Lille fell some weeks after the 7th of November, 1703, the day on which Eugène received the news of his mother's death. The Allied armies were now in France! Louis had lost all hope; he saw that peace was the only possibility for him. Since the defeat of his army in Italy he gave up the belief that he could hold the combined Spanish monarchy for his grandson. New regiments were on their way to Spain from both England and Austria; and they were led by Guido von Starhemberg, of whom Eugène had said, " Starhemberg understands as much about war as I do." " I am getting old," was Louis's thought; " Spain is won for the House of Habsburg."

He suggested that Holland should mediate between him and the Emperor. He offered to renounce Naples and Sicily to the Archduke Charles; the Netherlands should be converted into an independent State ruled over by the Elector of Bavaria; but the Spanish mainland was to be held by his grandson Philip.

The Allies refused all negotiations on this basis, and Louis went even further with his concessions. Then, in God's name, the Archduke should have Spain and all the other provinces if Louis's grandson might keep the Spanish territories in Italy! On this basis the Allies decided that they could begin negotiations, and Heinsius, the head of the Dutch Government, invited Eugène to come and discuss the peace terms at The Hague.

On the way he met the English head of staff, Cadogan, who, in the name of Queen Anne of England, declared that the Queen would never consent to a peace treaty unless, in the preliminary negotiations, the whole Spanish monarchy had been made over to the House of Habsburg. Eugène answered that Louis could never agree to such terms. Cadogan shrugged his shoulders.

Eugène's carriage drove through the war territory. He looked out at the landscape. He saw dead Frenchmen and Germans lying unburied in the ditches, corpses of horses, houses burnt and destroyed, trampled fields, desolate forests, and homeless people begging before the gates of the cities. In one relay station where he changed horses, a woman who recognised him came up with beseeching hands raised and implored for peace. His adjutant tried to drive her away, but Eugène held him back. " The woman is right," he murmured. " Peace must be gained at all costs ; the people cannot bear any more. And I ? "

He was tired, and had ceased to hate Louis. Olympia was dead. The great King was beaten, and begged for peace. He, Eugène, would grant him his wish !

But, two days later, he sat at the conference table with the Emperor's orders before him. He was to insist that the peace treaty should guarantee all the Spanish dominions to the House of Habsburg. Eugène had advised a compromise, but, instead of a reply, had received a draft of what he was to say in his speech. " I think that this King," he said, and looked around him, " I think," he repeated, " that Louis will think himself fortunate if, after renouncing that which is demanded of him, he is allowed to hold all the territories of the Netherlands and other States which he had previously annexed, without any justification whatsoever."

That was too much for Louis. His pride rebelled. In spite of the bad harvest and the costliness of warfare, in spite of the hard winter of the year 1709, he decided to continue with the war. He broke off negotiations and made colossal efforts. France must give him another army, an army of eighty thousand men. In spite of the distress, France would provide him with the necessary war materials, with munitions and provisions!

The supreme command of this army, the last which he could put in the field, Louis confided to Villars's hands.

Now here was the mysterious fellow out in the open once more! For some time he had ceased to remain behind the scenes in the world theatre: he had exchanged the diplomat's wig for the Marshal's bâton. But as a soldier he had had less luck than as a diplomat and had not succeeded in achieving more than a tepid success against Ludwig of Baden in the Rhineland theatre of war. He had again and again been forced to give up the command and to have it restored to him, according to whether he was in or out of favour with the King. Villars was not satisfied with his career: he had not proved himself indispensable. He had been called and then sent back again. While untalented Princes commanded armies against the enemies outside the frontiers, he had been delegated to suppress in the interior an insurrection of the Chamisardes, a rebellious sect who were causing unrest in France.

In his private life Villars was no more successful. He had caused married men a great deal of trouble in earlier days. Now he was himself a married man, and his younger officers courted his beautiful wife to such a degree that on one occasion he abandoned his army in order to surprise his wife in an intrigue. He came upon her serene and astonished at his behaviour. She said imperiously that he would never be able to adorn his head with a Duke's coronet if he were always imagining horns growing from it! Twice she had tried to get him raised to the peerage and twice Louis had refused. But when a party arose at Versailles the members of which called themselves the "Holy Ones," and wished to prevent the continuance of the war at all costs, Villars was the only talented Field Marshal whom Louis could send to the front for the last decisive campaign of defence. Villars was in favour of the continuance of hostilities. War gave him the only opportunity of satisfying his ambition.

He wished to become a Duke, Field-Marshal-in-Chief, and Connétable de France !

He was to meet both Eugène and Marlborough in the field, but Villars knew no awe. The combined armies of Eugène and the Duke were stationed before Tournay, the strongest fort that Vauban had built. The fortifications of the town were in perfect condition, and the stores were filled with provisions and armaments. Villars thought the capture of Tournay would be an impossibility. In his opinion, Eugène would not even attempt it ! The Marshal believed so little in the possibility of a siege and so firmly in the certainty of an open battle, that shortly after taking over the command he withdrew half of the garrison—in order to strengthen his army. But hardly had he, in a letter of extreme self-adulation, extolled his King's successful action than he learned with the utmost horror that the united enemy armies were marching in the direction of Tournay ! And it was now too late to obtain relief.

Another fortress lay before Eugène. He saw the walls ; his glance appraised the towers and the width of the moats. " It will be three weeks before the fortress falls," he said to Marlborough. The Duke nodded.

The famous Marshal of Saxony, who as a young man had served for the first time in the field under Eugène, explained some time later : " A skilled officer must be able to calculate the capacity of a fort's resistance to within an hour." Maurice of Saxony had learned with Eugène in the same school. On the 7th of July the siege had begun, and on the 30th, Marlborough and Eugène rode into the fortress.

Villars's reputation was at stake. Already Louis had sent him the Marshal Boufflers as counsellor and deputy. If things went any further, then Boufflers would take over the command and Villars would have to put up with his young wife's mockery. Instead of the wreath of laurels which he had promised her as a headdress, she would give him—— ! He would rather not think about it ! A battle—an open battle—and he would prove to the world that he was not only the most talented diplomat of his time, but the greatest commander as well!

Eugène and Marlborough granted his wish. It was a marvellous autumn day. Villars had entrenched his army uncommonly well and had heard that the two enemy commanders had decided to attack in spite of the adverse vote of the War Council. He galloped through the encampment, where loud cheers greeted him and caused his heart to beat faster. He was not only beloved at Court. Every soldier loved him. "Long live Marshal Villars!" Spies reported to him that the Allied armies had taken up their appointed positions in silence. He was just thinking that there was a lack of enthusiasm in the Imperial army when cannon-fire broke forth, and his left wing was forthwith attacked. It was reported to Villars that the Prince of Savoy himself led the battalions. "Then the left wing is lost," was the swift thought in Villars's mind. But shortly afterwards a courier galloped up to him and said, "Prince Eugène is wounded by a shot in the head and is only holding up with the greatest effort." At the same moment Villars groaned and collapsed. A cannon-ball had hit him in the foot. He had no time to hear that Eugène had been only lightly wounded and was once more leading the attack.

The battle of Malplaquet lasted into the night. The next day Eugène wrote to Victor Amadeus: "I cannot forgo reporting to you the great victory which we won yesterday over the enemy, who was entrenched between fortifications. The struggle was long, and cost much blood on both sides. There is no doubt that this victory will contribute much to the security and peace of Europe."

Eugène's war-tiredness was evident, and now he hoped that for the world, and even for himself, there would be rest at last. But the hope proved to be a false one. Malplaquet was a victory which increased the fame of both Eugène and Marlborough, but it was one which, in view of the terrible losses, they could not turn to account. A Pyrrhic victory? For all the Governments who had provided troops to take part in the battle—the English, the Dutch, and the German Princes—complained of the irrevocable losses. In England, Marlborough's opponents were gaining ground. In Siebenburgen, the insurrection had only been suppressed with effort. More preparations had to be made, more credit raised. The Allies threatened desertion. The King of Prussia wished to withdraw his troops from Italy, and the position of the Archduke in Spain was threatened. But the Court of Vienna refused to give way. Louis XIV continued to make offers which the Emperor as often rejected. Louis was even ready to relinquish the whole Spanish monarchy to the Imperial House. But then the Viennese Court demanded that the renouncement should be, not merely on paper, but that the French King should banish from Spain the grandson whom he had himself created King of Spain !

This Louis refused to do. He was over seventy years old and frail, but, if he was forced, then he would hold on—to his last breath and to the last man !

During these years Eugène was never for any length of time in his palace. There were always new campaigns, one after the other ; perpetual conferences about supplies, and munitions, plans of battles, reviews of troops ; he was ever in patient readiness " to go anywhere and everywhere where I am wanted, provided that by so doing I can gain a complete army equipped for battle."

Again and again Eugène, wearing his shabby brown coat, his sunburnt face turned in the direction of the enemy, took his place at the head of his troops. His opponent was Villars again, who had recovered from his wound. Cannon-balls flew over his head into the ranks of the infantry and, in the close fighting, drops of blood bespattered his wasted figure. He waged war, but he was tired. Why had the Emperor refused to accept Louis's peace proposals ? What more could anyone ask of the great King who fought on with heroic courage against the greater odds ? Eugène no longer hated his aged rival in Versailles. He had become his equal, and knew besides that Louis despised him no longer. Small occurrences, little acts of politeness, went to prove that Louis would like to make peace with him, and that he wished, by means of the son of his old friend, Olympia, to stop the bloodshed. Eugène's servant could not keep up with his master's pace as he journeyed to the army : with Eugène's wardrobe and some new furs, he fell into the hands of a French raiding-party. The news of the capture of Eugène's servant reached Versailles, and Louis at once ordered that the booty should be restored to Eugène with greetings from himself. Peace with Paris, peace with France ! Eugène had travelled in a wide circle over the whole of Europe ; but since the days at Gap, since the days of his advance into French territory, he had not set foot on the soil of the land of his birth. For he had fought in the Netherlands, on territories which Louis had conquered in his youth, which were not in the real France. Eugène was homesick for Paris ; he had not been there for thirty years. Why make war any longer ? The bloodshed appalled him. He was told of the atrocities committed by the French troops. He was sitting in a peasant house. The exhausted army was camping ; the wounded were being carried away. He knew the direction of the next advance, for his strategic faculties were as keen as ever. But the man was tired, and felt unable to go on any longer.

The next morning the French Marshal Berwick, a nephew of Marlborough (his mother was Miss Churchill, his father James II of England), found a letter on his table with the signature Eugène de Savoie. Did this letter of the Prince's contain an offer of peace ? The parchment was not that of a State document. The Marshal opened the letter, and read : " I am too convinced of your sense of right to be able to believe that outrages and atrocities have been practised with your knowledge. I assume that you hear of them with the same horror as myself, and that in the future you are ready to prevent their taking place. Even the calamity of war has its limits, and the laws of humanity should never be disregarded." Humanity ? The young Berwick had no use for such phrases. Probably the Prince was discouraged. Probably he had heard that Marlborough's position in London was already undermined for it was thought that the Duke would be recalled and that there would be a partial state of peace between England and France.

Eugène knew the story, but he did not believe that either the new English Government or Queen Anne would venture to dismiss Marlborough solely on the grounds that the Queen had quarrelled with the Duchess! But very soon proposals were made : whether Eugène would be prepared to join with the Elector of Hanover, the future King of England, whom Anne had appointed as her successor, to fight against the French? Eugène refused. He stated plainly that the Elector's arrival in the field, if he were to take over the command from Marlborough, would signal the moment of Eugène's departure. Marlborough was his trusted friend ; he would serve with Marlborough and with none other. Furiously he said : " The Elector shall not imagine that the English Crown is going to fall into his lap ! "

But Eugène's fierce partisanship could not prevent the Whigs, Marlborough's party, from being turned out of office and the Tories being put in power. " What we lose in the Netherlands," said the French Minister, the Marquis de Torcy, " we shall regain in England." Louis began to breathe again. The Duc de Vendôme commanded in Spain and was forcing the Imperial army to a retreat, and he himself had sent envoys to the Porte. He was not falling to his knees without making a stand first ! It was reported that the Ottoman troops were being assembled on the frontiers of Siebenburgen. With Hungary threatened, the Emperor would be forced to make peace !

Once more the Turkish peril? Eugène went to Vienna to get information about the Turkish mobilisation. He sat on a throne chair in the great hall of his palace as the ambassador from the Porte, Seifullah Aga, entered, and listened bareheaded to his greeting. His demeanour and his great name resulted in the Aga's promising to persuade the Divan to keep the peace. It was an empty promise, Eugène knew, but it meant at least a short delay.

An eye-witness of his interview with the Turkish

Ambassador reported that the Prince had enquired particularly eagerly as to the manner in which the Turkish guns were transported. It was a casual question, but one that had a hidden purpose, and the Aga answered it. Eugène was spared a spy in the Turkish arsenals, for, in spite of all the oaths and assurances of his guest, he held the war with Turkey to be unavoidable.

Marlborough was commander-in-chief of the English army again, and once more Eugène had the pleasure of intimate talks with his friend. They made common plans of how, by means of an overwhelming victory, they would march on Paris, dictate peace, and thereby strengthen Marlborough's position in England for ever. Then came the news of the death of Joseph.

Another new Emperor, another new master to whom Eugène must adapt himself! He did not know whether to ascribe the painful feeling which filled his days with sadness to the death of the young Emperor or to the tragedy of his own life. He was fifty years old, and, when honest with himself, had to admit that in the whole of his life he had known no real joy! What was the highest position in the State compared with the solitariness of heart or compared with the emptiness of his existence, which was filled with nothing but responsibility for millions of men in the country and hundreds and thousands of soldiers in the field? The Emperor was dead! Not so long ago they had rejoiced together over their successes, and had made plans to build up a greater German Empire from the Rhine to the Black Sea—a gigantic card-house which now, in view of Joseph's death, had collapsed.

The successor for whom Eugène must first secure the Emperor's crown was in Spain. He wished to be King of Spain; his heart was in Spain, and what lay outside the Iberian Peninsula did not interest him. At the same time Eugène was certain that he would lose Spain, for he knew that after the death of Joseph, who left no male heir behind him, the Allies would desert him in order to prevent the supremacy of the House of Habsburg in Germany and Spain being invested in one person. They feared the disturbance of the European Balance of Power, for the sake of which they had voted credits against Louis, and raised auxiliary troops. ... " My sorrow increases from day to day, for I loved the Emperor sincerely," wrote Prince Eugène. But his sorrow increased from day to day not so much because of any personal feeling for Joseph, nor because it was one more experience of a young man dying before his time ; no, his sorrowful brooding was concerned with the wrecking of his plans for the Empire. Count de Wratislaw's communication to the effect that the new Emperor was well disposed towards him drew from Eugène a weary smile. He was reminded of the fact that Charles had honoured his nephew Maurice of Savoy with the Order of the Golden Fleece. King Charles who would soon be Emperor, wished to convince Eugène of his love, gratitude, and affection : " of his true and sincere trust which was great enough to enable the two of them to depend one upon the other."

To depend upon one another ? Eugène knew how much that phrase meant ! But he had bound himself to the House of Habsburg, and he would remain true to the House of Habsburg. Charles should be chosen as Emperor of the Holy Roman Empire !

Eugène negotiated with the Electors to prepare for his election. In the meantime, Charles refused to leave Spain. With a great effort Eugène persuaded the young man who was to wear the crown to come to Vienna. Charles left his wife behind him in Spain, a separation that was very hard for him. He was head over heels in love with the mother of Maria Theresa. But the young wife was to be a hostage for him and a guarantee that he would not abandon Spain but return as the acknowledged King !

Eugène had arranged for a worthy reception for the new Emperor. He might have been satisfied with things had he not found Marlborough in a despairing mood. " We shall not be much longer together," said the Duke, and his handsome face clouded. He had had news from England. Louis XIV was losing on the battlefields and winning at the green table. The Whigs were out of power, and the Tories wanted peace ! Marlborough knew that he would be recalled. He clung to power ; he clung to the army ; he wished to go on fighting at Eugène's side, and to that end he even offered to go over to the Tories ; but they refused him.

A new shifting of scenes began in the world-theatre. Holland wished to make peace, and Queen Anne, who felt death approaching, wished to leave a peaceful England for her successor, the Elector of Hanover. The army under the English supreme command, and the German mercenaries in the pay of England and Holland, still supported the Imperial army. But Eugène knew that he must separate the Imperial troops from the others if he wished to prevent a recurrence of what had happened at the time of his first command under the Duke of Savoy. He wished to have a clear understanding and not to be taken unawares. The danger evoked once again his youthful elasticity. So they were going to recall Marlborough, and England was entering into negotiations with France ? Eugène went to The Hague in order to take the Allies to account. He found his glance was shunned, and that he was met with embarrassed looks. He decided to go to London. While making preparations, he received a letter from the English Chancellor of the Exchequer, a letter expressing great respect, but at the same time warning His Highness against coming to London. The population was indignant at the length of the war. They were in such an inflammatory state that the Prince's arrival might very well evoke hostile demonstrations. In England the desire for peace was so great that Eugène, who was known to stand for the continuance of the war, was likely to have a violently hostile reception. " Methods of unbelievable trickery are employed in order to hinder the journey of Prince Eugène to England," wrote the Ambassador, Count Gallas, to Field Marshal Guido von Starhemberg.

SE

In London it was feared that Eugène's personality would win over the Queen, and the Tories were afraid for their power. The Queen might be influenced by the arrival of the Whig leader's friend !

In London, an exultant crowd greeted Eugène with flags and flowers. He was accompanied by his nephew, a young man who, having won his spurs in service in Hungary, was now to be present at his uncle's diplomatic negotiations. He was to learn to be a worthy heir to Mazarin ! But during the journey over, the Chevalier of Savoy fell ill of a fever, and on his arrival was confined to his bed, and unable to be present at the Queen's reception of his great namesake.

The town was plunged in a fog. Eugène drove without pomp or ceremony to St. James's Palace, and was at once admitted into the Queen's presence. It was reported to the Emperor that " the audience did not last more than a few minutes," and Eugène himself relates that the Queen " was somewhat embarrassed and cold." The old woman cast a fleeting glance at the Emperor's message written in his own hand which Eugène presented to her, and said that in any case she had decided to let the matter in question be negotiated in Holland ! Eugène answered that that was what he had come to prevent. He wished for the re-establishment of the agreement between herself and the Emperor. England must not be allowed to negotiate separately ! Eugène was so determined in his speech that the Queen vacillated. She felt that she was not up to him, and, as he became more pressing, said that her health would not allow of her continuing the conversation. She was not permitted to discuss or confer with him as much as she could have wished. She must direct him to her Ministers. And with that the audience came to an end.

Before the doors of the palace, crowds waited who shrieked, " Peace—we want peace ! " as Eugène came out, and the cries rang in his ears for the rest of the drive to his house. Peace—he wished for peace too. But he feared that, just because of England's desertion, which was now a certainty, war would have to be continued. He appealed urgently to the Ministers once again, and begged the Queen for an answer.

Eugène's visit to London was not a fortunate one : a few days after his audience with the Queen he buried his nephew in Westminster Abbey.

At the time of his mother's death he had written letters in order to numb his sorrow. Now, after the death of his nephew, he read day and night, and waited for the Queen's answer. The fate of the House of Habsburg depended upon her. While he waited, he spent much time with antiquaries in the city, and bought books.

His friend Marlborough had fallen into disfavour, and was not permitted to leave his house. "You must see," Eugène declared, " that I cannot desert a friend in adversity, one whom I have venerated when he was at the height of his glory. Such behaviour would be contrary to my whole conception of honour."

At first the crowd yelled and whistled every time that they saw Eugène's carriage before the door of Marlborough's house. But in the end his perfect dignity and immovable calm won him the sympathy of the " gentlemanlike " crowd. They saw that he could not abandon a friend in trouble, and remembered that they had celebrated the victories which Marlborough and Eugène had won together. They ceased to hoot ; the men took off their hats, and Eugène was greeted with admiration and respect.

Bishop Burnet said : "His character is so universally known that I will only describe what I myself have seen of him. The Prince's nature is the humblest and most modest that can be imagined. He is embarrassed by the universal praise which the world justifiably accords him."

What was the use of the personal sympathy that was shown him ? Eugène looked across at Marlborough's handsome, hopeless face. They spoke of politics. "France's success is due to the fact that, when she is victorious, she follows up her victories in a completely ruthless manner, but when she herself is placed in a desperate position by the loss of life and strength, then all, or most, of her opponents fear to humiliate her to any great extent, not realising that in a few years she will have recovered and be again in a position to torment her neighbours." Eugène's genius knew his century and was able to see centuries ahead of him.

He knew that his stay in London was of no further use, and left before his appointed time. Alone and forlorn, he returned to the Continent.

The bells of peace rang all over Europe. England and Holland left the Coalition and made a separate peace. Eugène's presentiments were fulfilled. Marlborough's successor, the Duke of Ormond, the new commander-in-chief of the English army, marched out of Eugène's camp on the eve of the decisive battle and left him to his fate. Villars had a good time.

Before the Marshal had left to join the army, Louis XIV had discussed with him the measures to be taken in the event of a defeat. The aged King saw in imagination Eugène, his old, untiring, and terrible enemy already on the road to Paris, and declared that he was determined to die with his sword in his hand rather than allow the enemy to enter his capital. These words were the last expression of his resistance. Louis was inwardly broken. Both his son and his eldest grandson were dead, and his great-grandson so desperately ill that his death was expected at any moment. With the last breath of the two-year-old child, his grandson, Philip V of Spain, became heir to the French throne, and the European powers, who now declared themselves opposed to the investiture of the Governments of Spain and of the German Empire in the person of a member of the House of Habsburg, would for the same reason prevent a Bourbon from ruling over both France and Spain.

But when the Duke of Ormond left Eugène's camp, and peace was concluded between France, England, and Holland, Louis won new courage. His great-grandson was convalescent and Villars had had luck on the battlefields. With his weakened forces, Eugène could only place himself on the defensive and retreat!

A few months later, the successful Marshal Villars (now at last Duke and Peer of France) greeted Prince Eugène with low bows on the steps of the Castle of Rastatt, which Ludwig of Baden had rebuilt. The big man, already growing stout, had no need to stand upright in order to embrace the little Prince. He remained in a bent position as he put his arms round Prince Eugène. The meeting gave him a great deal of pleasure. He had not seen Eugène for thirteen years, and Villars's heart beat with pride to think that he could now meet him on an equal footing. He had revised his judgment. He no longer said: " The Prince of Savoy has more good will than understanding." He said instead : " I saw in front of me the greatest genius of my age."

But Eugène would willingly still have been the insignificant young man that he was at the time when Villars made his first report! The famous Prince Eugène who negotiated with the Marshal in Rastatt was a broken, discouraged man, who only maintained his dignity with a great effort. The expenditure of his genius and the superhuman efforts that he had made during his lifetime, and during the thirteen years' struggle, were all in vain. Why had the House of Habsburg not made peace three years before, at the time when he had urged it? Why had the Emperor overreached his demands, and insisted, not only that Louis should abandon his grandson, but that he should drive him out of Spain? Eugène went to Rastatt with the feeling that anything that he might accomplish for the House of Habsburg would be a gift from heaven, and that, whatever he did, he would be greeted by discontent on his return to Vienna. Charles VI, as the new Emperor was called, still clung to Spain, and now Spain could be gained for him neither by war nor by negotiations of any kind. More than that, if Eugène were not to succeed in making peace, then Savoy would fall away from Austria and a vexatious little war would break out again in the Po basin. Villars would invade the German Empire once more, and yet another army of exhausted men would have to be raised in the starving hereditary dominions. Would Eugène be capable of helping the Emperor Charles out of the chaos as he had helped Leopold? With dry lips, his nervous fingers taking the brown snuff out of his snuff-box and holding it to his nose, he sat opposite Villars at the conference table. Villars made suggestions, all of which he was obliged to refuse. The whole Spanish monarchy for France? Impossible! Eugène sprang up: war should decide the issue! He knew that he must bluff, and that he needed all the elasticity of his youth in order to win for the Emperor at least a part of Spain. He stared at the marble walls of the conference chamber as though he had not heard Villars's suggestions. Every now and then he got up and declared the conference at an end. Why did Villars wish to continue with the negotiations? He guessed the reason: Villars wanted to be the French national hero as he himself was the German idol. Villars wanted to bring peace to the French people. Was it that? Eugène began to stretch his demands; Villars began to plead. If Eugène would not agree for the sake of the House of Habsburg, would he agree for Villars's sake? He must go to Versailles with a peace-offering! With alarming exactitude he exposed the inadequacy of the Habsburgs to Eugène. So Villars was well informed, and yet he begged for peace? " Villars is anxious," Eugène reported to Vienna, " and wishes for peace with all his heart. As I see the state of affairs, if it depended upon him he would sacrifice anything and everything to that end. Only he would have to gain some advantage in order to be able to claim some reward from his Court. One thing is certain: the Marshal's ambition will impel him to bring about peace at all costs. For he imagines that just that is needed to crown his fame in France."

The two commanders-in-chief sat opposite one another

day by day for months, until at length Eugène succeeded in gaining the Netherlands and the Spanish provinces in Italy for the Emperor ; Louis XIV retaining for his grandson Spain, together with all the other colonies.

Eugène's genius had been victorious on the battlefields, but the diplomacy of Louis XIV had gained the disputed territories.

PART V
"Wide Horizons Within Narrow Frontiers"

CHAPTER I

IN THE YEAR 1710, ten years after the beginning of the terrible war of the Spanish Succession, a book entitled *Theodice*, written by a German, appeared in the French language. The famous philosopher Leibnitz felt the necessity of encouraging a world driven to despair by want and misfortune by the publication of a work devoted to nothing less than the vindication of God. This thoroughly optimistic book by a "Christian philosopher" became popular. Leibnitz's theories were not only discussed at the Courts of Berlin, Hanover, and Wolfenbüttel, where he had personal influence : he was already a figure of international repute, having published political, historical, and philosophical works under various pseudonyms, as well as under his own name ; and having been a diplomatic agent in Paris and Venice, as well as in a number of princely chanceries of the German Empire.

The great diplomatic plans that he had made in his youth were, of course, wrecked by his poverty and by the paltry endeavours which soon took the place of his lofty ambitions. The young man who started in poor circumstances needed a timely position, a title, and a secured income, and therefore, in spite of the prospects which the French Ministers, even Colbert himself, held out to him, he took the post of librarian and adviser to the Elector of Hanover. For thirty years he worked hard to gain rank and honours : for thirty years he served the House of Hanover for an insignificant wage, as an official in the State Chancery as adviser in all political and economic questions and as historian of the Guelph dynasty. The man with the wide horizons in his heart and mind sat within the narrow frontiers of Hanover, and in his free moments carefully added up his expenditure so as to make his appointed two hundred thalers cover his needs ! At first the noble gentlemen of the Guelph family had begged for his services, and had even sent couriers to Paris after him, in order to persuade the famous man to come to their Court. But, once he was there, they had the rare bird in the cage, and ever more diverted him from politics in the direction of science. These great men looked upon the librarian and historiographer as a serious buffoon who, for some inexplicable reason, was venerated by the rest of the world, but who was only interesting, in their opinion, when he made suggestions for the breeding of silkworms—and not when he wrote the *Theodice* ! Leibnitz was always having to become inventive in new fields ; he had to make calculating machines, to discuss mines which might be made productive, in order that he might at last gain an opportunity of becoming politically active. To be sure, his politics were those of peace and not of war ; also he had more success with women than with men. While the Princes of Hanover and Wolfenbüttel ordered him, in a superior and condescending manner, to confine himself to the work for which he was paid —namely, to writing the chronicles of their family—he became on more and more intimate terms with the Princesses who married and became Queens. The little man with the long lean legs, the pale face, and ice-cold hands, became the confidant of Liselotte of the Palatinate of the ready pen, with whom he kept up an intimate correspondence until the end of his life. He became also the intellectual friend of the new Queen of Prussia, wife of George of Hanover, the successor to Anne, Queen of England. The homely Princesses who had thus become great ladies sensed the genius in Leibnitz. They wished to do something for their kinsman's counsellor who was also their private adviser, and commended him to their cousin in Vienna—Elizabeth Christine, wife of the new Emperor Charles VI, who had at last brought her Spanish adventure to an end.

Leibnitz journeyed to Vienna.

In those days, however, a recommendation to the Empress alone was not enough protection at the Emperor's Court: it was necessary besides to find a means of access to the man of whom later Frederick the Great was to say that he had been the real Emperor.

At that time the war had not yet come to an end, and Prince Eugène was not easily accessible to the philosopher, even though the way to the highest dignitary in the State was paved for him both by chamberlains and by the Empress's lady in waiting, Fräulein von Klenk. Leibnitz arrived with a plan in readiness. He wanted to found an academy of sciences in Vienna to establish a Pan-Europe of the intellect; and it was not without a certain scepticism that he donned his gala cloak in order to visit His Highness. He felt that he would once more be confronted with a man who called himself a statesman because with his trusted sword he had been able to mark a diplomatic circle around him; he would be face to face with a war hero, a blustering general to whom he proposed to explain that the mutual spiritual understanding between the peoples of the earth was a far stronger weapon towards the maintenance of peace than the mightiest army in the field! Leibnitz did not expect much from the interview, although his general impression of Vienna was more favourable than it had been at the time of his last visit there twelve years earlier, to say nothing of his first visit in the year 1688. Incidentally, he remembered having met Prince Eugène already on that occasion, and now felt that it had been foolish of him not to have made himself acquainted with him then, when the Prince had not yet become the Emperor's highest dignitary. But Leibnitz did not reproach himself! How could he have guessed that the reserved, taciturn being of the year 1688 would become the greatest man of his time? Now, since Italy and Hungary had become the Emperor's possessions, people began to live in Vienna as they did in Paris! Leibnitz had prophesied this, and now verified his prophecy with satisfaction. But when he arrived at the palace in the Himmelpfortegasse, and was shown up the magnificent staircase into the reception-rooms he had to admit that the house exceeded in magnificence anything that he had ever seen. Even in Paris, Leibnitz thought. He first entered a vast *salon*, the walls of which were hung with pictures, where he was left to wait for a short time. He glanced at the pictures and saw representations of the battles of Zenta and of Hochstädt ! " Self-glorification ! " he said to himself. Evidently the Prince wished to be reminded of his own heroic deeds ! He would have to be flattered ! But, on the other hand, this contradicted the advice which Leibnitz had been given as to the manner of his conversation with Prince Eugène ! " Speak to him frankly of that which lies nearest your heart. The truth is the only method by which to win the sympathies of Prince Eugène," he had been told.

" His Highness awaits you." An adjutant showed the philosopher the way. He crossed two *salons*, hung with tapestry, and passed through a mirrored room. Here a mirror framed in grey marble attracted the far-seeing Leibnitz, who had heard that it had cost twenty thousand gulden ! Then he entered the library. A cry of astonishment escaped him. In gold-leaved Morocco and Turkey leather, arranged carefully in rows, the backs of thousands of books bound in red, yellow, and dark blue, shone with a dull radiance. It was a wonderfully reassuring sight ! Leibnitz, the bookworm, who had come with feelings of doubt and suspicion to see Prince Eugène, felt that all was well. For one moment, the thought went through his head that perhaps the rich man had set out a sham display : When he received a philosopher, he received him in the library ! Then he looked around once more. Over the chimney-piece was a picture let into the wall ; the portrait of an old man who was measuring the world, and the figure of a woman who pointed out the various places to the philosopher. Over the door through which Leibnitz had entered hung the portrait of a *medicus* studying a urine measure, and opposite was the portrait of a young man turning over the leaves of a book. " A beautiful room," Leibnitz felt rather than thought. Then he heard a dry staccato voice enquiring after "Monsieur de Leibnitz." He turned round, made the accustomed salutation, and saw with a stirring of emotion Eugène's masklike face. The conversation was in French. Eugène smilingly apologised that he was unable to speak German with the man who was propagating a unification of his mother-tongue. He said that he had so much to tell Leibnitz that he did not wish to mangle the language! He would do his best to protect and extend the frontiers of the German Empire; the philosopher must do his part by ensuring that within the frontiers the German language was spoken universally! He, Eugène, welcomed the idea, and would support it by all the means in his power.

Was this the celebrated silent, taciturn Prince speaking? Leibnitz saw Eugène's sparkling, animated eyes fixed keenly upon him. The Prince said that he was delighted with the philosopher's visit. It was a joy to him to know someone else who desired to inculcate in humanity a reconciliation of belief with reason. Leibnitz was right in spreading the doctrine that without the possibility of evil there could be neither perfection nor goodness. He, Eugène, had read *Theodice*; but even before he had read it he had himself come to the conclusion that the power and influence of goodness consisted in the triumph over evil: ". . . that it was an ethical parallel to the shadows in a picture and to the dissonances in music which, rather than disfiguring a work of art, co-operate in contributing to the harmony of the whole."

In their winter quarters, scattered over the Netherlands, on the French frontiers, on the Rhine, on Spanish territory, in Siebenburgen, and in the Po basin, the Imperial soldiers awaited with apprehension the first day of spring. When the sun appeared and the snow melted them, the drummers would seize their sticks and the trumpeters their instruments, and all would march in rank and file. Then the battalions, batteries, and squadrons would march out on to the battle-field, each division to its appointed place which Eugène had arranged beforehand. Then cannon-fire would begin and cannon-balls break up the order. The cavalry galloped with drawn swords, the infantry with muskets in their hands; and none who were fighting—neither the Imperial armies and their auxiliary troops, Prussians, Hanoverians, English, and Dutch—knew that the man who commanded them, and who was looked upon as the Mars of his time, the bloody War-God of his epoch, and was prized as such, spent all his free time in thinking about peace and harmony in the world!

Religious differences had shaken Europe. During the Thirty Years War, Catholics and Protestants had both endeavoured to let the might of arms determine the kind of religious doctrine to which each individual must subscribe. Louis XIV had persecuted and driven out the Huguenots; Leopold had sent those of the Reformed Faith to a tribunal of death in Hungary. Eugène congratulated himself that his master, Charles VI, whom he (as yet) dominated, left the Hungarian Protestants the freedom of their faith. He knew that the Jesuits had gained the ear of the Emperor's Spanish favourites, and that his own power was built on a sandhill which the fanatical champions of Catholicism were undermining. But, despite this, he determined to fight as long as possible for honesty, clarity, and freedom! Eugène was not a Protestant, and his Italian origin should have made of him a fiery champion of the Only Saving Church. But as soon as dogmas of belief contradicted reason he was unable to subscribe to them. When the Papal Bull *Unigenitus* was proclaimed, and when the Archbishop of Mecheln refused the sacrament to those of the dying in his diocese who had not recognised the Bull, Eugène said: " How can men who, in many cases, during their whole lives have never heard anything of the Bull, make a decision a few minutes before their death?" Eugène, who had been schooled in theology, saw in the decrees of the liturgy only a means to power; they were not, in his opinion, the means of pleasing the God of harmony in whom he believed. He had had dealings with the Pope in a diplomatic capacity, and could not bring himself to accept the fact that God's representative on earth refused the sale of corn to a starving army because His Holiness had made a pact with the enemy. Eugène asked himself whether " *ad majore majorem Dei gloriam.*" He felt with Leibnitz that God was present in the smallest things, and that God was supreme.

Whenever Leibnitz was in Vienna he was Eugène's guest. The man whom St. Saphorin describes as having been difficult in conversation, who was wont to interrupt discourse in a brusque manner, let himself be taught by the philosopher, and listened to Leibnitz with the same rapt attention with which as a young man he had listened to the mathematician Sauveur, who had instructed him in the art of fortification. Indeed, his veneration for intellect was so great that a general, the Count de Bonneval, who had fallen into disfavour, wrote in a jeering manner to Leibnitz : " He preserves your writing as the priests in Naples preserve the blood of St. Januarius ; that is to say, he allows me to kiss it, and then locks it away again in a small chest."

The writing which Bonneval described was the *Monadology*, Leibnitz's most famous work, which he wrote for Prince Eugène and dedicated to him. It was a thank-offering from the philosopher, not to the most powerful man in the Empire, and not to the Field Marshal and statesman, but to the philosopher Eugène in whose library Leibnitz had spent the happiest hours of his stay in Vienna. He said : " I am convinced that no man will advance the cause of science to a greater extent than Prince Eugène."

Eugène had started to collect books in a very modest manner. He was self-taught, and as a young man had made a great effort to satisfy his hunger for knowledge. During all his campaigns, and in all theatres of war, he had taken books with him—chiefly works of history, which assisted him in the comparison of the past with the present. He had his reading to thank for many strategic successes ; and although he had not had the express intention of making use of the material that he assimilated, it made an impression upon him, nevertheless, and, for instance, Hannibal's principle of luring a superior enemy on to dividing his forces—which had decided the issue of the battle of Cannæ—became Eugène's stategic principle. Eugène transferred the proven ideas of historical personages to his own period. They did not remain just dead theories in his mind, but suddenly came to life in decisive moments, released in lightning fashion by some chain of ideas in Eugène's mind, behaved as though they were the product of his own original thought, and determined his successes. In his conversations on the subject of leadership in war he never adopted the standpoint of having originated anything new.

Eugène's peculiar genius, reduced to a formula, amounted to his faculty for making complicated things simple, and his ability unconcernedly to circumvent difficulties in the shortest way and to put difficulties out of the way altogether. His writings on the art of war are, in the noblest sense, platitudes, as, for instance, this one : " In dangerous times, counsel and action consist in nothing else than in the army and in money."

To some degree he found Columbus's egg. His counsels and knowledge were expressed as briefly as possible. He could afford to tell the truth. Even in diplomacy, he had experienced that, in a world in which everyone lies, he whose word is believed is at an advantage. As a statesman he fought with his cards on the table. " Honesty in public affairs is far better policy than bad dissimulation. For in consequence of the method of secrecy mistrust will arise even in matters of the most harmless nature."

Eugène began his studies with the universal history of Marcus Justinus and the life of Alexander the Great by Q. Curtius Rufus. One who models himself on the lives of great men is apt to find that his character is affected by their habits ; all the more, as all great men have like characteristics. Prince Eugène differed from the leaders of genius of previous history, and from the leaders of ancient history, above all in his character as an idealist among conquerors : he had never wished to win for himself since the time in his youth when his need of proving his own worth was satisfied.

He had given himself to the service of the Habsburgs, and remained in their service, until his life's end, without any ambition to attain for himself what he attained for them. It is possible that not personal humility, but rather the knowledge of circumstances, lent him his humility in service. With Wallenstein died the last condottiere who raised his own troops and put them at the disposal of some ruling power. Eugène was never in Wallenstein's position. He always commanded foreign troops, never those who swore loyalty to him personally. His powerful position in the State did not depend upon the physical power of an army at his back ; his power consisted in the might of intellect and of genius ; it was the bodiless power which subjugates leaders as well as armies. He was the first commander of a new age, and, through intercourse with his troops, the first to recognise the necessity of a social relationship between soldiers and their leaders. At the beginning of his career he had looked upon the men as so much cannon-fodder, and had treated them no differently than did Ludwig of Baden—who was known in Germany as the greatest waster of human material—for whom a strategic victory was worth more than a thousand men ! Through the lack of men and material, Eugène came to recognise the necessity of sparing both men and material ; and by this means the individual, who in his time had been looked upon merely as an armed and movable uniform—the common man—entered into his consciousness. The connection between the activity of the individual and his success as a commander became so clear to Eugène that he cared for the individual in order to further his own success. And soon this lonely man felt a sense of well-being only when he was in an encampment in the atmosphere of common weal and common woe in the world of men whose sympathy made him happy. First, bread for the men and hay for the horses ; then, and then only, did Eugène go to rest, and only then did he sit late in the evening to read by the light of a candle, either in his tent or in a hastily repaired and ordered peasant house.

At his death, the value of Eugène's library was estimated
TE

at a hundred and fifty thousand gulden. The immensity of this sum can only be realised by comparison : the palace in the Himmelpfortegasse, with all its art treasures, was valued by the experts of that time at only one hundred thousand gulden ! There were a vast number of books in the library, but Eugène had read them all ! That fact is authenticated by the poet Jean Baptiste Rousseau, more friend than librarian, to whom Eugène confided the care of his library. He wrote that " Eugène's library consists of many good and beautifully bound books. But the astounding fact is that there is hardly a book which the Prince has not read, or, at least, looked through, before sending it to be bound. It is hardly believable that a man who carries on his shoulders the burden of almost all the affairs of Europe—that the highest Commander in the Empire, and the Emperor's first Minister, should find as much time to read as though he had nothing else to do. He understands a little of everything, but shows no predilection for anything special. Since he reads entirely for recreation, he understands how to gain advantage from his reading just as he does from his official duties. His judgment is extraordinarily accurate, and his conduct of the most endearing simplicity."

After the peace of Rastatt, Eugène returned to Vienna, to his palace in the Himmelpfortegasse, in the hopes that he might be able to live there for a time as a private individual. He had no intention of retiring from his official duties, but after thirty-one years of almost uninterrupted service he would like to have taken a holiday from public life, and to have made out for himself a programme of private study. For thirty years the Prince, who up till the time of his mother's flight from Paris had been brought up in French luxury, had only enjoyed the amenities of life such as riches, rank, and prestige during short intervals. With almost childish exactitude, this mature man copied all the luxuries which Mazarin had enjoyed and which he knew of by hearsay. It cannot, however, be imagined that the influence of heredity in Eugène's distant relationship with the Cardinal can have extended to include his hobbies, although it is certain that the liking for the display of wealth was common to both of them, due to their Italian blood quite apart from their relationship. All Vienna had to be aware of the fact that Prince Eugène lived in the most magnificent of palaces —and not only Vienna, but the whole of the rest of the world ! In tales and descriptions of travellers, adventurers, and cavaliers accounts are to be found of Eugène's wealth, with, even during his lifetime, an exact and detailed description of his palaces. For instance, it was recounted that one chandelier had cost twenty thousand gulden—and one rare book or manuscript, in his library, six thousand gulden ! Men of no consequence and of no name were permitted access to Eugène's private apartments, even to his bedchamber, the private garden, and the menagerie which, like Mazarin, he had acquired, and for which he had had birds sent from India in the same way as he must have heard from Olympia that her uncle had done, and for which he begged friendly rulers to contribute rare animals which in some way had come into their possession. Eugène was always regretting that he had not more time at his disposal to devote to his possessions. A contemporary calculated that his income amounted to three hundred thousand gulden a year, most of which sum he spent, not knowing to whom to leave his fortune. His favourite nephew had died in London, and, two years before that, another had died in Barcelona. He had married the last surviving one to a Princess Liechtenstein, but he was untalented and gave Eugène no pleasure.

Eugène was unexpectedly plunged again into work, and work that represented for him the reflection of world events in his thoughts, and his reactions to them. The peace treaties of Utrecht and Rastatt had ended the world war of the Spanish Succession. Projected upon the map, the treaties showed the boot of Italy for the most part Habsburg, the Netherlands and the greater part of the Netherlands belonged to the Habsburgs, while the Spanish Peninsula itself and the colonies were Bourbon. The head of the House of

Savoy, Victor Emmanuel, had acquired the right to a kingship. The kingdom of Sicily had been granted to him, but was later exchanged for that of Sardinia. Max Emmanuel, the Elector of Bavaria, somewhat disappointed and ill-humoured, reigned once more in Munich. For what had come out of the promises of his friend the Marquis de Villars? Where was the division of Spain between himself and Louis? England had gained the most, not only by having acquired Newfoundland, Nova Scotia, and the Hudson Bay lands, as well as Gibraltar and Minorca, but chiefly because the domination of France in Europe had been destroyed.

The two rivals for Spain, Charles and Philip, made peace only on paper. The Emperor of the Holy Roman Empire would willingly have exchanged the insignia of Charlemagne for the Spanish Crown. Spain remained his unlucky love for the whole of his life. He was Emperor only very unwillingly, and his party adherents from the time of the Spanish campaign remained his favourites at the Court of Vienna. They were the rival party to Eugène, who, after the Peace of Rastatt, demanded that Charles should put the interests of the Empire before those of Spain. But he urged in vain ; for Charles continued to call himself King of Castile, Aragon, Legion, Granada, Navarra, Toledo, Valencia, Galicia, Mallorca, Mauritius, Algarbia, Algeciras, Gibraltar, of the Canary and Indian Islands, and of the *terra firma* of the Oceanic Sea, as well as Margrave of Catalania and Asturia ! Philip of Spain, to whom all these titles *de facto* and *de jure* belonged, raised a claim, on the grounds of the hereditary rights of Charles II of Spain, to be called Archduke of Austria. Eugène, who only called himself plain Eugène of Savoy, and no longer Margrave of Saluzzo and Piedmont, and did not even sign himself with his princely title, had the greatest difficulty in preventing a war which had the object of satisfying his Emperor's love of titles !

As his great-uncle had done before him, Eugène tried to divert His Majesty by distractions. But he had not inherited the necessary talent for such diversions, and, although there are reports of festivities in his palace, every description of such an event shows that Prince Eugène was ever serious and deliberate. He had no aptitude as a *maître de plaisir* in the grand style, and was in no wise inclined for noisy company. After such festivities his name would be found in the list printed in the hand-written *Wiener Zeitungen*. All the other noble guests at the Royal festivities were mentioned in company with a lady, and at the end of the row of the princely and noble couples there was the name of Prince Eugène of Savoy—alone. Lonely until the end of his life ? No ! First there were his numberless friends, good-humoured adventurers from all over the world, whose company he preferred to that of the stiff, conventional Austrian nobility. They were all men who had crept into his confidence, seekers after a protector, Bohemian natures—who attracted Eugène because he found them easier to get on with— such as the Count de Bonneval, the Marquis von Westerloo-Merode, and St. Saphorin. They had all remained unmarried, like Eugène himself. A young sculptor called Mariette was the Prince's favourite, and in unauthenticated writings a young Italian female was mentioned as having won his favours. It seems much more likely that this Marietta was in reality the young Mariette ! The son of the famous Parisian copper-engraver was hardly twenty years old when he came to Vienna first. At the instruction of his father, who did a trade in pictures, he called on Prince Eugène, and stayed for several years in the palace in the Himmelpfortegasse. In the Royal archives in Vienna there is a letter from Prince Eugène to his adjutant-general, the Freiherr von Hohendorf, in which he commends the young Mariette. Eugène made it possible for the young man to make a journey to Italy in order to educate himself in his art. Eugène also recommended the unknown sculptor to the kindness of heart of Count Tarini. The young artist whom the Prince of Savoy had taken under his protection should have every advantage !

Ten years later Mariette wrote to Prince Eugène from

Paris. Now he had become the executor of Eugène's piety, his trusted emissary whose business it was to protect the late servitors of the House of Soissons from want.

Still Eugène did not erase the past. He had humbled Louis XIV in fact, although the peace had ceded territories to the King's grandson. Eugène learned with satisfaction that the frontier of the Pyrenees, which, when he seized Spain for his family, Louis had wished to wipe out—just because of the near relationship—had proved to be an unsurmountable barrier between France and Spain. The great King had sacrificed prestige in his own kingdom ; his grandson, the King of Spain, did not obey him. Only in his own phantasy did the Roi Soleil rule over a kingdom upon which the sun never set. He was a very old and lonely man. His only successor, apart from the King of Spain, his grandson, was his great-grandson, a child two years old. When this child died, according to the treaty of peace which excluded Philip V from the succession in France, Philip of Orleans, the son of Liselotte of the Palatinate, would rule over the French kingdom. And if the ailing child survived his youth, then after Louis's death Philip of Orleans would become Regent. Louis hated the Duke of Orleans. He was a free-thinker without respect for the Church and for the dignity of kingship and without restraint; he was a dissolute character, and cynically exposed all his debauched habits to the public eye. Louis XIV lay in bed : his illness was known by the name of altersbrand, a putrid fever of the limbs. But he maintained his dignity and calm, and the outward appearance of Majesty which, since the death·of Mazarin, he had worn with such grace ! That even Eugène was not entirely reconciled with his life's enemy is shown by a remark of his, concerning the office of commander-in-chief of the Swiss Guard in the French army. He said : " My father had occupied this post, and at his death we hoped that my brother would have it. But the King preferred to give it to one of his natural sons, instead of granting us the favour. He is the ruler, and one cannot oppose him," he added with a gentle irony. And then : " But sometimes one is glad to be in a position to cause a demonstration of contempt to be regretted."

France was no longer a rival to the Emperor in whose name Eugène ruled. The twenty-nine years of war during Louis XIV's reign had cost his country, on the battlefields and in the hospitals, one million two hundred thousand men and fifteen hundred million livres; and, in addition to that, a national debt of two hundred and eighty-three million livres had been incurred, of which the half was a floating debt for which the creditors could at any moment claim repayment. The balance of French finances seemed to be shaken for ever. Eugène could, with a quiet conscience, counsel the Imperial diplomats to propose a better relationship between Austria and France! He did so in an impersonal manner, abstracted from his attitude to Louis XIV. How much longer would that ancient in Versailles continue to live? He had *made* himself immortal, but he was not immortal!

Eugène was opposed to the action advised by the Emperor's Spanish friends, namely, the support of the Catalanians against the Castilians, on whom the power of the kingdom of Philip rested. But the Emperor had not officially renounced Spain. The fact that the Catalanians called him Charles III was enough reason for him to found in Vienna a Spanish Council or a Chamber with the function of administering those Spanish provinces on Italian soil and in the Netherlands which had been ceded to him at the Peace of Rastatt. Each of the fifty Spanish aristocrats drew an allowance of ten thousand guldens. Charles VI was far more like his father Leopold than his brother Joseph. He was not a German in his mentality. As his father had preferred to speak Italian, so he preferred to speak Spanish, and longed for the sunny peninsula. There he had dreamed the dreams of his youth, and there, as a young man, he had fought and hoped. What had he to expect from his position as Emperor of the Holy Roman Empire? The Germans were repellent to him. They did not adhere to the strict Spanish etiquette. Charles VI did not understand that Eugène wished to exchange the Netherlands for Bavaria in order to strengthen the Emperor's power on German soil, and thereby to further the realisation of his plan for the greater German Empire. Give up the Netherlands and ancient Burgundy, which had given birth to Charles V, whose worthy successor Charles VI wished to become? The Emperor was astonished. He felt injured in his family pride. The Spanish Council had an easy game against Eugène. The Jesuits and Spanish councillors intrigued, and carried through the suggestion that Eugène be deprived of his post of Governor-General of Milan ! In the Spanish circle it was even asked whether Eugène was in any way indispensable. This stranger and immigrant, who was neither German nor Spaniard ? They decided that he was not indispensable, and demanded his banishment, or, at least, his resignation from all offices.

This was the thanks of the House of Austria !

CHAPTER II

In the witty biography, written a hundred years ago, in the autobiographical form, by the Prince de Ligne, the author makes the Prince speak of himself thus : " The short years of peace were more exhausting for me than the war. The time was taken up by conferences with the Ministers of England and Holland, concerning the Peace Treaty, and conferences with the Emperor's Ministers concerning methods for putting the State finances in order ! The finances were in an unbelievable muddle. I had to pay the Army when and how I could ; often my guarantee would be questioned, and often, just as one pawns diamonds, I was obliged to pawn whole provinces. However, gradually, and in spite of the Ministers' stupidity, I succeeded in increasing the State revenues." Even though the autobiographical form of Ligne's little book is fictitious, yet it proves to have been correct in its dates. The sentences quoted above, refer, very shortly, to those of Eugène's activities, after the Peace of Rastatt, which were concerned with the disposition of finances. The problem was made the more difficult for him, inasmuch as not only the Emperor and his Spanish clique, but the administration also, offered passive resistance to all his measures.

The national debt consisted of two parts : some of the creditors had either made loans of money to the Emperor, or had delivered goods on a contract basis. The others demanded arrears of payment in the form of honours and pensions. These were chiefly civil servants and military officials who, over a period of many years, had served the Crown in special ways. Eugène and Gundacker von Starhemberg evolved a scheme for the foundation of a State Bank in Vienna. The city of Vienna received the customs duties and all taxes on provisions, both in Vienna and in all the Austrian hereditary dominions, and with these revenues, had to ensure the payment, within fifteen years, of the first group of creditors. For the second group, the pensioners, and recipients of gifts of honour from the Emperor (which last were only registered on paper), there was no provision for payment of capital within any given term. These creditors were *rentiers* of favours, and received five per cent interest. At some later time, when Austria and the Emperor were rich once more, the capital would be at their disposal !

The most difficult of the monetary negotiations were with the heirs and creditors of the Jew Oppenheimer, who had died during the War of the Spanish Succession. After his death, Eugène wrote to Count Starhemberg : " Oppenheimer's death is a new trial. All the merchants are involved in the affair, and they have declared their inability to enter into further contracts before the Jew's affairs are settled." Gundacker replied that France could have thought out nothing more efficacious for her own benefit, and for the discomfiture of the Emperor, than the death of Oppenheimer !

The " Imperial Oberfactor," as Oppenheimer was entitled, was an old acquaintance of Eugène's. In the existing correspondence, letters are constantly found which testify to the relationship between Eugène, the father and son Oppenheimer, and their successor Wertheimer. " The recruitment must be hastened and the soldiers must be given their pay. For only if they receive money will they achieve anything." Eugène had insisted upon this point when he was quite a young general, and he knew that he could only obtain money with the aid of the Jew. He protected Oppenheimer, and wrote : " Therefore, the necessary arrears in the payment of provisions must be made, for the Jew Oppenheimer protests that he cannot continue, if he is left in the lurch as regards money."

Eugène's recognition that provisions, munitions, forage —in short, all necessities of equipment—constituted the foundation of success in war differentiated him from all the other commanders of his time, who behaved in a dilettante fashion when it came to the economic side of war. " Your Majesty, the Crown is tottering on Your Majesty's head, the sceptre is threatening to fall out of your Majesty's hands, and the whole monarchy is threatened with a downfall." Eugène had raised a warning finger, and had overstepped the boundaries of respect towards the Emperor, only because not enough money was forthcoming for the troops !

He had reason enough for his haughty, imperious attitude ! It is only necessary to turn over the leaves of a so-called Court and Honours Calendar of the time of Charles VI to confirm the fact that the Emperor was claimed so much by religious and representational duties, which demanded his presence from early morning till late evening, and from the first to the last day of the month, that there was no time left over for him to think of work, or to reflect on the duties connected with his Government. Nearly every day in the year offered an occasion for devotional exercise followed either by a monastic repast or a gala reception. There were the Golden Fleece celebrations to which only the Knights were invited, appearing at Court and in church in their red velvet gold-embroidered doublets, cloaks, and hats ; there were days dedicated to the consecration of candles, birthdays and name-days of Royalty when the élite in Spanish gala dress were admitted at Court to the " hand-kiss." A note in parenthesis remarks that on such days only compliments were served, but nothing to eat or drink ! From this and from the office records of the Court exchequer, which entered large sums even for the monastic repasts of their Majesties, it can be perceived that on every other occasion there was eating and drinking, even after those processions in which the Emperor and his wife were requested to appear " on foot." The editor of the Calendar added to the data, the following remark : " From this long list of solemnities it can be seen how their Imperial Majesties are almost daily engaged, and that they are obliged to spend much time at both spiritual and worldly ceremonies."

Eugène would have granted their Majesties the time. But

the vast Court apparatus, which was perpetually in motion, cost money—two million a year—while for the Empire's military concerns, ranging from the Netherlands to the southernmost point of Sicily, from the frontier forts of Tortona and Novara to Wallachia, only eight millions had been put aside. Was Eugène expected to stand in readiness for war with this sum only? He told the Emperor that he must cut down the Court expenditure. Reduce the Court expenditure? The Emperor looked at him angrily. Very well, he would economise! He kept his promise, inasmuch as he passed Eugène over at the next distribution of property! The Emperor's sense of dignity was injured, and he came more and more to the conclusion that his Spanish councillors were right—the tiresome Savoyard must go!

Undoubtedly Eugène would have been put on the shelf, indeed, he would have been dismissed, had not the war in the East—which had begun almost simultaneously with the war in the West—persisted after the Peace of Rastatt. The eighteen-year-old King of Sweden had turned against Peter the Great, had undertaken a wild invasion of Russia, and had nearly forced his way into Moscow. He had, however, then been beaten almost to the point of destruction by the great Russian Czar. He fled into Turkey, and succeeded in stirring up the Porte against Russia. Peter was shut in on the Pruth by the overwhelming Ottoman forces and purchased peace by bribing the Grand Vizier. A condition of the treaty was that Charles XII should go back to his own country. He returned by way of Vienna; but Eugène did not receive the Swedish King. He had no use for commanders who made war for war's sake. The fact that Charles rode up staircases on horseback, and that he galloped to the chase mounted on captured stags made no impression on Eugène. His pact with the Turks had roused the Prince to indignation against the Swedish King. "The Prince is as furious with the King of Sweden as it is possible for anyone to be," wrote General von Schulenburg in his memoirs. Eugène had given vent to his indignation. Thanks to Charles XII, the Turks were stirred up again. Did it mean

CONTEMPORARY REPRESENTATION OF EUGÈNE'S MENAGERIE

another war? When he heard from the Swedes of the increasingly energetic mobilisation of the Turks on land and sea, Eugène redoubled his preparations. Already a Turkish fleet had passed through the Dardanelles : already a Turkish army had landed on European soil. The Imperial Ambassador intervened ; but the Porte declared that their measures were directed against the Republic of Venice only, and that the mobilisation in no wise purposed the invasion of the Emperor's country.

That was not a declaration of war—rather the reverse ! But could the Turks be trusted ?

In Eugène's library stood a newly invented *machina planetarum*, " a system of planets arranged according to the theory of Copernicus." It was a remarkable construction, which was meant to represent the mechanical movement of the world. Eugène set up this apparatus, again and again making the great world, raised on the small frame, go through its performance for his pleasure. The earth turned itself round the sun when the machine was set in motion, and the planets moved in circles as long as the clockwork functioned. Then the world stood still—Eugène could hear the beats of his own heart. He called his adjutant. After a few moments, with clanking spurs, the Baron von Hohendorf appeared. The Prince was in the library, and the general, who was a cultivated man, looked forward to a learned conversation. Was the Prince planning a new purchase of books ? For some time now, he had been Eugène's agent and buyer at the antiquaries. But he only procured for his master the books that he could not purchase himself ! " The maps of Serbia, of Smyrna, and of Banat," ordered Eugène. Without a word von Hohendorf retired, and came back again accompanied by servants who spread out the maps in front of the Prince. The adjutant stood aside and watched while the little man sped from map to map, supported himself on his elbows, gesticulated, and traced the course of the Danube. " War again," thought Hohendorf. Soon maps were spread over the whole *salon*. The course of the Danube from Vienna to the Black Sea was divided into squares. "The list of troops," commanded Eugène, and commanded that the Jew Oppenheimer be sent to him.

The son of the famous *Oberfaktor*, who to a certain extent had succeeded to the rights and duties of his father, stood before the Prince. "Ask him," said Eugène to Hohendorf, pointing with his finger to Oppenheimer, "whether he can undertake the delivery of provisions for sixty thousand men and forage for twenty thousand horses."

"Whither?" asked Oppenheimer in reply.

"The Danube," replied Eugène shortly. Oppenheimer wanted to haggle; he hesitated as to whether he could undertake the whole supply.

"Yes or no?" asked Eugène. His face had lost its fresh colour, he was deathly white.

An hour later, Gundacker von Starhemberg was with him. "How much money can you realise?" asked the Prince.

"None at all," Starhemberg answered.

But a few days later the necessary money was produced. Eugène desired the war. He gave himself no time for pangs of conscience to remind him that there would be more dead, more wounded, and more devastated territories! Was it merely arbitrariness and wantonness to begin another war, or was it really a necessity? The Turks had gathered together two hundred thousand men on European soil; their Danube flotilla was assembled at Belgrade ready at any moment to transport provisions for the Turks up the Danube.

The Danube flotilla? Had Eugène forgotten it? After all, he thought, I ought to have taken the advice of St. Saphorin, the adventurer and nobody, of twenty years earlier, now Resident to the English Government, at the time when he had made his suggestions for the building of a Danube flotilla. "I not only need soldiers, I need ships as well," Eugène decided, and commissioned them to be built.

He knew the country in which he intended to make war. He knew every stone and tree, every rise and fall of the land. He knew the course of every river, and every piece of stagnant water in the neighbourhood of Peterwardein. Would it be possible to hold the fort if the Turks were to arrive there before him ? he asked himself. As yet the Emperor knew nothing : he believed the promises of the Porte. Eugène would have to coerce him. He called General von Hohendorf. " Will you announce to His Majesty that I wish for an audience ? "

There were difficulties. First of all, Charles VI did not wish to receive the tiresome Prince ; then, when pressed, he agreed to do so. Eugène explained with cool politeness that he wished to betake himself to the army in Hungary : the Turkish preparations had caused him to fear the worst, and he wished to take defensive measures. That was all ! !

Eugène took upon himself the sole responsibility of making contracts with Oppenheimer, to which he forced Gundacker to agree, collected his General Staff, distributed the army commands, and wrote to the German Princes saying that the moment had come in which to drive the Turks from European soil. Yes, there would be war, with sacrifice of life ; but the hegemony of the Unbelievers in Europe would be ended for ever !

Louis XIV had died a few months earlier. His courtiers who, in his lifetime, had crowded in hundreds round him—rejoiced if a glance even fell upon them—now left his remains alone. Five of them accompanied his heart to the Jesuit chapel to which he had left it in his will. In order to save expenditure of money and time, his funeral procession was of the simplest. Cursing and reviling, and casting stones and dirt, the populace of Paris followed the great King's coffin through the streets.

While Eugène was preparing his campaign of conquest, he was overtaken by thoughts of Louis. Was it not his love of adventure and the Bourbon blood of invaders, which through his grandmother, the Princesse de Carignan, flowed in his veins, that drove him in his old age into the battlefield ? Was it this blood which urged him to wage war in the east because his enemy in the west was dead ? Would his plan, his youthful plan, which had arisen like a phantom in his mind on that long-ago ride to Regensburg, be realised in the east as well as in the west? He had conquered Louis XIV. Was he now to bring about the downfall of the Turkish world-empire? And then? Then—— Latterly he had breathed with increasing difficulty. As long as he was in the field his chest trouble was not so noticeable. The doctors had ordered him good air. But in Vienna he was always poring over books, and was never in the open air. When the war came to an end, when his plan had succeeded and he had in reality extended the frontiers of the Empire as far as the Black Sea—just as he could extend them now on the map with a stroke of the pen—then, and then only, his breath might be allowed to give out!

Unceasingly he pressed tobacco to his nose and inhaled the aroma. He was shaken by a fit of coughing. To live no longer——!

Eugène once more demanded an audience with the Emperor. There he stood, confronted with a younger edition of Leopold I—a dilatory, indecisive creature; a weakling who was incapable of making a decision—who asked him what he should do if his wife, the Empress (who was awaiting her confinement), should give birth to a daughter, instead of a son and heir to the Throne! "Raise an army and fill the war exchequer, Your Majesty," was Eugène's answer. "Prepare in time, and, instead of negotiating, act! Incidentally, Your Majesty——" He was about to set off; he had come to take leave of the Emperor, and here was a paper. "My will, Your Majesty." He had only one relation, his nephew Emmanuel. "No, not the Turks, Your Majesty; my chest trouble!"

Charles's underlip, damp and heavy, hung down to his chin. He did not know whether to wish that Eugène should go to his grave in this detestable Hungary—or whether he ought to hope that no misfortune befall the Prince. In the one case he would be at peace with his courtiers. But then— the threatened frontiers? In the other case the frontiers would be secured. But then—his domestic peace? And

Spain? Who would conquer Spain for him once Eugène was dead? He bade the Prince take care of himself. Why did he wish to betake himself to the army at all?

Eugène evaded the question, and answered coolly: "I will devote myself to the care of the army and to Your Majesty's service with the uttermost devotion and obedient loyalty."

The Emperor was defenceless: Eugène had ignored his question. Well, he must go then, but Charles added that "he would constantly suffer from the lack of Eugène's person."

Now Eugène had to decide upon the subordinate commanders! he turned to Guido von Starhemberg. But Starhemberg had had enough of the Emperor's service. He was as much in disfavour with the Spanish favourites as his commander-in-chief. He was not going to be tormented any longer. When Eugène pressed him, he wrote to his nephew: "Whoever attempts to rob me of my rest and quiet has no affection for me. I only ask to be forgotten, and pray that no one may remember that I am still in the world. My approaching sixty years and my broken body refuse to work any longer."

Nearly sixty years old? Eugène himself needed only seven more years to attain that age. He straightened his thin figure. Old and worn out like Starhemberg! He? Not yet!

In July 1716, with a staff of twelve ordnance officers and cavalry generals, Eugène entered a small place near Peterwardein. Sixty-five thousand men, of whom twenty thousand were cavalry, were waiting for him. These troops were his achievement as President of the War Council! He had never yet led such a well-equipped army. But of the enemy there was nothing to be seen. The corn was growing thickly in the fields, and the landscape was steeped in peace. Had all his preparations been in vain? Accompanied by Count Pallfy he rode through the country, reconnoitring; and sent out spies. But even on the Turkish side of the Danube all was peaceful. Whenever Eugène saw the Danube he saw Belgrade before him. As long as that fortress was standing the

Empire was not secure from Turkish invasion. A war must ensue : the fact of the preparations proved that the Turks had planned it. This time Eugène was determined to attempt the capture of Belgrade. Twenty-five years earlier it would have been impossible to hold, on account of the threatening Power in the west, but now he would have the power to hold it. " It seems," he wrote to the Emperor, " that this barbaric nation is for superstitious reasons determined to await the outbreak of hostilities without an official declaration on the part of Your Majesty." But, he went on to say, he would advise disregarding this superstition on the part of the barbarians, and would like to undertake without hesitation those actions which might be expected to lead to successful results.

That was not clearly expressed. Eugène did not directly ask for authorisation to wage war. But, when he received full powers from the Emperor, he wrote to the Porte.

For answer he received a bloodthirsty letter from the Grand Vizier, threatening that the shameful violation of peace " would cause the ignominious downfall and everything unholy to overtake Eugène's children and grandchildren." Well, then, it should be war ! Eugène was content. His nervousness vanished. With complete calm, he observed the movements of the Turkish army, which crossed the Save —two hundred thousand men strong—marched to Carlowitz, and set itself up around the so-called Chapel of Peace which had been built to commemorate the battle of Zenta. Pallfy offered to take one thousand five hundred men and reconnoitre the positions of the enemy, so as to make certain from which side they were to be reached. The Count's patrol was attacked by some twenty thousand Turkish cavalry, and Pallfy succeeded, only with the greatest difficulty, in getting back to Peterwardein. The Turks pursued him, and in the night built fortifications, a chaos of deep trenches which were extremely difficult to see over and more or less high earthen walls. Did they intend to invade Peterwardein ?

Eugène crossed the Danube with his army, and likewise

occupied a fortified encampment. Hardly, however, had he fortified it, than the Turks began to fire upon the camp with *Mortars* and heavy guns. He was in a difficult situation, and decided to return across the river and defend Peterwardein with a strong garrison. His generals believed that the strength of the Turks would be broken in the attempt to storm the walls of the stronghold, and that the Ottoman army, with considerable losses and without having attained its objective, would be forced to retreat into Turkish territory again. But just that was what Eugène wished to avoid. He wanted neither to remain in the entrenchments nor to effect a long-drawn-out manœuvre. The soldiers were in the most satisfactory condition, having just come out of barracks, and having suffered no distress, he declared. They desired a battle just as much as their commander did, he added. Barely seventy thousand against two hundred thousand—three to one again? The disproportion was confirmed by the generals with anxious consideration. But " *Jung gewohnt, alt getan* " is an Austrian proverb. Eugène stuck to his plan, he allowed every foot soldier fifty cartridges, every cavalryman twenty-one. The baggage was left behind. Each man was allowed to take with him only that which he needed for the battle. The artillery was ordered to be ready before daylight, the entire cavalry and the infantry, which had remained on the left shore of the Danube, was to be transported across the river, on the two ships, at dusk on the evening of the 4th of August, in order that the attack might begin in the early morning.

The fortifications which General Caraffa had set up in earlier campaigns constituted the base in Eugène's plan of battle. They were protected on both sides by steep banks and were difficult to attack. Behind them lay the fortress of Peterwardein, the guns from which were able to range across the ramparts. Eugène placed his army in front of the fortifications: on the left it was protected by a morass, and on the right by another steep bank.

Everything was ready for the attack, when suddenly a storm broke forth. A furious tempest tore several shipmills from their anchors on the Danube, and drove them with such force against the bridges that confusion arose, and the attack had to be postponed for two hours. During the night and day preceding the attack, Eugène had retained his calm ; but the storm upset his plans. Two hours delay ? He saw that during these two hours the Turks had observed his preparations for the attack. The ground was covered by the lines of their massed troops extending further than the eye could reach ; their horsemen stood in readiness facing the Imperial cavalry, and their trenches were filling up with janizaries. Fifty thousand against two hundred thousand—and the psychological moment lost ! A retreat ? He glanced once more at the battlefield ! The first cavalry attack must succeed ! The mailed horsemen were in reserve for the protection of the infantry ! It was seven o'clock in the morning. " Forward ! " Eugène gave the word of command. Dragoons and hussars fell into a trot, and in one offensive put the whole of the Turkish cavalry to flight. Was victory already achieved ?

The outcome of the battle would have been determined in that first half hour if the infantry had advanced in order. But Eugène was obliged to send forward the closed line of his mailed horsemen—a part of the armoured cavalry—to their protection. In the meantime the disorder amongst the infantry increased. The Turks pressed forward, and opened their flanks.

From his elevated standpoint Eugène saw that the battle was won. It was the moment of genius. He still had a few thousand cavalry held in reserve, and now threw them forward. The Turks, in terror, hesitated in their pursuit, and at that moment the Imperial infantry turned about and advanced to the attack. Closed in on all sides, the Turks could not hold out.

The Grand Vizier Ali made one further attempt. During the entire battle he had been standing beside his tent, in front of the sacred flag, and now he dashed forward towards his troops in order to prevent their flight. He drew his sword against his own men. But nothing was of any use ; they fled.

Then, with his bodyguard, he threw himself upon the enemy. A few minutes later he was hit in the forehead by a bullet, and fell from his horse.

The loss of their commander increased the confusion amongst the fugitives. Bulwarks, tents, guns—everything was abandoned : the Turks only thought of saving their own skins, and fled in disorder, along the shores of the Save, towards Belgrade.

It was still only mid-day when Eugène rode towards the Grand Vizier's tent.

He was conscious of a feeling of strength : now he would undertake the capture of Belgrade.

Once again he sat in his tent, bent over a map. From outside, in the camp, came the sounds of rejoicing. He had given over the booty to the troops. Its value was so great that a contemporary chronicler related that some of the soldiers could have had a satisfying nest-egg for the rest of their lives if the spoils had been sold for their real worth. . . . " But it is a strange fatality that spoils of war are never of any real use. They are always either destroyed or squandered, and very soon no one knows what has become of them ! "

Four days after the battle, Colonel Count Khevenhüller entered Vienna bearing the news of victory. Postilions trotted in front of him, and the streets were full of people, who held up the messenger. So great was the excitement of the crowd that, as Khevenhüller himself relates, he was obliged to repeat over and over again the description of the battle. He was the only one who could give an exact report, for Eugène had forbidden the War Council to publish the circumstances of the battle : he did not wish the Turks to see through his plans.

The bells were rung and the streets illuminated. Everyone rejoiced : the Christian faith had triumphed over the unbelieving Turks ! Up to the present Rome had not been friendly to the Prince, but the Pope was obliged to take account of this victory. As a " recognition of marvellous war services for the cause of Christendom and the Catholic Church," he sent Eugène a hat, and a sword richly set in diamonds blessed by himself.

The news of the conquest of the Turks spread like wildfire throughout the world. Already, twelve days after the battle, Monseigneur le Duc de Villars, Marshal of France, wrote Eugène a letter : " This is a great day for the Emperor and for his famous general. I renew my prophecy, and set the Black Sea as the goal of your victories ! "

In Vienna everyone was in favour of the termination of hostilities, and for the conclusion of peace : the spur to further achievement and the belief in Eugène had to come from Paris ! Would he really be able to press forward to the Black Sea ? He proceeded to capture Temesvar, and refused to be content with insignificant victories. When General Mehmed Pasha begged for an unhindered retreat for the Hungarian rebels who had served under the Turkish flag, Eugène wrote with his own hand on the agreement of surrender : " *La canaglia puo andare dove vuole !* " When he was in a good mood Eugène liked to speak Italian ! What did the hundred discontented Hungarians matter to him on his Alexandrian march to the east ? The Black Sea was his goal ! Oh, if he were only younger ! He sent the border captain, Dettin, with twelve hundred men into Wallachia. Everywhere the country people declared themselves on the side of the Imperial soldiers, and greeted them with joy.

Dettin pushed into Bucharest, and brought Prince Maurokordato with his family to Hermanstadt. A large number of Bojars wandered out of Wallachia into Siebenburgen. A raiding party undertook an expedition to Moldavia, and succeeded in reaching Jassy. Was it much farther now to the Black Sea ? Would Eugène succeed in reaching it yet ?

During the campaign a letter arrived from Max Emmanuel of Bavaria, Eugène's old friend and the first conqueror of Belgrade. He begged the Prince, " in consideration of the old-time understanding between them, of their blood relationship, and of his appreciation of Eugène's qualities, to allow him to offer his good wishes," at the same time soliciting Eugène's influence with the Emperor to allow his son to come to Vienna and serve under him.

This humble request on the part of the man who had once been such a power in the army proved to Eugène the alarming heights to which he had risen in his career. He remembered his youthful, ambitious remarks, at which Max Emmanuel had smiled at the time. "Everything can be achieved by persistence and determination!" he had said. Even the capture of Belgrade!

The Powers intervened in favour of a truce with Turkey, but Eugène did not believe that the Porte was serious in its desire for peace. The Turks only wished to gain time, and to gather their strength in order to start the war again with greater zest. He heard that, in Turkey, troops were being assembled, and also that every pretext was being used to excite insurrection in Hungary. Cautiously, almost too cautiously, he gave instructions to the Imperial Ambassador in Poland to ensure that there the insurgents received neither assistance nor support. Louis XIV was dead, but his diplomacy still lived. The precautions in Poland were all the more necessary, declared Eugène, "because there, as is well known, the channel has always existed by means of which evil machinations against Hungary are secretly instigated and attempted."

On no account must a premature peace be made, and on no account must he be behind the Turks on the battlefield! In order to capture Belgrade, Eugène would have to be able to cross either the Danube or the Save unhindered; and for this purpose more money was necessary, as well as new equipment and fresh provisions. But, it was no longer so difficult to obtain the *nervus belli* as in former times. Pious Roman Catholics subscribed half of their property, the Jews in the Habsburg hereditary dominions collected, by taxation, half a million gulden, and the German Empire contributed fifty "Roman months"—Oppenheimer was now able to deliver the necessary equipment ! The Danube flotilla was enlarged, new guns cast, and then followed the advance to the theatre of war.

Two days before Eugène's departure from Vienna a daughter was born to Charles VI. She was christened Maria Theresa. The Prince congratulated the Emperor, who accepted the congratulations sadly. No son—was he to be the last male in the Habsburg line ?

On the day on which Eugène took his army across the Danube near Peterwardein, he received a letter from Mr. Wortley Montague, from Adrianople. The English Ambassador made peace proposals in the name of the Sultan. He said that it had never been the wish of the great ruler to wage war with the Emperor. Ali, the dead Grand Vizier, had acted in a despotic manner and in disobedience of the Sultan's commands. Turkey was desirous of peace.

The Prince sent on the letter to the Emperor, with the remark that, undoubtedly, the Englishman in sending such a letter was actuated by fear of the Turks. God forbid the necessity of concluding peace !

In Eugène's camp, sixty-one battalions and one hundred and seventy-six squadrons were ready for the battle. He had the youngest brother of the King of Portugal quartered in his tent, a young Prince of a reigning house, who was on hostile terms with his family (as Eugène himself had been thirty years before !), twenty years old, without means, and ambitious. Eugène took the good-looking boy under his wing, and kept him at his side for the whole of the campaign. He had other guests besides—French Princes who wished to learn the art of war from this French-born general. They were all spectators waiting for the play to begin : the play of the siege of Belgrade.

Eugène debated whether he should once more ride with a patrol, in the direction of Belgrade, to reconnoitre. But a picture of the town, and of the neighbourhood, had impressed itself upon his memory in such detail that the

PRINCE EUGÈNE'S TRIUMPH AFTER THE CAPTURE OF BELGRADE

expedition was superfluous. He saw the mountain before him, framed in red-brick walls and roofed in terrace-like form, the walls washed by the waters of the Save and the Danube; and he saw the sharp line which marked the joining of the two streams. The picture was unchanged, but spies had reported that morasses had arisen which rendered difficult the passage across to Banat to fetch provisions. Eugène laid his encampment so that, like the fort opposite, it was surrounded by a chain of trenches and defence works, in order that in the event of a defeat he could set his army up again and venture upon a second battle.

But most important of all were the bridges which he threw across the Save, and the Danube bridge—the historical Danube bridge—which he protected on both sides by ships.

Eugène was cautious. Belgrade was the strongest fortress in the east. Thirty thousand men, the cream of the janizaries, lay in the defences. The report that the Porte had raised an overwhelming army to save the town was proved to be correct: the new Grand Vizier Chalil advanced from the east with two hundred thousand Turks.

Once again, just as before the battle of Peterwardein, a hurricane raged. The bridges which Eugène had thrown across the Danube and the Save were broken, and most of the boats on which they had been built were carried off by the current. The Turks did not mean to lose the advantage of the confusion which they thought certain to have been caused in the Emperor's camp by the storm. Ten thousand of their men marched against the Danube bridges, in order to complete their destruction. With great noise of shouting they pressed forward, but, with only sixty men, a Hessian captain, whose name history has forgotten, withstood the onrush until help was forthcoming. A few days later the janizaries broke out of the fortress and stormed Eugène's camp; but they, also, were driven back.

Need makes of speed a necessity. Eugène learned that the preliminary attacks had been undertaken, in the first place, to prevent the setting up of batteries from which the bombardment of the town was to begin. The Turks wished to delay the siege preparations. That was, in itself, enough reason for Eugène to hasten them. Five days after the attack the bombardment began. The garrison answered fire.

Gradually, however, the Turkish firing was lamed, and on the 30th of July, Belgrade, viewed from the riverside, had all the appearance of a vast ruin.

But on that same day there were great jubilations in the town, for, from the battlements of the castle, the vanguard of the Turkish army was sighted.

On the 31st of July the Turks began to build an encampment quite close to Eugène's. An eye-witness reports that the vast numbers of the red and green tents presented a variegated, almost festive, spectacle.

Eugène knew that the Turks would attempt the attack within the shortest possible time, chiefly because they could not supply enough provisions in their encampment; and thus it was clear to him that he was suddenly put into an extremely critical position. His army was shut in on both sides by the two rivers, which could not be crossed in full view of the enemy; in front of him was a mighty fortress, and behind him the Turks, with twice as strong an army as that which he had at his disposal. The generals advised their commander-in-chief to retreat: the Imperial army must break through on one side otherwise it would be lost.

In the commander's tent there was breathless silence. All eyes were fixed upon the mask-like face, which remained unmoved. Why did the Prince not answer? Was he not convinced of the relevance of their suggestions? Would he follow their counsel, and go out of the way of the overwhelming power and save himself from the trap into which he had fallen? With astonishment they saw come over his face an inexplicable expression of cheerfulness. Eugène smiled. " Either I take possession of Belgrade or the Turks take possession of me! " he said. It was madness; he knew that actually he was lost. Looked at from the strategical point of view, three possibilities were open to him.

But they were only possibilities for a desperado. He explained them. In the first place, he could stay in his encampment, stave off the Grand Vizier's attack as best he might, and at the same time continue with the siege and capture Belgrade in full view of the Turkish army. As a second alternative, he could convert the Grand Vizier's attack into a battle, defeat him, force him to a retreat, and take the town unmolested. Finally, he could first attack and defeat the Turks, and thus put an end to the difficult position in which he found himself.

Should he stay quietly in his entrenchments, stand fast and repeat the method which he had so often practised when faced by superior forces ? Would Eugène be able to hold out in that case ? The generals doubted it. The bombardment was so fierce that no part of the encampment was safe. Dysentery had broken out, due to the bad nourishment, and there was a danger that within a very short time the Imperial army would be reduced to half its original numbers. The men were restless—what was Eugène waiting for ?

At last, on the 16th August, 1717, the generals received their battle orders. An offensive ? Yes ! They were content, and studied the points which they were to observe and obey both before and during the action. The instructions were chiefly for the benefit of the officers, who were told to distribute their orders calmly and in cold blood " without noise or impatience," to leave the soldiers time so that they were not confused by undue haste. No one, neither officer nor man, without explicit orders was to depart, even to a hair's breadth, from his appointed post, and no one on pain of death was to plunder or go out after booty. The cavalry were to fire in the last resort only : the infantry, however, because they were everywhere mixed up with the cavalry, were to maintain a constant fire, experience having shown that the Turks were more alarmed by a continuous, uninterrupted fire than by the fierceness of the bombardment. Everywhere the troops were to keep together in the closest formation, and to show blind obedience and trust in Eugène ! Only thus could their purpose be achieved.

Like a motor which feeds a thousand wires with its prodigious forces, Eugène held his troops together. Security and victory were only to be won when no single nerve in his own body refused to function, when the army remained steadfast and every man moved in accordance with his will.

It was midnight. In deep silence, avoiding the slightest sound, the cavalry rode in two wings out on to the open field, and formed a battle line. An hour later, the infantry followed. The night was light and clear. Eugène feared that the march would not long remain unnoticed by the enemy. He thought of retreating. Then, suddenly, a thick fog descended—so thick that he himself could not distinguish anything at a distance of ten paces. Heaven had laid its mantle of invisibility on the army which slowly advanced towards the enemy fortifications.

But the fog made it impossible to keep to the direction that he had ordered. The cavalry of the right wing missed the way, and suddenly fell into one of the newly made Turkish trenches. Rifle fire began. In the Turkish camp, the alarm was given. "Keep together—keep together." Eugène's command was handed on from man to man; the ranks were closed, but the infantry had received the order to keep close to the cavalry, and thus, in marching behind Pallfy's cavalry, they lost their direction also.

In the centre there was an empty space. Then, suddenly, gusts of wind cleared the fog away. Eugène saw the enemy positions and those of his own army. His heart stood still at the sight of the terrible danger! He saw the Turks thickly massed in the centre. Lost! Lost! the thought went through his head. Now they are penetrating our flanks. But the weakness only lasted for a moment. "Forward!" he shouted. The infantry ran rather than walked behind him, and hurled themselves with fury upon the Turks. "Cavalry! Forward! To the attack!"

Eugène surveyed the battlefield. Whence came the firing that was mowing down his infantry? He saw a mound from which eighteen guns were unceasingly firing! "Storm!" he commanded. With flags flying, and drums beating, ten companies of grenadiers, in close formation, together with four battalions, covered on the flank by two cavalry regiments, attacked the battery. Now they had surrounded the mound ! The guns were silenced.

By nine o'clock in the morning, Eugène with his army was able to occupy the stormed heights which commanded the surrounding country. The thunder of his cannons broke forth. The cavalry galloped forward ! The Turks were beaten !

On the 22nd of August, Eugène entered Belgrade.

Now it would have been possible for him to advance further still. Now Eugène could have marched, unmolested, down to the Black Sea ! But then news came from Vienna that the Spanish Government had manned a fleet and were sailing against Italy. While the Emperor was fighting the Turks, Louis XIV's grandson was planning to attack him in the rear ! The Italian possessions would have to be protected. Eugène was ordered to hold an army corps in readiness at once to send to Italy to their protection.

Were they going to hold him back again ? Had they forgotten that he could calculate ? He wrote that His Majesty's dominion in Italy must be in a very bad state if five to six thousand Spaniards could effect its downfall. Eugène knew which way the wind was blowing. This was the work of the Spanish Council, his enemies at Court, who wished to prevent him from gaining fresh victories, and from becoming indispensable.

For the first time he decided to rebel. He would, under no circumstances, permit a single man to be sent to Italy until peace with Turkey was concluded ! The conquest of Hungary, Italy, and the Netherlands seemed to satisfy the House of Habsburg : it did not wish for any more possessions. But these were countries which he had conquered, and which he refused to set at stake. He was determined upon that point.

In Vienna they did not desire a greater German Empire, he knew. They dissipated themselves in small intrigues. No one was in favour of great undertakings ! For thirty years

Eugène had combated Austrian futility, and had fought against it more violently than against any other enemy. As long as he lived, the frontiers confided to his keeping should remain untouched. But—afterwards ?

When the Sultan advanced peace proposals, Eugène agreed to them. He further arranged for the fortifications of Belgrade to be rebuilt " so that the town should not only in words, but in fact—as its geographical position alone was enough to indicate—represent the bulwarks of Christendom."

It was a sacrifice for him. All hope was lost of reaching Constantinople. After this victory, the Turks would nevermore venture to attack the Roman Empire of German nations—never again, as long as he lived ! And in Vienna, now that he had shown his despotism and proved his determination not to subordinate himself to the Emperor's will when it disagreed with the dictates of reason, the Court would never venture to entrust him again with the supreme command of the army. He was feared; and he knew that, had he not become a philosopher, there would have been good reason to fear him.

He took leave of the army, and ordered that the strictest discipline should be observed during the demobilisation. But not even all the commands that were to ensure the maintenance of order and tranquillity could prevent his farewell from giving rise to a whisper in the army, which, becoming louder, rose into song. A melody had arisen. Wearing his plain brown coat, his mask-like face inclined, his dark eyes fixed upon the ground, he rode away. Behind him, a choir of thousands upon thousands of voices rose and swelled ; and for long afterwards the sound of their singing stayed in his ears. A folk-song had been born, and was sung throughout the land. And while Eugène rode slowly from fort to fort, from garrison to garrison, through the territories that he had conquered, back over the whole long road of his campaign, past Zenta towards the plain which came to life before his eyes on that clear September day (over there was the Imperial provision store, the Turkish encampment, and the sandbank in the river from which Starhemberg had decided the issue of the battle) past Petronell, the place where his brother had fallen : while, still with bent head, he drew near Vienna ; the song spreading like wildfire or a wild alarm, had reached and penetrated the town. As he entered the city, women and children, soldiers and officers, all took up the refrain to greet him :

"*Prinz Eugen der edle Ritter* . . ."

CHAPTER III

WHENEVER a gilded coach drawn by Isabella-coloured horses stood before the gates of the Batthyáni palace on the Freyung, a square in the centre of Vienna, the passers-by knew that a card party was in progress in the illuminated reception-rooms, where piquet or l'hombre was being played ; and that Prince Eugène of Savoy was to be found amongst the players. There are very few details known concerning the hostess whose honour it was to count Prince Eugène amongst her daily guests. But the many letters, diplomatic reports, and memoirs in which she is described, or briefly mentioned, provide colour and brushes with which to paint her portrait.

Countess Batthyáni, widow of an officer who had fallen in battle during Eugène's last campaign, was the daughter of the Imperial Minister Strattmann, an official of bourgeois origin who had been recommended to Vienna from Germany, and who had risen high enough during the reign of Leopold to receive the arms and coronet of a count. This influential man had conducted negotiations with the rebellious Hungarians and had married his daughter to a leading Magyar magnate, so as to win his support for the Emperor.

The Countess had inherited her father's ambition, and after his death wished to play a part in politics at the Viennese Court. As she herself could not be the Emperor's favourite, since, besides his beloved wife, he already had a mistress—the wife of his friend, Count Allthan—she became the Countess Allthan's friend. But the friendship was not of long duration. It was not enough for her. She intrigued against the Allthans, and that was equivalent to intriguing against the Spanish Council and circle of friends about Charles VI.

If the Countess Batthyáni wished to find support in this Court war, she would have to acknowledge the man who was the chief object of her enemies' ill-will, namely, the Prince Eugène. Having inherited her father's mentality, she could do so with all her heart. The Prince had always been intimate with the Count von Strattmann, and his daughter, who pursued politics with passionate fervour, had no difficulty in establishing contact with Eugène. A warm friendship arose out of their mutual interests.

Every evening cards were played in her *salons*. Surrounded by her guests, she stood under the shining chandeliers and awaited the illustrious members of the German and Austrian Court party who attended her receptions. A major-domo in the livery of the Batthyánis smote three times with his stick upon the parquet and called out the historic names of those who entered the *salon*. Then the Liechtensteins arrived, the Windischgrätz, the Coloredos, the Lodrons, and the Auerspergs, and stood in the room in watchful groups to converse. They all seemed to be waiting for some further event before sitting down to play. At last the major-domo announced : " His Highness the Prince of Savoy ! "

With his hollow, death-like features unmoved under the vast wig, Eugène, bending slightly forward, entered the room with quick steps. The picture before his eyes reminded him of the most cherished scene of his childhood. The Countess stood and received him, as his mother had received Louis XIV in the Palais Soissons. The similarity in character of the Countess Batthyáni and Olympia attracted Eugène to her. She was not merely an elegant Court doll like the others, who only thought about clothes, the chase, and Court ceremonial. For the first time since his mother's death Eugène had the opportunity of discussing his plans with a woman whom he admired, of offering his schemes for criticism to a subtle feminine understanding, and apparently, also, of learning in an unobtrusive manner everything that went on at Court. Often when he sat with her at the card-table, for the space of half an hour no card would be played ; instead, in an inaudible voice the Countess told the Prince what, for

WE

instance, the Lord Chancellor of Bohemia, Leopold Schlick, Eugène's notorious enemy, had said to the Emperor about Eugène; how the Allthans had preened themselves on hearing it, and how the Count Allthan had said openly that he could not tolerate anyone higher in rank than himself at Court. "He is the Emperor's favourite," said the Countess, "because his wife is his mistress!" For instance—as St. Saphorin himself wrote to London—Count Allthan had caused Count Daun to be recalled from his governorship of Naples solely because Eugène had protected him; he wanted to demonstrate that his influence was greater than Eugène's. That the Prince had taken no notice of his action drove Count Allthan to desperation. He longed to meet Eugène and to insult him openly, so as to force him out of his undisturbed calm into a quarrel which should be his downfall—since the Allthans were indispensable to the Emperor! Eugène had often occasion to remember something that Villars had said to him in Rastatt: "We two are friends. Our enemies are: mine in Paris and yours in Vienna!"

While the populace, even at that time, created a myth around the figure of Prince Eugène and wrote poems about his battles, extolling him as the genius of his age, in the Emperor's private apartments more and more voices were raised in protest against his manner of government of the Spanish Netherlands and against his decrees in the War Council. The Emperor himself was already worked up to the point of being ungracious to him openly. He said nothing to Eugène to his face: but, for instance, when he saw him snuffing tobacco, he said aloud that the tobacco habit was a repulsive one. Charles VI himself bespoke all political questions with the Countess Allthan; but he said openly, in order that amongst the listeners there might be one who would report it to Eugène, that he would gladly dispense with the Prince's counsel, all the more willingly as he was convinced that they did not originate in Eugène's own brain! He, the

Emperor of the Holy Roman Empire of German nations, King of Spain, and so forth, felt himself in no wise under an obligation to govern his Empire according to the wishes of a Countess Batthyáni ! London demanded further information concerning this speech, which became generally known, and St. Saphorin reported that : " Prince Eugène's influence is dwindling from day to day. The Emperor has been successfully persuaded that the Prince's attitude is determined for him either by the Countess Batthyáni herself or by her advisers."

There were many like reports, the worst being that of Count Bonneval, who recounted in his memoirs that : " Since the Hungarian war, he [Prince Eugène] has become entangled with a woman, the wife of a cavalry captain." Bonneval did not appraise the Countess in a kindly fashion, although he was said to have fancied the voluptuous type. " A large bosom is the only pleasing quality about her," he wrote. " She was no longer young, ugly rather than handsome, but she had a great deal of intelligence, and understanding of the ways and weaknesses of men and of how to lead them without their being aware of the fact. He [Prince Eugène] was often in her company in a castle in the neighbourhood of Vienna which he possessed : here he spent the greater part of his free time. . . . It was obvious that this woman had possessed herself of his personality, that she dominated him, and shared most of his cares. Every manner of thing happened to incur general disapproval."

All those initiated in the Court intrigues wondered how Eugène managed to administer his duties as President of the War Council as though nothing threatened him, and how he continued to govern the Netherlands through his representative, the devoted Marquis de Prié. All the while he was being maliciously criticised he declared undisturbedly : " I hope that everyone will recognise that the object of all my efforts is to fulfil my public duties to the general well-being." At the Court of Vienna the ministers attacked one another on every occasion, each one trying to undo the measures of the other. But Eugène did not seem to notice this. Or was it that he wished to educate the Imperial Ministers by this roundabout method ? He wrote to Prié : " One must endeavour to rule in peace and quietness ; nothing advances the public service so much as harmony and the mutual assistance of Ministers as heads of the administration, and their inferiors."

Every one of these statements and every exchange of letters between Eugène and Prié was known to the Court. Eugène's coolness and calm increased his opponent's discomfort. Was he *quite* unaware of what was being prepared for him ? Was he too superior to take any account of it ? Was he so proud that he looked upon them all as too insignificant for their pricks to harm him ? Or was he already too old to fight any more ? None of these assumptions was the right one. Eugène's enemies forgot that they had to do with a strategist of the grand style, with the man who had worn out Vendôme in the swamps of the Po basin, and who, in spite of the weak support at his disposal, had been strong enough to defeat the strongest armies ! Just as Eugène had received reports through spies and agents on every military action of his late enemies, so he now received news of all the intriguers' schemes which were aimed at him. He let the chase continue, knowing that it was in his power to destroy the miserable hunters at one blow. To be sure, apart from his feeling of superior power, the thought influenced him of how pleasant it might be perhaps if his enemies were to bring him low, and he were to be deprived of office. Then at last, as an old man he could live for pleasure in the warmth of the Countess' friendship, give himself up to study, surrounded by the manifestations of wealth in the peace of his country estates. He expressed the thought in the remark : " With an income of ten thousand gulden, I can live in peace to the end of my days ; and my supply of books is sufficient for me not to be bored."

He would have laid down his arms and have submitted himself, smiling, either to favour or to disgrace, if he had not been withheld from doing so by two incentives : the ambition of the Countess Batthyáni, and, at weak moments, the breach in the harmonious spirit of his own life's wisdom, created by his own ambition. He aspired to nothing for himself: he was beyond that. A man who could declare that his own philosophy of life did not permit of his wearing a crown or filling the rôle of a sovereign had no ambition for himself! His ambition was idealistic, abstracted from his ego. As a statesman, he felt so much at one with the German Empire, which in its final manifestation he considered to be a new creation of his own mind, that he did not wish to retire from his appointments and leave the Empire in the incapable hands of Charles VI and his Ministers.

The problem that chiefly occupied the attention of the Court of Vienna was that of the succession, after the death of the Emperor. His wife had borne him daughters only, and his predecessor, Joseph, had also left a daughter. Which of these girls, Joseph's or Charles's eldest daughter, was to inherit the Habsburg lands after the death of Charles? In order to decide this question during his lifetime, Charles made a family statute, which is known by the name of the Pragmatic Sanction. It was to be acknowledged by the German Princes and by the other Powers, and was to guarantee the succession of Maria Theresa, Charles VI's eldest daughter. The decree was opposed by the majority of the Powers, whose opposition was partly serious, and partly a manœuvre intended to force the Emperor to offer counter-concessions in return for a declaration of agreement. Envoys extraordinary rode through the whole of Europe, from Court to Court, haggling and bargaining. When Eugène was asked by the Emperor as to what measures he should take in order to carry through his decree of succession and establish it firmly, the Prince advised him not to negotiate so much, but rather to provide his daughter with a well-filled exchequer and a well-equipped army. Then he would be able to dispense with the promises of the individual Powers, which, in any case, would not be kept!

The Emperor took this cool, commonsense advice amiss: the relations between him and Eugène had become insupportable. Then it happened that Victor Amadeus, Eugène's cousin, bethought himself of making use of this juncture in affairs. Was not this a crisis in the world which might be turned to advantage? Was not this the longed-for opportunity of winning Milan for Savoy? Victor Amadeus declared his agreement with the Emperor's plans : he would acknowledge the Pragmatic Sanction, and, in order to set the seal on his acknowledgment, he begged the hand in marriage of the Emperor's niece, a daughter of the late Joseph, for his eldest son. He wished to ally himself with the illustrious Habsburg family! The Emperor, to whom nothing seemed more important than winning such a mighty supporter for the maintenance of his decree of succession, was in favour of the plan with his whole heart and soul. But Eugène advised against it ; he swore to Charles that Victor Amadeus was not to be trusted. He explained that the marriage had been proposed solely for the purpose of having, later on, a pretext for a claim on Italian territory. When Charles was dead, then the King of Sardinia would be the first to support the annulment of the Pragmatic Sanction, and would make the marriage of his son with Joseph's daughter a pretext for possessing himself of Milan. Eugène advised against the proposal? In spite of—or, rather, just because of—his opposition, Charles was determined to fulfil Victor Amadeus's wish.

Count Allthan's brother-in-law, Count Nimptsch, was agent to the ruler of Savoy. He was a frivolous young man, with a love of good living, who had taken up politics merely in order to satisfy his desire for the life of a *grand seigneur*. Eugène was aware of this. One morning Nimptsch awoke without having been called by his servant. The man had disappeared, and the secret letters which Nimptsch had received from Victor Amadeus were missing out of the secret drawer of his writing-table. On that same morning, Count Allthan, Master of the Horse, was compelled to announce Prince Eugène for an audience with the Emperor, and had to yield him precedence. He expected to be present during the audience ; but Eugène said briefly that he wished to speak to the Emperor alone. The Count remained at the door. He heard voices raised in excitement. Had the reserved Prince lost his self-control at last ? Was he quarrelling with the Emperor ? Allthan leaned upon the door to listen, and assured himself with satisfaction that they really were quarrelling.

In Charles's private cabinet, Eugène announced, in raised tones, his intention of resigning his position. He resigned from the posts of Governor-General of the Netherlands, and President of the War Council, as Field Marshal and Lieutenant-General of the Holy Roman Empire. He refused to serve an Emperor who permitted him to be slandered after he had brought the Empire out of a condition of dire need to its highest state of development. He had won thirty-five battles for the House of Habsburg. He renounced his salary ; his personal feeling of self-righteousness was sufficient for him for the rest of his life. He would leave Austria ; but he would summon the whole of Europe to judge of the mortification that he would be forced to undergo, if the Emperor left unpunished those who had insulted the Prince of Savoy !

All was now quiet in the Emperor's private cabinet : Count Allthan heard no more. Had Eugène really spoken of slander ? The Count no longer felt comfortable. The letters which were missing from Count Nimptsch's writing-table lay before Charles VI. The Emperor read them. Was he suffering from a delusion ? he wondered. There before him, in black and white, was what Allthan and Nimptsch had told him about Eugène. Was the whole thing a concoction, planned to bring about Eugène's downfall ? The Emperor read on very carefully. So Victor Amadeus had instructed them to say all that about Eugène ? Nimptsch was to bring to the notice of the Emperor the fact that Eugène was opposed to the marriage of Joseph's daughter with the son of the King of Sardinia, because the Prince wished to marry her to the Crown Prince of Bavaria. Eugène, the letter went on to say, was well aware of the Austrian nobility's favourable attitude to the Electoral House, and with Bavaria's help he planned to dictate laws to the Emperor. Was none of it true ? Charles wondered. He read it once again.

Eugène had warned him against Victor Amadeus, and now he was shown to have been right; the King of Sardinia was bribing his best friends even—Nimptsch and Allthan——

Eugène saw the Emperor's altered attitude, and saw how Charles was searching for words by which to bring about a reconciliation between them. Should he refuse the reconciliation and become a homeless old man—lose his intimate friend, the Countess Batthyáni—be deprived of his beloved home, the Belvedere with all its art treasures, the palace in the Himmelpfortegasse—and renounce all his political plans? The Emperor held out his hand to Eugène, and asked whom he should punish. Eugène expressed no wishes. The Emperor asked whether the House of Habsburg and the Empire could still count on his services. Eugène saw the sad eyes fixed upon him—like Leopold's, he thought. In a hard, dry voice Eugène stated that he would not resign so long as he could rely on being unmolested in the performance of his duties to the Emperor and to the Empire! Charles sprang up and embraced him. He hoped, he said, that he and Eugène would remain the old friends that they had been in earlier days.

On the same day Count Nimptsch was arrested.

The Emperor kept his promises. After that agitated audience, Eugène was restored to favour. His influence in all affairs of State rose so rapidly that soon, from every standpoint, he occupied the post of Prime Minister. The Emperor discussed nothing of the slightest import with the Ministers of portfolio until Eugène was initiated in the matter. Gradually the most secret correspondence went through his hands, and foreign Governments consulted him unofficially before they presented their wishes or grievances to the Court.

The work increased. Every day Eugène sat in his conference chamber and received diplomats and generals, besides the secretaries of the War Council and of the Council of Secret Service, to whom he dictated schemes for State treaties which were afterwards sanctioned in the Emperor's private cabinet. He was so busy that he had to arrange for an exact division of his time. It was difficult for him. He tried to work out a system that would fit his many-sided work into the framework of his days. " Regularity," he decided, " is the secret of all achievement. One only needs to neglect it for a very short time, in order to lose it for ever. The best method of despatching business is to deal with the items in the order in which they come. This method makes for a quiet spirit and a contented world."

In spite of his strict adherence to routine, Eugène could not surmount the whole of his work. Besides the affairs of the Court, the Government of the Netherlands, which he administered through his representative, the Marquis de Prié, gave him more and more to do. As is the case after all great wars and upheavals, an age of innovation had set in. One who contributed much to the change was the Scotsman, John Law, who, in Paris—and, by a curious coincidence, in the Palais Soissons itself—founded the first bank to issue notes for circulation. The basis of this undertaking, which issued shares for the first time, was the territories in the New World, on the Mississippi, which were to be exploited. The well-known financial crash which resulted from the experiment known as Law's bank-note swindle is well known to everybody. The effects of this adventurous example extended beyond Law's lawsuits. In every corner of the Netherlands promoters appeared, who endeavoured to extract capital from this *fata Morgana* of distant lands. The Imperial generals who were stationed in Brussels, and heard accounts of the riches which their comrades in France had gained as the result of their speculations, stormed Eugène for permission to undertake similar enterprises. Eugène replied very briefly that : " It is enough for someone to appear as a promoter for me to lose my good opinion of him. For, in most cases, I have found very little worth and sincerity in people who concern themselves with such things." His system was one of solidity, and in the place of wild speculation he advocated deliberately weighed possibilities. He was a political economist who never lost sight of foreign policy. Certainly the age demanded economic innovations, he agreed; but he would only approve of those which were honourable and were for the benefit of the whole people rather than for the benefit of individual speculators, and which did not tend to increase mutual envy and competition between neighbouring countries.

Only when the Dutch captured, by force, ships belonging to private owners, despatched from the Imperial Netherlands to the East Indies, did Eugène agree to the foundation of a State trading company. He founded his agreement on general economic opinions which prove his startling comprehension of economic questions. The East Indian Company was founded. Eugène himself subscribed for sixty thousand guldens' worth of shares, the entire nobility followed his example, and the enterprise flourished. Eugène was, however, quite convinced that this prosperity was only transient. The two interested sea Powers, England and Holland, feared the keen competition of the Austrian Netherlands, and demanded, in return for their agreement to the Pragmatic Sanction, that the Emperor renounce the Netherland sea trade and dissolve the East India Company. When Charles VI refused to do so, they joined with Spain and declared that, if Spain were to stand on their side against the Emperor, they would assist her to recapture her earlier possessions in Italy. This meant a world alliance against Austria, and a covenant of which the members were neighbours of the Empire—for Hanover belonged to the King of England, and Prussia was allied with him! The Emperor's difficult situation was relieved by the ambition of the Queen of Spain. Elisabeth Farnese, Philip V's second wife, wanted to marry her own two sons—the youngest sons of Philip V— to the Emperor's daughters. In Madrid, the Queen alone was influential. She would force Spain solemnly to guarantee the Pragmatic Sanction, if the Emperor would give his consent to the double marriage. Charles did so at once. He did not consider his eldest daughter, Maria Theresa, who, according to the new dynastic law, was to inherit all the States of the House of Habsburg, as an indivisible whole :

he only thought of his younger daughters, and, by his agreement to the marriages, won the alliance with Spain.

Here was another complicated situation which had arisen in the world without; and still there was no united Germany under Habsburg rule to deal with the chaotic state of affairs. To gain the support of Prussia—to be in agreement with Prussia—that was Eugène's credo. Prussia must secede from England ! At first he had a difficult task. The first Prussian King, Frederick William, had been influenced against Eugène, both by false reports and by a former partisan of the Count Rakoczy's. These attempts at slander went so far that it was even whispered to the King that the Prince planned to kidnap him, either during a journey or at the chase, and have him imprisoned in Vienna ! The slander-conspiracy was brought to light; but, in spite of this, Frederick was still inclined to believe in the possibility of a planned piece of bravura on Eugène's part. He wrote to him that he was anxious to unearth the truth, but between the lines of his letter mistrust showed itself. The Prussian Field Marshal, Count Flemming, brought the letter to Vienna. He was received by Eugène in the great conference hall of the Belvedere. The magnificence of the room made an impression on the Field Marshal. But just its vast dimensions made such a violent contrast with Eugène's insignificant appearance. *This* little man was said to be the great man of his age ? Was this feeble-looking creature the boldest cavalry officer of his time ? Flemming looked at the Prince with unconcealed irony. It would be impossible to put Eugène beside the tall fellows in his monarch's service, he thought ! He smiled self-confidently. Then—suddenly—Frederick William's letter was thrown violently on to the table that stood in the middle of the room ! Eugène had turned round and made as though to leave the room without a word of farewell. Then he pulled himself together. Flemming saw the small, keen eyes directed upon him : the mask-like face was turned towards him. The voice, which, during the greetings, had been smooth and flattering, was now dry and hard. Eugène spoke in staccato tones. " It is true that I am no monarch," he said, " but I stand second to no one in the possession of a keen sense of honour. I am not the man who would do otherwise than march against Prussia at the head of an army and at the Emperor's command."

Involuntarily, Flemming drew his heels together in a salute.

Eugène's answer had effected the execution of the slanderers in Prussia. Flemming had made a true report of his interview, and at once the good relations between his King and Eugène were re-established. Frederick even invited him to Berlin. But, even at the time of the slander, the report had spread in Prussia that Eugène thought more of the destiny of the Holy Roman Empire than any other statesman of his time, and had encouraged a closer relationship between Austria and Prussia. " The alliance between Austria and Brandenburg must be concluded for all time, with the conditions that neither party is to break it off separately." That was an expression of opinion which pleased Frederick William. If Austria were to maintain a state of constant peace, then Prussia would have time and opportunity to develop ! And then ! Then—it would remain to be seen—— !

Personally, Eugène was not in sympathy with Frederick William, least of all with the personal aspect of his life. The private life of the Prussian King repelled him. It differed from his own chiefly in that Frederick William led a coarse life, and, above all, enjoyed collecting his smoking confederacy together for coarse drinking-bouts, while Eugène himself, with his increasing wealth, was ever refining and spiritualising his existence. Nevertheless, in politics, personal antipathies and sympathies should not be allowed to count ! Eugène found, amongst his officers, a suitable man to send to Berlin—Count Seckendorff. He sent him as ambassador to Frederick William's Court, and through him gained more influence than any statesman had ever achieved by means of an ambassador. Seckendorff sympathised with the King, and yet remained true to the Imperial Crown and to Eugène. He was truly enthusiastic when Frederick William paraded his tall fellows; he applauded and cheered, and missed none of the military parades and manœuvres which filled the King's days. Eugène was not in sympathy with these military games, and always criticised them unfavourably in his letters. But, in spite of his personal aversion for the Prussian King, he succeeded in gaining Frederick's support for Austria. " His Majesty's confidence in Your Highness is so great," Seckendorff was soon able to report, " that, in comparison with Your Highness, he despises all his other friends and enemies." And another time : " One word from Your Highness meets with greater belief on the part of the King than the most violent representations of the evil-minded." Whenever a quarrel arose between Frederick William and his son, afterwards Frederick the Great, Count Seckendorff intervened on behalf of the Emperor—but really on behalf of Prince Eugène. Eugène wanted to secure feelings of gratitude towards the House of Habsburg, on the part of the young man, for the benefit of its future sovereign, Maria Theresa. Surely that must follow, if Frederick had every reason for gratitude towards Charles, her father. His favourable opinion must be won, even if he were to request an alliance with the hostile combination of England and Hanover by wishing to marry the English Princess. Such a marriage must be prevented without Frederick's becoming aware that Eugène was frustrating it ! Prussia must be allied with Austria, and not with Hanover. The intrigue was successful. Frederick William forbade the marriage of his son with the English Princess. Would it be a good move to marry Frederick to Maria Theresa ? he wondered. The plan was considered and weighed. The Crown Prince got wind of it, and at once wrote to Lieutenant-General Grumbow to say that he was ready, if the King wished it, to enter into a family relationship with the House of Habsburg through a marriage with the Archduchess Maria Theresa. With the flair of genius, Frederick foresaw all the objections and declared with the manner of an experienced diplomat that, as it was to be expected that a union of the Austrian and Prussian hereditary dominions under a single ruler would endanger the European Balance of Power, and would call forth the jealousy, or rather the open resistance, of all the foreign States, if the marriage were to come to pass, and he were to be guaranteed a suitable sustenance during the lifetime of the Emperor, he would renounce the throne of Prussia in favour of his brother !

Eugène had observed for some time the affectations of the hypocritical young man and saw through his plan : " To gain the Habsburg dominions by marriage and the Prussian by force ! " He did not trust Frederick, and, when the Prince's suggestion was brought to him, he said prophetically : " Just as by means of this proposal it can be seen that the Prince is not to be trusted, so also can the width and comprehensiveness of his ideas be perceived ! However immature and transient they may be in themselves, yet they show that he lacks neither energy nor understanding. And, therefore, the more dangerous he will prove for his neighbours if he is not to be moved from his present principles of conduct."

Eugène refused Frederick's suggestion. He was to be allowed to marry neither an Austrian nor an English Princess ? That fox Frederick saw himself caught in his own trap. But his time would come ! It was suggested that he should marry a Princess of Braunschweig-Bevern, the daughter of a friend of Eugène's ? He acted as though he approved of the plan, married—and only denounced his bride's lack of taste in clothes.

Politics know no truce. Every day brought new reports and news of fresh events, which forced Eugène to take up an attitude towards world affairs. He did so calmly, with a superior enlightened understanding. The philosophy with which in the last years of his life he examined the political conditions of the world was of value beyond his own time. His human wisdom is most clearly expressed in a few lines out of a letter written to his friend-enemy Villars, with whom he still corresponded. " As regards the general position," he wrote, " now, as at all times, it is concerned with many plans, great schemes, and secret machinations, which are there for the purpose of disturbing the public peace and of destroying the happiness which Europe could so easily enjoy if only people would not take pleasure in preventing it ! "

Yes ! Without politics the world would be a wonderful place ! The old man Eugène felt this more and more every day as he walked through the rooms of his palaces. He loved the winter in his palace in the Himmelpfortegasse, amongst his books and friends, and with, every evening, his game of cards at Countess Batthyáni's palace on the Freyung. In the spring, the gardens of the Belvedere blossomed, and from the windows of his bedroom Eugène could look out over the town to the Kahlenberg in the background. He enjoyed the summer in Schlosshof, the new property, not far from Vienna, which he had bought and altered to his taste. It was only a half-day's journey out there, with good horses, and the roads were so even that he could be driven without any jolting through the countryside. He would not admit it to himself, but he needed a constant change of place. Was it that he had never lost the sense of homelessness ? He did not attempt to account for it. He journeyed from one castle to another, staying in none of them for any length of time, despite the fact that every room in his palaces was furnished in the most luxurious manner possible. No reigning Prince outside France—not even the Emperor himself—possessed such magnificently furnished and decorated palaces as Eugène. All the walls were draped in gold and silver brocade, ornaments and pictures adorned the *salons*, the ante-chambers were of gleaming marble, and the floors laid with exquisite taste. All his palaces were surrounded by gardens, reminiscent of the parks in Paris, and orangeries, pavilions, and statues ornamented the avenues. His menagerie was the largest, his conservatories the finest, in Austria. From the ironwork in the gardens to the window pediments, every detail was artistically carried out. For Eugène, luxury was a necessity.

Old age overtook him with rapid strides; he had very little leisure. But, whenever the hours were not taken up by the dictation of writings of military and diplomatic purport or by interviews with generals, politicians, and the ambassadors of the countless German States with which he was in constant negotiation, Eugène buried himself in literature, added to his collection of copper engravings and to his picture gallery, and devoted himself to beautifying his palaces. In Paris, Mariette had to superintend the manufacture of fire-dogs and fire-screens of gilded bronze, and to choose the marble for each individual fireplace. There were fireplaces even in the summer palace of Schlosshof; for Eugène was an old man now, and began to feel cold, even in the summer; so that, behind the finely arched framework of red, black, or yellow marble, a fire had to be kept perpetually burning. All the living- and reception-rooms were hung with Venetian mirrors, for, although Eugène had no desire to see his own reflection, yet, in whichever room he sat, tired, and tormented by incessant fits of coughing, he liked to see reflected in the mirrors the whole room, with the beauty which he had gathered around him! The man who, during his lifetime hitherto, had never spared himself, now wished to pamper his eyes. He was hungry for beauty; but only for beauty in his surroundings. This old man, who was almost a spendthrift when it was a question of satisfying his need of luxury, spent nothing at all either on himself or on his clothes! Baron Pöllnitz, who knew him personally, recounts in his memoirs that " Prince Eugène was generous and luxury-loving in everything but in his clothes!"

The years passed set in the mosaic of the marvellous surroundings which Eugène had created for himself. He would have liked to travel; but he was too old and frail. He longed for the wide world. He collected engravings, views of towns, and maps; all the works of art in the world which he was unable to see in the original were reproduced for him by the engraver's needle. He was chained to one

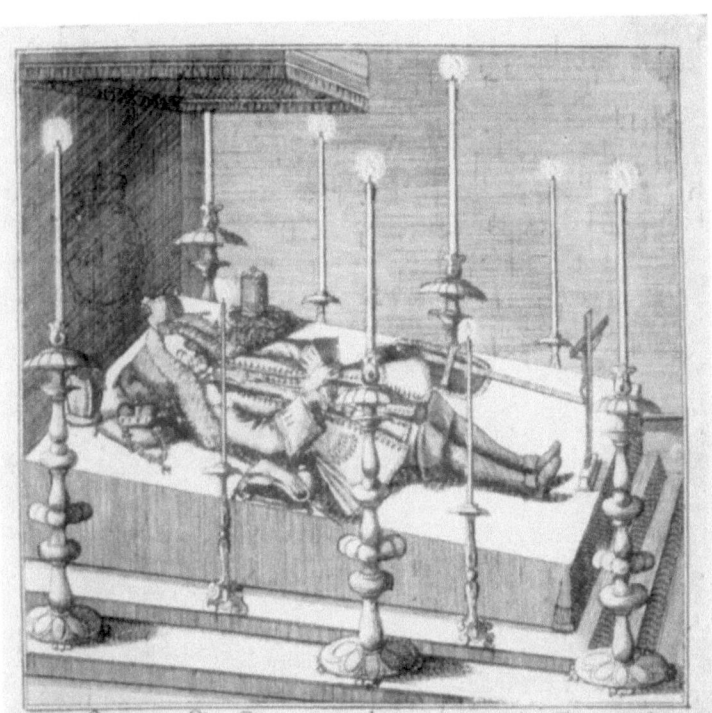

PRINCE EUGÈNE LYING IN STATE

place; but, when he visited his menagerie, he was able to realise in imagination the size of the earth. He studied the countries whence came all the animals that he possessed: the lions, golden eagles, monkeys, Angora goats, and the birds of every colour from all parts of the world. In the small room in which he lived, limited by the radius of a day's journey, he experienced the whole world. A wide circle of men in all parts of Europe supplied him with books, besides which, he received historical records, contemporary chronicles, and critical writings which paid tribute to himself. But, whenever such works were dedicated to him, he refused the dedication. Every exaggeration was painful to him. " Because you praised my person to a degree which I have in nowise earned, I could gain no satisfaction from the publication of the poem," he said on one occasion when the poet Curini read a poem of praise aloud to him. " I hope that you will make use of other opportunities of proving your talent! " Eugène had no faith in the objectivity of his contemporaries. He was mistrustful, and warned the poet Rousseau against becoming a historian. " It is far more difficult to write history than it is to write poetry," he said, " for, when one wishes to write the history of past epochs, it is only with the greatest difficulty that one obtains the material with which to complete the task satisfactorily; and when one tries to write contemporary history, then it is difficult to satisfy the whole world at once. One should say neither too much nor too little about any one subject, and that is a most difficult task when one is writing about living persons." Eugène feared neither contemporary criticism nor the chronicles of history; but, the older he became, the more fiercely he fought for truth and for that objective opinion in the light of which he himself wished to be described. He was seen more and more seldom in Vienna, and no longer either on foot or on horseback. He drove through the streets in his coach, and the populace acclaimed him; but he never went to Court now, except for the Golden Fleece celebrations, when he appeared in the full dress of a Knight of the Order. He preferred society in a small intimate circle to the life at Court, and did not even attend the larger receptions at the Batthyáni palace, but appeared only at the small card-parties.

The friendship between the old man and the still youthful woman continued, having outlasted both the intrigues which attempted to separate the couple and the exchange of political differences. It was the friendship of a man for the woman in whom he believed to have rediscovered the beloved mother. Eugène's relationship with the Batthyáni was the return to the mother.

Eugène was over seventy years of age when he was forced to lead an army, for the last time, into the battlefield. He did so unwillingly, for, in spite of his warnings, the military machine, having been neglected, was in a bad state of repair, and in any case only a small contingent was equipped. The pretext for the war was the death of the Elector of Saxony, who was at the same time King of Poland. The successor to the great Louis, his great-grandson, Louis XV, who was married to the daughter of Stanislaus Lesczynski, the former King of Poland, wished to restore his father-in-law to the Royal dignity, while the Emperor had concluded a pact with the new Elector of Saxony, whereby the Elector was to acknowledge the Pragmatic Sanction in return for the Emperor's support of his candidature for the Polish Throne. Russia had lent her support to the agreement. Eugène was invited by the Emperor to express his opinion on the political situation. In a memorandum, which, by its lucidity, reflects the illuminating quality of the Prince's statesmanship, Eugène raised two leading questions. Firstly, whether the interests of the House of Habsburg were such as to justify its concerning itself in Polish affairs ; and, secondly, whether the Emperor ought to oppose the conquest of Lorraine. The last question was relevant, in view of the death of the Duke of Lorraine, both of whose sons had been brought up at the Viennese Court. Franz of Lorraine was even looked upon as the future husband of Maria Theresa, the Emperor's heiress. Louis XV laid claim to the Duchy of Lorraine.

Ought Poland to fall into the hands of the French Stanislaus? Should Lorraine be left to be seized and occupied by France? Eugène replied to both questions in the negative. The Emperor would have to defend himself! This memorandum decided the war. Supported by an Imperial army corps, the Elector of Saxony was able to crown himself Augustus III of Poland. That was a success, but then both Spain and Sardinia took sides with France on behalf of Stanislaus and declared war on the Emperor!

It was now too late to mend the situation. There was war in the south, in Naples, and in Sicily—where the Spaniards conquered—and in the Po basin, where the united armies of France and Savoy captured Milan, and where Austria lost all her conquered territory with the exception of Mantua! Was Eugène's life work to be destroyed? Had all his efforts been in vain? He felt old; he could not do anything to help, for he must hurry to the north as quickly as possible. On the right bank of the Rhine, he found himself faced with superior enemy forces, and was unable to venture upon an offensive. How could he attack with an army of twenty-five thousand men against one hundred thousand Frenchmen? Of what use was it that the soldiers acclaimed him? He saw amongst them his veterans of Zenta, of Höchstädt, of Belgrade. He saluted them, knowing that all their efforts and courage would be in vain. Their Prince Eugène would never again lead them to victory! By means of judicious marches and well-chosen positions, he managed to hold the enemy in check; but to win a victory was impossible! During the weary, tedious operations on the battlefields, the Crown Prince of Prussia, later Frederick the Great, accompanied him. Eugène was not victorious, but the young man, with clear perception, declared that the shadow of the great Eugène, by his last campaign on the Rhine, had presented the world with a masterpiece out of the *haute école* of strategy.

Tired and thoroughly ill, Eugène returned to Vienna. After his return from the army, he altered his daily régime entirely. He pleaded his age as an excuse not to appear at Court—not even for the Golden Fleece celebrations. He drove out only to visit the Countess Batthyáni. There is a legend which says that his Isabella-coloured horses used to find their own way every evening from the Himmelpfortegasse to the Freyung. For a long time, no one descended from the coach, for the old man Eugène, his coachman, the Haiduck, and the footman—the total of whose ages counted over three hundred and ten years—all slept on peacefully, although the coach had been stationary for some time !

When Eugène's counsel was absolutely necessary, then the sessions were held in one or other of his palaces ; but he no longer pursued politics with any pleasure. He lived to see the Pragmatic Sanction guaranteed by nearly all the European Powers, the marriage of Maria Theresa to Franz of Lorraine, and the peace with France, which he had advised the Emperor to conclude despite all his losses. Austria had a part of Italy restored to her. So, after all, not all that Eugène had conquered was lost ! His life had not been useless ! He received a letter from the new Grand Vizier assuring him that the Porte was determined to maintain the peace which the Prince had concluded with Turkey eighteen years before. Eugène had given peace to Europe, but, for himself, he longed for the peace of another world.

" Health and good humour," he wrote in the first week of April 1736, " constitute together the greatest human happiness. My friends are fairly satisfied with my humour, for I set peace of mind above bodily health in value."

On the 20th April, a secret conference took place at Eugène's house. Some questions still remained to be discussed when he broke up the session, with the words : " That is enough for to-day. To-morrow, if I live as long, we will continue ! " At mid-day he had guests in his palace in the Himmelpfortegasse, and in the evening he drove, as usual, to his card-party at the Countess Batthyáni's. But he talked less than usual, and breathed with greater difficulty. The Countess begged him to take some physic. " There will be time enough for that to-morrow," he said, and drove home. He went at once to bed, leaving an order that he was not to be awakened before nine o'clock on the following morning. As his servant entered the bedroom at the appointed hour, he found his master lying motionless, and thought he was still sleeping. But when he returned at ten o'clock he saw that the Prince was dead.

The exact hour of Eugène's death was never determined.

CONCLUSION AND BIBLIOGRAPHY

PRINCESS ANNA VICTORIA, the daughter of Eugène's eldest brother and his only surviving niece, was his sole heiress. This elderly old maid found two hundred thousand gulden in cash, and as much again in the bank, awaiting her; but to Prince Frederick von Sachsen-Hildburghausen, who had become engaged to her directly after the announcement of her inheritance, this sum did not seem large enough to compensate for her revolting ugliness and cantankerous humour. When, however, he had once made up his mind to shoulder this unpleasing burden, he determined to indemnify himself by all the riches.

The entire fortune left by Eugène was valued at eight hundred and seventy thousand gulden. Some idea of the purchasing power of money at that time can be gained by taking the fact into consideration that the Belvedere with its menagerie, orangery, and gardens was valued at one hundred thousand gulden only! Prince von Sachsen-Hildburghausen had achieved something—he had made a good match! His wife Anna Victoria sold everything—the palaces, the country estates, the art treasures, even the library! She was burdened by no sentiment. All that she wished to keep in remembrance of her uncle was expressed in the form of cash! She kept nothing personal that had belonged to him. That which she failed to realise in so much coin, she squandered with such openly demonstrated impiety that all Vienna was roused to indignation, and a slanderous piece of verse was attached to the gate of the palace on the Himmelpfortegasse:

> *Est-il possible que du Prince Eugène, la gloire*
> *Soit ternie par une si vilaine Victoire ?*

But the ugly Princess Victoria cared nothing for public opinion. She was likewise quite indifferent to the fate of Prince Eugène's private documents, his personal correspondence, and his notes and autobiographical writings, which, if certain references can be relied upon, he had, in all probability left behind him. There would exist to-day very few writings from his own hand, and very few letters and documents to prove his history, if most of the writings concerning Eugène's public activities had not been preserved in the family archives of persons who had stood in any kind of relationship to him ; and, above all, preserved throughout the centuries by conscientious recorders in the State collections of records. The whole comprises a vast amount of material concerning diplomacy and the science of war. In the present work, the author has only used as much of this material as he has deemed necessary for the portrayal of Eugène, the man—and his epoch. Those persons who came into personal contact with Eugène have described the meeting either in letters or memoirs, and such notes, intended either for private use or for publication, complete the material of the archives.

With a few exceptions, the passages quoted from Eugène and from his contemporaries have been translated into modern phraseology in order to render the understanding of them easier in a work of this kind.

In the following Bibliography, only the more accessible sources are listed. They will serve as works of reference to the reader who is interested either in the various representations of Eugène which have been published up to the present day, or in the details of particular historical events.

Vienna, *February 1933*.   P. F.

A r n e t h : Prinz Eugen von Savoyen, Druck und Verlag der typographisch-literarisch-artistischen Anstalt, Wien 1858.
A r n e t h : Das Leben des kaiserlichen Feldmarschalls Graf Guido von Starhemberg, Carl Gerold und Sohn, Wien 1853.
A r t a n v i l l e : Mémoires pour servir l'histoire du Prince Eugène.
B a n c a l a r i : Prinz Eugen, Dieter, Salzburg 1898.
B e c k : Prinz Eugen von Savoyen, Konegen, Wien 1907.
B e k e r : Prinz Eugen als Förderer von Kunst und Wissenschaften, Kathol. Lehrerseminar, Wien 1902.
B e l g i j o s o : Histoire de la maison de Savoye, 1869.
B e r g m a n n : Leibniz in Wien, K. K. Hof- und Staatsdruckerei, Wien.
B i o g r a p h i e n berühmter Staatsmänner in Frankreich, Hof 1797.
B ö h m : Sammlung der hinterlassenen politischen Schriften Eugens, Herdersche Verlagsbuchhandlung, Freiburg im Breisgau 1900.

Bonneval, Memoires du Comte de —, Chapell et Renaud, Paris 1806.
Brechler: Die Büchersammlung des Freiherrn v. Hohendorf, Generaladjutanten des Prinzen Eugen.
Burnet: Histoire de ce qui c'est passé de plus mémorable en Angleterre, 1735.

Carutti, Domenico: Il cavaliere di Savoya e la gioventù del principe Eugenio.
Chelmecki: König Johann Sobieski, Braumüller, Wien 1883.
Chernel: Histoire de France pendant la minorité de Louis XIV, 1879/80.
Choisy, Abbé: Mémoires (ed. Lescure, Paris 1888).
Claretta, Gaudenzio: Le relazioni politiche e dinastiche dei principi di Savoja coi margravi di Baden.
Coxe: Memoiren des Herzogs von Marlborough, 1820/22.

Dangeau: Memoires (ed. par le comte de Cosnac et Bertrand).
Dolfin: Acta Eugenii Francisci Sabaudiae ducis, Viennae 1735.

Eckstein: Die Flucht in das Unendlichkleine, eine Leibniz-Studie, Internationaler Psychoanalytischer Verlag, Wien.
Engerth: Prinz Eugen nach der Schlacht bei Zenta.
Engerth: Feldzüge des Prinzen Eugen in Ungarn.
Erbe: Zinzendorf und der Adel seiner Zeit.
Eugen von Savoyen, Feldzüge des Prinzen —, herausgegeben von der Abteilung für Kriegsgeschichte des K. K. Kriegsarchivs, Verlag des K. K. Generalstabs, Wien.
Eugène, Vie du prince —, écrite par lui-même, Michaud, Paris 1810.
Eugenii, Des grossen Feldherrn —, Herzogs von Savoyen und kaiserlichen Generallieutenants Heldenthaten, Riegel, Nürnberg.
Eugenii, Leben und Thaten des grossen siegreichen —, Schmidt, Nürnberg 1736.
Eugenii von Savoyen, Sonderbare Nachrichten von dem ruhmwürdigen Leben und Thaten des Feldherrn —, Nürnberg 1738.
Eugens Korrespondenz, Haus-, Hof- und Staatsarchiv, Wien.
Eugens Korrespondenz, Nationalbibliothek, Wien.

Eugens Leben und Thaten, Degen, Wien 1791.
Eugens von Savoyen, Neueste und in Kürze gebrachte Lebensbeschreibung des Prinzen —, Gröbl, Prag 1779.

La Fare: Mémoires (ed. Raunié, Paris 1884).
Fehr: Prinz Eugen, Feldherr und Staatsmann, Broschürenverein, Frankfurt 1899.
Fitzpatrick: Great Condé and the period of the Fronde, 1874.
Folkmann: Die gefürstete Linie Kinsky, André, Prag 1861.
Fuhrmann: Alt- und Neues Wien, Prasser, Wien 1738.

Grunwald: Geschichte der Wiener Juden, Selbstverlag der israelitischen Kultusgemeinde, Wien 1924.
Grunwald: Samuel Oppenheimer und sein Kreis, Braumüller, Leipzig 1913.

Haller: Geschichte von Schlosshof, Hölzl, Wien 1903.
Hammer: Geschichte des Osmanischen Reiches, Hartleben, Pest 1836.
Hammer: Wiens erste aufgehobene türkische Belagerung, Hartleben, Pest 1829.
Haymerle: Prinz Eugen von Savoyen, Verlag des Wiener Kaufmännischen Vereins, Wien 1890.
Hegemann: Das Jugendbuch vom grossen König, Hegner, Hellerau 1932.
Heigel: Beziehungen des Kurfürsten Max Emanuel von Bayern zu Franz Rakoczy.
Hennes: Prinz Eugen von Savoyen, Mainz 1856.
Herchenhahn: Geschichte der Regierung Kaiser Joseph I, Crusius, Leipzig 1786.
Hofmannsthal: Prinz Eugen der edle Ritter, Seidel, Wien.

Ilg: Prinz Eugen von Savoyen als Kunstfreund, Gräser, Wien 1898.

Jorga: Geschichte des Osmanischen Reiches, Perthes, Gotha 1911.

Kaufmann: Nachlese zu den Auszügen der Korrespondenz des Fürsten M. K. von Löwenstein mit dem Markgrafen Ludwig von Baden und dem Prinzen Eugen von Savoyen.

Kausler: Das Leben des Prinzen Eugen von Savoyen, Herder, Freiburg im Breisgau 1839.
Kematmüller: Das Dragonerregiment von Savoyen.
Keym: Prinz Eugen von Savoyen, Sammlg. historischer Bildnisse, Serie 1/4.
Klopp: Leibniz' Plan der Gründung einer Societät der Wissenschaften in Wien, K. K. Hof- und Staatsdruckerei, Wien 1868.
Klopp: Türkenkrieg bis zum Frieden von Carlowitz 1699, Hannover.
Küchelbeckers Allerneueste Nachricht vom Römisch-Kayserl. Hofe, Förstl, Hannover 1730.

Landmann: Prinz Eugen von Savoyen, Kirchheim, München 1905.
Ligne, de: Mémoires du prince Eugène.

Macaulay: Kleine geschichtl. und biograph. Schriften, Weigel, Leipzig 1853.
Macaulay: Kritische und historische Aufsätze.
Malleson: Prince Eugene of Savoy, Chapman and Hall, London 1888.
Maurer: Prinz Eugen von Savoyen, Russell, Münster.
Mauvillon: Histoire du prince Eugène, Wien 1790.
Mayer: Geschichte der Stadt Wien, Verlag des Altertumsvereins zu Wien, 1914.
Mazarin: Lettres pendant son ministère (publ. par Chernel).
Montagu: Reisebriefe.

Noorden: Europäische Geschichte des XVIII. Jahrhunderts, Buddens, Düsseldorf 1874.

Oncken: Allgemeine Geschichte in Einzeldarstellungen, Grote, Berlin 1879.
Orléans, Aus den Briefen der Herzogin Elisabeth Charlotte von —, an die Kurfürstin Sophie von Hannover, Hahn, Hannover 1891.
Orléans, Briefe der Herzogin Elisabeth Charlotte von —, Inselverlag, Leipzig 1908.
Orléans, Briefe der Herzogin Elisabeth Charlotte von —, Bibliothek des literarischen Vereins in Stuttgart, Tübingen.

Orléans, Briefwechsel zwischen Leibniz und der Herzogin Elisabeth Charlotte von —, herausgegeben von Bodemann in der Zeitschrift des historischen Vereins für Niedersachsen, Jahrgang 1884.

Pauer: Prinz Eugen von Savoyen, Berühmte Österr., Heft 5, Wien 1880.
Perey: Le roman du grand roi, Calmann-Lévy, Paris 1894.
Perrin: Histoire de Savoy, 1900.
Pezzl: Eugens Leben und Taten, Wien 1791.
Pflugk-Harttung: Ullstein-Weltgeschichte, Ullstein, Berlin 1908.
Plaisance: Histoire des Savoyens, Chambery 1910.
Platz: Markgraf Ludwig Wilhelm von Baden-Baden, Reiff, Karlsruhe 1908.
Pöllnitz, Mémoires de Ch. L. Baron de —, London 1735.
Proschko: Prinz Eugen von Savoyen, Manz, Wien 1887.

Quichenon: Histoire généalogique de la royale maison de Savoye.

Renée: Die Nichten Mazarins, Kuntze, Dresden 1858.
Renner: Wien im Jahre 1683, Waldheim, Wien 1883.
Richter: Prinz Eugen von Savoyen, Hölder, Wien 1872.
Riedler: Österreichisches Archiv, Jahrgang 1831/33.
Rinck: Leopold des Grossen, römischen Kaysers wunderwürdiges Leben und Thaten, Fritschen, Leipzig 1709.
Rinth: Kurfürst Max Emanuel von Bayern, Ganghofer, Ingolstadt.
Robiquett: Le cœur d'une Reine, Alcan, Paris.
Röder: Des Markgrafen Ludwig Wilhelm von Baden Feldzüge wider die Türken.
Röder: Kriegs- und Staatsschriften des Markgrafen Ludwig Wilhelm von Baden, Österr. militär. Zeitschrift, 1834.
Rosenlehner: Die Stellung des Kurfürsten Max Emanuel von Bayern zur Kaiserwahl Karls VI., Lüneburg Verlag, München 1900.
Rousseau, J. B.: Gesammelte Dichtungen, Schlesinger, Berlin 1845.

Salvandy: Histoire de Pologne, Paris 1829.
Sartori: Eugenius Princeps Sabaudiae.

Schulenburg, Des Reichsgrafen, Joh. Mathias von der — Leben und Denkwürdigkeiten, 1834.
Schulte: Die Jugend des Prinzen Eugen, Mitteilungen des Instituts für Österreichische Geschichtsforschung, Band 13, 1892.
Schulte: Markgraf Ludwig Wilhelm.
Sourches, Mémoires du Marquis de —, ed. par le comte de Cosnac et Bertrand, Paris 1852.
Suchier: Prinz Eugen als Bibliophile, Hempe, Weimar 1924.
Sybel: Prinz Eugen von Savoyen, Cotta, München 1861.

Tessé, Lettres du Maréchal de —, publ. par de Rambuteau, Calmann-Lévy, Paris 1888.
Thürheim: Feldmarschall Ernst Rüdiger Graf Starhemberg, Braumüller, Wien 1882.

Vansca: Geschichte der Stadt Wien.
Vauban: Der Angriff und Verteidigung von Festungen, Bergmann, Berlin, 1744.
Villars, Mémoires du Maréchal de —, publ. par Vogué, Renouard, Paris 1887.

Wellenhof: Der Winterpalast des Prinzen Eugen von Savoyen in Wien.
Woldershausen: Das Leben Zinzendorfs.
Wolf: Fürst Wenzel Lobkowitz, Braumüller, Wien 1869.
Wundt: Leibniz, Leipzig 1917.

Zimmermann: Prinz Eugen der edle Ritter und seine Zeit, Lieschnig, Stuttgart 1838.
Zimmermann: Prinz Eugen, Stuttgart 1838.
Zschakwitz: Joseph I., Leipzig 1712.
Zschakwitz: Karl VI., Frankfurt 1723.

www.ingramcontent.com/pod-product-compliance
Lightning Source LLC
Chambersburg PA
CBHW022048160426
43198CB00008B/154